Enigma Books

Also published by Enigma Books

The De Valera Deception
Lenin and His Comrades
The Decision to Drop the Atomic Bomb
Target Hitler
Truman, MacArthur and the Korean War
The Eichmann Trial Diary
Working with Napoleon
Election Year 1968
American Police I (1845-1945)
American Police II (1945-2012)
Deadly Sleep
Islam and the West
The Last Testament of Lucky Luciano
Spy Lost
My Fault: Mussolini As I Knew Him

Robert L. Miller
and
Dennis Wainstock

Indochina and Vietnam

The Thirty-Five-Year War
1940–1975

Enigma Books

Published by Enigma Books, New York

Copyright © 2013 by Dennis Wainstock and Robert L. Miller

First Edition

Printed in the United States of America

ISBN: 978-1-936274-65-9
e-ISBN: 978-1-936274-66-6

Publisher's Cataloging-In-Publication Data

Miller, Robert L. (Robert Lawrence), 1945-
  Indochina and Vietnam : the thirty-five-year war, 1940-1975 / Robert L. Miller and Dennis Wainstock. -- 1st ed.

  p. : ill. ; cm.

  Issued also as an ebook.
  Includes bibliographical references and index.
  ISBN: 978-1-936274-65-9

  1. Indochinese War, 1946-1954. 2. Vietnam War, 1961-1975. 3. Indochina--History--1945- 4. Vietnam--History--1945-1975. I. Wainstock, Dennis, 1947- II. Title.

DS526.7 .M55 2013
959.05/3

Contents

To those who served

Introduction

The Indochina and Vietnam Wars followed one another over a thirty-five-year span, lasting from 1940 to 1975; yet these two closely related conflicts are usually treated separately, usually in isolation. For most Americans, in fact, the Vietnam War begins in 1965, as a consequence of the Tonkin Gulf Incident. This book attempts to recast the reconstruction and interpretation of both conflicts into a single historical event for the student and the general reader. The mass of material now published—including archival documents, memoirs, and individual studies in various countries and as many languages—is so vast that an attempt at a comprehensive yet manageable account of the long war in Southeast Asia has become a far greater challenge.

The authors have attempted to solve this problem by offering a succinct and useful overview that doesn't omit important details and takes the latest and mostly excellent scholarship into account within the space available. With the opening of new archives, particularly in North Vietnam, to a certain extent, the reader is offered access to far more complex background on the subject than was previously possible. No longer can we rely upon an exclusively America-centric narrative in discussing Vietnam and Indochina. This new information both enriches and complicates our understanding of the broad evolution of the conflict and it's far reaching consequences. The authors have chosen to remain close to the facts, avoid excessive interpretation, and concentrate on the issues and personalities, while taking into account the most significant recent studies available.

The Indochina and the Vietnam War taken as a single conflict from 1940 to 1975 resulted in two to six million casualties in the Indochinese peninsula, namely Vietnam, Laos, and Cambodia. That same area in 1945 had a population of about 25 million that never included more than 40,000 French nationals. The bulk of the fighting took place in the northern part of Vietnam, known as Tonkin, and to a lesser extent in the south and the Mekong Delta during the French period; then within South Vietnam after 1961 with incursions into Cambodia. Both Laos and Cambodia remained marginal to the fighting between the Vietnamese, French, followed by the Americans later on.

The United States actually began its direct involvement in Indochina in July 1940, within days of France's defeat by Nazi Germany, as a reaction to Japan's military expansion into Southeast Asia. Almost ninety years of French colonial rule in Indochina were suddenly in jeopardy with the collapse of the French army and the armistice of June 22-24, 1940, with Nazi Germany and Fascist Italy. The shattering national trauma had a devastating psychological impact on all the colonies in the French Empire. While Laos and Cambodia would remain consistently favorable to French presence, Vietnam, with its highly cultured elite that had already shown its impatience with colonial rule and was longing for independence, saw the events in Europe as a golden opportunity.

The background and the context of the French colonial experience remains the cornerstone to understanding the origins and development of the Indochina War and the American entry into the Vietnamese conflict. Most histories of the war begin with a token mention of the colonial past, usually limited to the battle of Dien Bien Phu, in order to concentrate exclusively on the American War. French colonialism is mostly the object of sweeping condemnations on ideological grounds, without the benefit of adequate analysis. That approach, while expedient, offers an incomplete view of the complexity of traditional Vietnamese nationalism and its communist variant. This overview uses a selection of published sources to reconstruct the context and the development of the long war while providing an objective picture of the colonial past.

Catholic missionaries and French traders and adventurers established themselves early on in Southeast Asia, where the path to colonial conquest began haphazardly in the seventeenth century. Until the 1850s France's contacts with Vietnam remained the stuff of a small number of daring individuals rather than the product of any single government decision. After 1852 a colonial plan for Southeast Asia was drawn up in the French naval ministry and carried out with some success in Indochina, mostly by the French navy. After the defeat of France by Prussia in 1870 colonial expansion lay dormant for over a decade. By 1880 France was again aggressively acquiring territory and imposing its rule in Asia and Africa. In 1939 the French saw no reason for undue alarm regarding their Asian possessions.

Indochinese nationalism was considered a negligible quantity by French colonial administrators just before the Second World War:

> ...it was not a danger taken very seriously by the French colonists and administrators...They felt that France was strongly implanted in Indochina, its contribution was expected to last and its tutelage could count on the loyalty and support of the population.[1]

Following the beginnings and the consequences of colonization, the roots of the Indochina War are examined along with the increasing American involvement. America's Vietnam War that immediately followed the Indochina War is reconstructed as thoroughly as possible on its own merits and without any ideological assumptions.

---

1. Yves Gras, *Histoire de la guerre d'Indochine* (Paris: Plon, 1979), p. 275. [Our translation]

Indochina and Vietnam

Part I

An Imperial Conquest

1.

France in the Far East

In 1619 a ship named *Santa Teresa* sailed from Lisbon bound for the Portuguese settlement of Goa in India. The voyage took six months and four days, circling the Cape of Good Hope where it almost ended in disaster because of a terrifying storm that lasted many days. What made this particular trip remarkable was one of the several Jesuit missionaries on board, Father Alexander de Rhodes (1591-1660), a member of the newly founded and very zealous Society of Jesus. Asia, along with the vast colonies of Central and South America, was considered a new fertile land for the conversion of vast numbers of Asians to the Catholic faith. Apart from possessing an extraordinary vocation as a missionary, de Rhodes had a sharp ear and a keen interest in languages, possibly because of his Spanish mother, who had emigrated to France, and was thought to be of Jewish origin, escaping persecution. In any case de Rhodes was born in Avignon, then part of the Papal States, and therefore not technically a subject of the Kings of France, a fine point that would have some importance when a few historians claimed that his early mission was proof of early French colonial designs over Indochina. After leaving Goa for Macao in 1623 and the cancellation of a mission to Japan where missionaries were being persecuted and expelled, de Rhodes was ordered to Cochinchina in 1624. Located on the southern tip of Vietnam, it was already a transit point for other European merchant traffic. De Rhodes set out to learn the Vietnamese language in order to make as many converts as possible. He described how he was fascinated by the unusual bird-like sounds of Vietnamese and spent many days learning from a 12-year-old boy and later from a Portuguese priest who taught him the basics of the spoken language. Soon he traveled north to Tonkin and founded the first mission in what is now northern Vietnam in 1627.

Apart from successfully converting thousands of Vietnamese, including the sister of King Trinh Trang, de Rhodes began studying the culture and history of the land. Constant strife and religious suspicion forced him to leave Tonkin in 1630 and return to Macao, where he remained teaching and studying for ten years. In 1640 he returned to Cochinchina to continue his missionary work until he was finally recalled to Rome in 1649. In 1651 he published his most important book: a Latin-Portuguese-Vietnamese dictionary that revolutionized the knowledge of the language and set the basis for transliterated Vietnamese using Latin letters, known as "quoc ngu." Without a doubt that early effort served as an inspiration to French explorers and naval officers later on who saw in his efforts the establishment of early cultural and religious ties in Vietnam that were to endure for four centuries. However, it would be mistaken to ascribe to Father de Rhodes' missionary work the signs of an early plan of colonial expansion in the seventeenth century when no such designs for a permanent French presence in Indochina existed.

After the French religious wars and the internal strife of the Fronde, France was poised to become the most powerful nation in Europe. Intent on competing with the other great colonial powers, mainly England and Spain, France was eager to have a vigorous presence in Asia. The first decisions were the establishment of trading posts and ports of call in India and China. The motivations were complex and may best be described as the convergence of a Catholic zeal for the propagation of the faith, the expansion of French trade, and the projection of a great nation state's power around the globe. Faith,

military might, and commerce would remain the fundamental moti-
vating factors from those modest beginnings to the tragic conclusion
of the First Indochina War in 1954. Yet the establishment of a colonial
presence was not the result of a master plan carefully hatched by the
government in Paris. As events will demonstrate, colonization appears
to have been the product of converging factors at specific moments of
opportunity when a small adventurous group of men made those conquests possible.

The first half of the seventeenth century was a strategic moment,
not of vast conquests of territory but in establishing the outposts and
contacts that would encourage the bold attempts at colonization later
on. In 1624, with the rise to power of Cardinal Richelieu as King Louis
XIII's prime minister, the era of French supremacy began in Europe.
Later on, under Louis XIV and following the treaty of Westphalia in
1648, many initiatives indirectly affecting Indochina were to follow: in
1658 the French religious Society of Foreign Missions (Société
française des missions étrangères) was founded in Paris to train and
dispatch religious and lay missionaries to foreign lands and make as
many conversions to Catholicism as possible. Obviously French
missionaries were also loyal subjects of the King of France and many
played an important role as informants once they became involved
with local society. Almost at the same time, in 1663, Prime Minister
Jean-Baptiste Colbert was authorized to establish the French East
India Company (Compagnie des Indes orientales) to compete in the
Asian trade. It was inspired by both the British East India Company,
founded in 1600, and the Dutch East India Company created one year
later.

The French company was state-run rather than private, and
focused on trade rather than imperial conquest. Although destined to
fail early in the eighteenth century, the company confirmed France's
determination to carve out a significant position among the large
colonial powers already present in Asia. Most of the efforts of the
French were concentrated on India during the early part of the eighteenth century, giving rise to brutal conflicts with England and the
Netherlands. The British eventually prevailed. France was left with a
few trading posts on the eastern Indian coast that became important

way stations for ships stopping in Cochinchina en route to Macao and Hong Kong. Indochina was at the time a remote backwater, bypassed by the British and Dutch who found more fertile lands to conquer elsewhere. Most of the Europeans present along the coast were Portuguese traders. The early years of French presence were almost exclusively characterized by a growing number of vibrant Catholic missions that often required, and called for, help and protection. As of 1710 the newly established secretariat of the colonies was attached to the ministry of navy, an administrative decision that would involve French naval operations in Asian colonial ventures that were to follow. Naval officers were to play an essential role in the conquest of Indochina.

The modern ministry of the colonies was a creation of the Third Republic. Vietnam and the other countries of Indochina had a long and rich history behind them when France began expansion in Asia. From 110 BC to 939 AD, Vietnam endured almost one thousand years of subjugation under Chinese colonizers in its northern half. The Chinese rulers finally departed Tonkin after a long period of revolt and bloodshed but their presence would leave its imprint on Annam and Tonkin forever. The southern part of Indochina, located roughly below the 18th parallel, which included southern Laos, Cambodia, and Cochinchina, was under Siamese and Hindu influence. For seven centuries northern Indochina managed to discourage Chinese attempts to reestablish control. Yet at the same time Vietnam had assimilated Chinese Mandarin culture within its elites while rejecting China's political domination: a love-hate relationship that remained as a permanent backdrop in Vietnamese history. The constant fear of a Chinese invasion was discouraged by indomitable Vietnamese pride and fierce attachment to independence. Chinese warlords would always hesitate to take on Tonkin because they knew it would be a long and costly struggle.

In the endless sparring between kings and warlords that punctuate the history of Indochina, Catholic missionaries managed to carry on their work and convert considerable numbers of Vietnamese. This provided a compelling reason for the French navy to visit the ports of the Vietnamese coastline, besides protecting merchant shipping and a few French trading posts. In a familiar scenario the local kings and warlords would at first welcome the missionaries and after a relatively long period—once it was felt that there had been too many conversions or under the pressure of other events—they would turn against the foreign priests and order them expelled, imprisoned, or killed, often after having been cruelly tortured. During the colonial period the missionaries remained a key link to the local population, or at least to the vibrant Catholic minority that was mostly located in Tonkin. National spirit always played an important role in Vietnam far more than in Cambodia and Laos: the Vietnamese had a stronger and older culture and deeply resented all foreigners, whether they were Chinese, French, or in more recent times, Americans. Conflicts would drag on for long periods with extreme cruelty and brutality inflicted by all sides.

An important precedent was created by Monsignor Pineau de Behaine, a French missionary who went to Cochinchina in 1767 but soon had to flee to Macao. In the Portuguese colony where he spent a few years and became fluent in Chinese and Vietnamese, Pineau, emulating Alexander de Rhodes, also compiled an Annamite-to-Latin dictionary. He returned to Cochinchina and in 1777 King Nguyen Ahn (who later became Emperor Gia Long of the Nguyen dynasty) took refuge in Pineau's monastery to escape a revolt. The priest became an advisor to Nguyen Ahn, and helped the Vietnamese ruler recapture Saigon. Later, Pineau would travel to the court of Versailles where he presented young Prince Nguyen Phuc Cahn to King Louis XVI and requested military assistance to help Nguyen Ahn. He obtained very little since, as the King of France personally explained to the Catholic bishop, France had allocated huge sums to back the expedition to help the American insurgents and could not afford any further financial strain. Pineau finally returned to Vietnam after many delays in India, where a fleet was assembled to help Nguyen Ahn regain power. The expedition arrived in 1789 and was the prelude to almost constant fighting engaged in by the Nguyen dynasty to remain in power. Pineau who in the end had become more of a politician than a man of the cloth, died in 1799 and was buried with honors by the Vietnamese. French involvement even in this case cannot be labeled a colonial enterprise but rather a limited intervention that ended once its initiators had left the scene. What did remain was the legend and the myth associated with the relentless missionary work carried out in Vietnam, often under the protection of the French flag.

After the loss of India to the British in 1757, the Revolution and the Napoleonic wars, France had mostly abandoned colonial expansion and had even disposed of important territories, such as Louisiana, which was sold to the United States by Napoleon in 1804. From the revolution in 1789 and the reign of Napoleon until the end of the monarchy in 1848, the only major French conquest was the expedition to Algiers in July 1830 and the related campaigns inland to the Sahara desert. The French kings from 1814 to 1848 were careful to avoid foreign adventures and preferred to concentrate on internal control. The attack and conquest of Algiers, originally to be found among Napoleon's many unfulfilled plans, stands out as the exception during the restoration period.

The Second Empire and the Conquest of Annam (1852–1870)

After 1852 French colonial expansion became a pressing issue under Napoleon III during the Second Empire (1852–1870). The new French Empire, proud of its Napoleonic military tradition and ushering a period of unprecedented economic prosperity, was decidedly aggressive overseas. Napoleon III hesitated at first about foreign interventions: the Crimean War, the Italian War of independence of 1859, the expedition of Maximilian and Carlotta in Mexico with the support of French troops—all these adventures were fairly limited in scope and appeared to be timid attempts by the emperor to emulate his illustrious uncle. The expeditions into the Far East and Indochina were not carefully planned invasions, even though several study groups were set up recommending such action. The decision to send a naval squadron was delayed at first by long bouts of hesitation on the emperor's part, until he made it a matter of policy. The Second Empire was also a strongly Catholic regime that proclaimed itself as the privileged defender of the Catholic Church and the Papal States— Empress Eugénie was of Spanish origin, very religious and close to the Papal States—until its defeat by Prussia in 1870. Helping French missionaries in Asia was therefore of great symbolic value and became part of France's civilizing mission during the Second Empire that was to be the last openly Catholic political regime in France.

The execution, after cruel torture, of Father Auguste Chapdelaine in China in 1856 provided the kind of horrific incident that prompted France to join with Britain in what is commonly known as the Second Opium War. The expedition ended after the defeat of the Chinese and the signing of the treaties of Tientsin in 1858. In that same year Admiral Rigault de Genouilly attacked the harbor of Tourane (Da Nang) to prevent the expulsion of Catholic missionaries. When he was unable to hold on to Tourane, Genouilly turned southward and occupied Saigon in 1859, followed by most of Cochinchina. In 1863 Cambodia also became a French protectorate extending the reach of colonization further to the west. The French soldiers newly dispatched to Southeast Asia were neither prepared nor properly equipped to fight in the kind of tropical humidity of those regions—a huge handicap during the campaigns in Indochina in the 1850s and 1860s when the troops landed wearing thick woolen uniforms in temperatures of over 90 degrees. The nonexistent sanitary conditions caused rampant diseases such as cholera and dysentery, making any expedition more a struggle for basic survival than any battle. Many casualties in the French army and navy were caused by those terrible conditions.[1]

In those early campaigns the impressions written by the officers and soldiers in letters to their families or in personal journals provide a vivid picture of what they were experiencing thousands of miles from their homeland. Around 1860 one reads:

> Over there nothing links the soul to the earth. The meaning of life is missing. The soil gives way, it's all mud; only thoughts can float above this infinite greenery. That is precisely where at the end of a long happiness you find perfect annihilation, the end of all sadness, of every memory…[2]

And the Annamites, according to Commander Pallu de la Barrière, like other Oriental races seemed to have "lesser will" with "changing and unpredictable personalities composed of secrecy and cruelty

---

1. Philippe Franchini, *Les Guerres d'Indochine, Vol. I* (Paris: Pygmalion, 1988).
2. Ibid.

behind their peaceful disposition." Captain Grammont, some years later, would note that the Vietnamese were "superstitious without being fanatics, anchored to tradition without having a political faith, they place the respect for the old ways above their attachment to the land and the worship of the family ahead of religion…they are eager to please you to avoid having to serve you…and are indifferent to the threat of death…" Those nineteenth century impressions were to remain virtually unchanged in the eyes of the colonizers during the one hundred years of French presence in Indochina.[3]

The northern Tonkin region that borders China, known as the Viet Bac, was by far the most difficult part of the Indochinese peninsula to conduct military operations. The Annamite Empire and the Chinese warlords lived in fractious harmony but came together when they were faced with incursions by the French navy. The first major attempt to establish even a modest presence came with Captain Francis Garnier, a naval officer stationed in Saigon in 1862 who set up an expedition to explore the source of the Mekong River from Cambodia that took him deep into China. His feat of exploration was celebrated in Paris where he was received by the Empress Eugénie. He returned to Indochina after the war of 1870 and took part in a new expedition in Tonkin in 1873 when he captured Hanoi but was confronted by the Black Flags (Pavillons Noirs), a mercenary Chinese army led by warlord Liu Yongfu. Garnier was killed in a firefight with Black Flag soldiers in December 1873 and his plans to occupy Tonkin had to be set aside for the time being.

The Third Republic Creates Indochina (1870–1940)

In 1882, less than ten years after Garnier was killed, Henri Rivière, another French naval commander overstepping his orders, forced his way into Hanoi. Again the Vietnamese, knowing that they were too weak to offer adequate resistance, called on the Black Flag army and the Chinese for help. Chinese troops moved into Tonkin and the French negotiated a truce that would divide the region. But Commander Rivière was not satisfied and with reinforcements

---

3. Ibid.

managed to move beyond Hanoi. He had the backing of the government of Jules Ferry in Paris that was set on establishing a French presence in northern Indochina. But the Black Flags defeated Rivière, who was killed in action in 1883, prompting Paris to dispatch Admiral Amédée Courbet with a fleet to first attack the imperial capital of Hué, forcing the Vietnamese imperial government to accept France's protection over Tonkin. However, the fighting between the French and the Black Flags was not over and Courbet prepared another major offensive to force the Chinese to withdraw. With increasing anti-European protest in China the French decided to move and Courbet launched an attack on the fort of Son Tay, flatly defeating the Black Flag army, mostly because of intense artillery fire. By May 1884 an agreement was reached recognizing France's protectorate over Annam and Tonkin and the withdrawal of Chinese troops. However, the agreement was immediately denounced by China and fighting resumed in Tonkin. A new campaign began in January 1885 aimed at expelling the Chinese from northern Tonkin as French expeditionary troops went beyond the Chinese border and blew up the famous Gate of China customs house, a symbolic structure separating the two countries. Several battles ended in stalemate or minor defeats for the French forces, causing the sudden fall of the government of Jules Ferry on March 30, 1885. The French chamber of deputies was not at all unanimous about the conquest of Tonkin and Radical Party leader Georges Clemenceau led the anti-colonial forces that were defeated by just three votes, virtually splitting the deputies in two. In the end Annam and Tonkin would both become part of French Indochina.

Peace talks with China finally ended with France obtaining control over Tonkin while French troops evacuated Formosa and the Pescadores Islands.

With the fall of the Second Empire and the proclamation of the Third Republic, French politics were relentlessly divided between factions on the left and the right. But as the republic was proclaimed on September 4, 1870, the regime effectively remained without a constitution until 1875. A majority of politicians on the right wanted to restore the monarchy but they were outvoted by the republicans, who finally won the day by a single vote. During that period colonial expansion remained politically in limbo. The republican and radical left took a strong anti-clerical position, seeking to limit the power of the Catholic Church in every aspect of national life and primarily in elementary and secondary education and the religious orders. This would eventually lead to strict laws separating Church and State in 1905, championed by the radicals.

Moderate republicans such as Jules Ferry were also both Freemasons and imperialists, much like many Tories in Great Britain during the same period. Ferry embodied France's will to expand and civilize, as he stated very clearly in a landmark 1885 speech: "The duty of the superior races [...] is to civilize the inferior races." But there was also a much more ambitious agenda: "France must, thanks to a colonial empire, be present everywhere the future of the world is being decided. ... Colonial policy is the daughter of industrial policy..." He made the strongest argument yet for modern imperial expansion, and major action followed with the establishment of a protectorate over Tunisia in 1881, the occupation of Madagascar in 1885, the exploration of the Congo, and the planned conquest of Annam and Tonkin. Most of these initiatives were taken in a semi-secrecy that irritated the left-wing radicals, who resented being repeatedly placed in front of the fait accompli of an incident involving French nationals, missionaries for the most part, or hard charging naval officers. Actually the political struggle was taking place between the republican majority in France, with Ferry and the colonialists on the right and Clemenceau and the anti-colonialist radicals on the left.

In his famous speech in the chamber of deputies attacking Jules Ferry, Clemenceau proceeded to criticize each argument used by the colonialists as if he were in a court of law.

Point one: colonies are desirable for economic reasons because they provide markets and investment opportunities—wrong, because the cost of acquiring colonies may never be amortized by the future benefits and the newly acquired lands will drag the country down into debt.

Point two: the humanitarian argument, also known as the "civilizing mission" (*mission civilisatrice*) or the "white man's burden" of Kipling's poem, later on drew scorn from Clemenceau: "The conquest you call for is quite simply the abuse of power of scientific civilization over rudimentary civilizations to grab and torture man and squeeze out any strength he has for the benefit of the so-called civilizer... To call this civilization is to add violence to hypocrisy."[4]

Point three: the political and military justifications offered by Jules Ferry were that the French people needed to move beyond their borders and set out into the world, to take over and acquire territory and become an energized and dynamic, imperial nation. Clemenceau's reply was that this took soldiers and energy away metropolitan France at a time when the French people should be thinking about the threat coming from Germany and being ready to fight to retake the lost provinces of Alsace-Lorraine.

The two powerful schools of thought in France after 1870 included the nationalists and the imperialists that were to be found in most political parties, including the Radical Party and the Bonapartists who remained influential until the First World War. The main political and ideological goal of the nationalists was to seek revenge on Germany because of the loss of Alsace-Lorraine. But the expected settling of accounts with the Germans couldn't happen for many years to come because of France's military weakness. Nationalist agitation amounted to a long propaganda campaign to prepare French public opinion for a war against the "hereditary enemy." The military argument that colonies would detract from the main goal of defeating Germany was in part resolved by the creation of a professional colonial army trained to handle local contingencies and not having to rely on troops needed in France itself. The monarchists opposed imperial expansion during that early period and remained averse to any foreign adventures.

The imperialists on the other hand, were impatient for action, eager to compete with the British Empire in extending France's control over vast territories in Africa and Asia. A powerful financial and business lobby was represented by over 80 colonial investment companies based in Paris at the turn of the century, some of them highly successful with stock listed in the Paris Bourse.[5] The third component on the far left, prior to 1914, were the socialists who remained too few

---

4. J.-B. Duroselle, *Clemenceau* (Paris: Fayard, 1988), p. 225.
5. Raoul Girardet, *L'idée coloniale en France de 1871 à 1962* (Paris: la Table Ronde, 1972).

to make a difference politically but had a growing voice in French political narrative. Their main spokesman was Jean Jaurès (1859–1914), who made pacifism his trademark after 1900 and rejected both positions. He denounced colonialism as capitalist oppression created by "crooked financial speculation." Imperialism was also regularly criticized by the Marxists, who called it "the final stage of capitalism," a slogan that Lenin would repeat before and after taking power in Russia. In spite of all the opposition colonial policy remained popular. mainly due to the spectacular acquisitions of territory and the perceived wealth created for France.

From 1880 to the First World War a lively debate on imperialism was taking place in almost every major Western country, and France was no exception. The United States had its brief imperial moment during the Spanish-American War and the Philippine Insurrection when William Jennings Bryan and Mark Twain bitterly criticized President McKinley and later Theodore Roosevelt for their policy of imperial expansion. France was actively pursuing a vigorously expansionist colonial policy as the land mass and population under its control, multiplied several times until half of the African continent, Indochina and after 1920 the Mandates of Syria and Lebanon in the Near East were flying the French flag. After a brief conflict with Siam, where Britain and France forced the Siamese to give up Laos and claims to other territories with Thai populations, France proclaimed a protectorate over Laos in 1893 that became part of French Indochina. The vast newly expanded area was considered a key strategic link between India, Indonesia, and China and was destined to become a major issue during the Second World War and later the Cold War.

After the big push for Annam and Tonkin the governments of the Third Republic settled into the administrative task of organizing Indochina. By contrast with the naval officers of the Second Empire, all the new leaders the Republic sent to the colony were civilians: top politicians, usually Radical party members and Freemasons or career civil servants and diplomats. But the colonial organization remained a byzantine mosaic of responsibilities: a ministry of the colonies was created in 1894 and the government also had a secretary of state for the colonies along with the minister. A Superior council of the colonies was also created, which included the senators and deputies representing those territories having enough of a voting population. But the administrative responsibility of the various components of Indochina remained fragmented: the protectorates such as Cambodia, Laos, and Annam were administered by the ministry of foreign affairs that sent over career diplomats. Often the nuances of policy were different or even contradictory, depending on which government ministry was in charge. Power in Indochina resided with the Governor General, a true viceroy who ran the colony as an autocrat with the limitation that he could be recalled at any time by the government in power.

It was the arrival of a dynamic politician, Paul Doumer, in 1897, that changed the face of colonial Indochina in a lasting way.[6] In many ways the Left Radical Doumer brought with him ideas typical of the early Third Republic: a mixture of liberal reforms, republican ideals, and a pragmatic, positive approach to economic growth. His method was to enhance administrative control through centralization in a land that was a mosaic of small territories and kingdoms. From the start French civilian administrators took over from the old mandarin class at all levels of power and Doumer set the tone by moving the colonial capital north to Hanoi rather than staying in Hué, the imperial capital of Annam. It was a highly symbolic choice, since Hanoi was located in Tonkin, the most difficult part of Indochina to administer because of its fractious population. Ministries were organized and modeled on the government in Paris and a vast program of public works was quickly approved to build the infrastructure of the colony: roads, bridges, railroads, irrigation and drainage canals, and modern port facilities at Haiphong, Saigon, and Tourane. A new legal system was imposed and accepted by the kings and emperors ensuring the protection of French property owners, private and corporate. This typically colonial legislation encouraged investment by French farmers and doubled the number of farms in less than five years. For Indochina a major development came early on in 1875 when the Banque de l'Indochine was

---

6. Paul Doumer (1857–1932). Professor of mathematics and provincial journalist, Doumer was a Freemason and joined the Radical Party. Minister of Finance in 1895 before his appointment as governor general of Indochina (1897–1902). The Pont Doumer (Doumer Bridge, now named Pont Long Bien) was built under Doumer's administration over the Red River near Hanoi in the Tonkin Delta. President of the Chamber of Deputies (1905–1906) and president of the French Republic (1931–1932). He was assassinated by a mentally ill Russian émigré on May 6, 1932.

founded in Paris with capital from other major French banks but without any state intervention. Within one year the bank had obtained the right to issue banknotes locally, known as the piastres. From its main offices in Saigon the Banque de l'Indochine quickly became the center of dynamic economic growth for the colony, with several branches in Asia and other French colonies.

The negative effect of Doumer's initiatives came with the need to balance the budget, which was mainly achieved by heavily taxing the poorest Indochinese. State monopolies were instituted on salt, opium, and alcohol, quickly enriching the treasury but creating harsh resentment among the population that remained largely impoverished, particularly in Tonkin. Small farmers and peasants were mercilessly squeezed in their meager earnings, often by a corrupt mandarin class that continued to collect property taxes alongside the French administrators. Everyone blamed the French for the inequities of the system and that resentment became almost universal when coupled with the natural xenophobia of Vietnamese society. By the early twentieth century a new nationalist movement was emerging as a reaction to the blatantly abusive colonial system. Xenophobic sentiment found its model in China, where the reformist movement was gaining strength and in Japan that had just defeated Imperial Russia in 1905, thereby demonstrating that Asians could win when fighting a war against Europeans. The key to Japan's success had been its rapid and relentless modernization and several Vietnamese intellectuals, inspired by Japan, took the lead by creating new nationalist movements.

Phan Boi Chau (1867–1940), an early nationalist, had fought the French before fleeing to Japan with Prince Cuong De (1882–1951), a direct descendant of Emperor Gia Long and a pretender to the imperial throne of Annam. By 1906 a number of associations that rejected French presence had been created in Japan and weapons were purchased and shipped to Vietnam through secret societies. French authorities were intolerant of any attempts by the nationalists and used every opportunity to show they were firmly in control. In Hué the old emperor of Annam, Thanh Thai, was declared insane and deposed by French colonial administrators, then replaced with his eight-year-old son Duy Tan in 1907. That show of force was to have vast repercussions in Vietnam and across Indochina. Confucian respect for the father had been violated and served as a catalyst for protest, along with the harsh taxation inequalities that sparked the revolt of 1908. The French army reacted brutally against the protesters: firing into the crowds and the administrators made sure that those mandarins considered the moving forces behind the protests were swiftly brought to justice. Several leaders were executed by decapitation and the others were imprisoned. France also pressured Japan to end the activities of Phan Boi Chau and Prince Cuong De, who were promptly expelled and took refuge in Hong Kong. The French chamber of deputies took up the issue and a commission analyzed the problems that Doumer's rapid growth had created, but few corrections were made and the resentment of the Vietnamese remained and would increase later on. Several nationalist and communist movements began to emerge, including one that would eventually dominate all the others, led by Ho Chi Minh.

Between 1890 and 1914 the results of colonization in Indochina were truly spectacular and explained, in part, the lack of urgency about reforms and greater modernization. In 1877 a new rubber tree imported from Ceylon was introduced in Cochinchina and by 1898 the first plantation had been created with 15,000 trees. Soon after, a small number of companies and individuals began planting rubber trees on an industrial scale. The results were impressive and by the late 1920s French Indochina became one of the world's largest producers of rubber, a commodity increasingly in demand because of the universal success of the automobile. The Michelin rubber plantation near Saigon would remain active well into the mid-1970s, during the American phase of the Vietnam War and was a battleground on several occasions.

By 1928 rubber plantations employed over 80,000 Vietnamese coolies who came mostly from Tonkin and were paid a pittance. The degree of human mistreatment and exploitation was similar to that of other colonial countries rich in raw materials. By the 1920s investigative reporters were publishing articles about the poor treatment those workers were subjected to. Rubber plantations also entailed large scale deforestation and harmed traditional farming creating further discontent among Indochinese peasants. Most other colonies in Southeast Asia were harvesting rubber trees as well after 1900 and experienced much the same problems as French Indochina.

The development of agriculture and commerce yielded few tangible benefits for the Vietnamese population at large, even though it did lead to vast public works, improved education, and medical assistance. Wages remained very low and taxes on the peasantry were collected with great efficiency and complete disregard for human suffering. With a crisis looming the French government decided to appoint a new governor and selected Albert Sarraut, who was also a prominent member of the chamber of deputies and a Radical socialist party leader.[7] He would later serve as prime minister and as minister of the colonies in several governments of the Third Republic during the 1920s when he held meetings with Ho Chi Minh. The wealth that colonial possessions and Indochina in particular provided to France became clear and a new argument finally convinced the most hard line French nationalists when they were told that the vast human potential in the colonies would actually help defend France itself. Clemenceau the longtime opponent of colonial expansion finally changed his mind and joined the now popular movement supporting the vast imperial project. As governor general Sarraut initiated liberal reforms of the penal system, abolishing the cruelties inherited from the distant past that included torture, death by strangulation, and slow death by one thousand cuts. He opened the representative councils to more Vietnamese representatives and emphasized public health and education.

Vietnamese nationalists, however, remained skeptical and the secret societies pursued their struggle to shake off French colonial rule. Phan Boi Chau and Prince Cuong De had relocated to Canton under the protection of Sun Yat Sen and the Kuomintang, setting up in 1912 an Association for the Restoration of Vietnam. The reaction from

---

7. Albert Sarraut (1872-1962). Born in Bordeaux, was a Radical party politician from southwestern France, appointed governor general of Indochina (1911-1914), and again (1916-1919); he was also minister of the colonies in several governments and twice prime minister in 1933 and 1936. Like many other civilian colonial governors he was a Freemason and a firm believer in liberal democracy. Sarraut retired from politics in 1940 to edit the family newspaper *La Dépêche* in Toulouse but was arrested by the Gestapo in 1944 and sent to a concentration camp in Germany. He returned to elective office in 1946 and became the president of the Assembly of the *Union Française,* where he played a moderating role. Sarraut made a positive and constructive impression in Vietnam and Indochina; a high school bearing his name still operates in Hanoi.

French authorities in Hanoi came swiftly and both leaders were condemned to death in absentia: Phan Boi Chau was ordered out of China and Prince Cuong De was placed under arrest by Chinese warlord Yuan She Kai. When Albert Sarraut left Indochina in 1914 the colony was calm and few French soldiers were required to maintain law and order. An attempted uprising by the young Emperor Duy Tan in 1916 failed and he was exiled by the French with his family to the island of la Réunion. Nationalist agitation continued and Phan Boi Chau was arrested in Shanghai and turned over to French authorities, his death sentence was commuted to hard labor and he spent the rest of his life under surveillance in Hué. Prince Cuong De supported the Japanese during World War II and died in Tokyo in 1951.

With the outbreak of the First World War, the French government reappointed Sarraut for a second tour as governor general in 1916 to emphasize the policy of association between France and its colonial subjects. His promises gave hope to the Vietnamese elites that they might achieve self-government in some ways similar to that of the Philippines. The Indochinese participated in France's war effort by paying even higher taxes and sending 50,000 troops and as many workers to France. However, when Sarraut left Hanoi for the second time in 1920 to become minister of the colonies, no significant progress had been made toward a more liberal arrangement in Indochina. One of his projects to bring American investors into the colony was bitterly criticized by the opposition.[8] The idea of repaying France's war debt to the United States by handing over a number of its colonial possessions had also been discussed in the press of both countries. Indochina was even mentioned as a possible barter with the United States to erase the gigantic French war debt but nothing came of those rumors, except that they probably sharpened Franklin D. Roosevelt's curiosity when he was running for vice president in the 1920 election.

The new hope for the Vietnamese intellectuals and many other colonial subjects was that France would adopt Woodrow Wilson's Fourteen Points and in particular the right to self-determination.[9] The

---

8. Franchini, p. 123.
9. See Erez Manela, *The Wilsonian Moment* (New York: Oxford, 2007), which reconstructs the rising expectations created by the Paris peace conference and Wilson's liberal ideas in 1919-1920 quickly frustrated by the victors of 1918.

turbulence of the Russian Revolution and France's perennial lack of direction in its colonial policy ushered a new era of uncertainty. The main fear that communism would spread to the poor villages of northern Annam began to take hold, an area where Nguyen Ai Quoc (Ho Chi Minh) was originally from. Those problems were exacerbated by falling world commodity prices of rubber following the Wall Street Crash and the Great Depression. The new hardships sparked growing resentment among a population that was increasingly open to revolutionary ideas. The government in Paris and the colonial authorities never considered implementing a master plan to improve the living conditions of the Vietnamese population. During the 1930s the French administration did attempt to make a major effort to improve the livelihood of the coolies on the plantations and the Institut Pasteur, which was in charge of public health, made significant inroads in the battle against malaria and other deadly tropical diseases.

The interwar years were a time of great ferment in Indochina as economic progress had brought many Indochinese, and mainly the Vietnamese middle classes, into the French educational system. Some top students had traveled to France where they were impressed by the ferment of new ideas, including socialism and Marxism, and the freedom of expression that existed in the universities and in the press. When they returned they gathered in small groups that quickly became very critical of the heavy-handed authoritarian colonial system and eventually decided to seek its overthrow. A number of incidents took place with the rise of the nationalist parties such as the VNQDD, led by Nguyen Thai Hoc. In February 1929 in Hanoi a French recruiter of coolies, Hervé Bazin, known for his brutality, was assassinated: the police placed the blame on the nationalists. One year later the VNQDD took part in the mutiny of Yen Bai and Hoc was captured and executed. After the death of their leader the VNQDD crossed the border into China where they joined Phan Boi Chau. The murder of Bazin was seen as a blow against French colonialism although it may simply have been revenge for the innumerable cruelties the man was known for.

The same ambiguity may have been behind the 1928 murder in the Rue Barbier in Saigon, where personal and sexual rivalries may have been behind the killing of a militant nationalist by three of his comrades. All three were condemned to death and executed. In this case, once again, French justice came across as inflexible and indiscriminately brutal, giving added fuel to nationalist propaganda.

Besides the political movements there were also home grown religious and political sects such as the Cao Dai, Hoa Hao and Binh Xuyen, for example that were engaged in all kinds of profitable illegal activities from smuggling to gambling, prostitution and assorted crime. But the French, always in need of allies, decided the Caodaists and Binh Xuyen would have official status as decided by the Minister of the Colonies Georges Mandel in 1938, carving out small empires mainly in southern Vietnam. Contacts were also made through Prince Cuong De with Japanese business groups such as Mitsubishi setting the stage for future economic collaboration with Japan during the occupation.

In the second half of the 1930s as the deficit of the colonies was growing and becoming more of a burden for the French treasury, renewed suggestions surfaced to exchange colonial territories for peace with the Axis powers. The idea was even endorsed by President Franklin D. Roosevelt who was becoming a firm anti-colonialist in the American tradition going back to the revolutionary war and long standing anti-British sentiment. But once more it became clear that no colonial exchange would stop the greed and expansionist policies of the Axis powers and of imperial Japan in Southeast Asia.

In the 1930s Indochina was clearly not the kind of colony where excess European population could be transferred. Such a policy made no sense to France following the bloodletting of World War I when she suffered from exceedingly low birthrates and actually opened its borders to immigration.[10] Indochina was a colony that prospered because of its commodities and raw materials which as in all colonial situations, mostly benefited the colonizers with a small 'trickle down' effect on the indigenous population.

---

10. The First World War cost France 1.3 million men killed in action and 4.2 million wounded. Of the 20,000 Indochinese recruited into the French army for the war, 12,000 were killed in action. The French suffered from desperately low birthrates after World War I and welcomed hundreds of thousands of immigrant men and families to repopulate certain regions.

The Exposition Coloniale held from May to November 1931 at Vincennes just east of Paris, received a record number of seven million visitors and greatly enhanced the image of the French colonies in the public mind. At the height of the Depression in the United States and with the world economic crisis, the conservative government of André Tardieu proclaimed the idea of "the Empire as salvation." The colonial possessions would save France from the economic distress that so many other countries were experiencing and provide manpower from a reservoir of 70 plus million subjects. This idea remained powerful during the prewar years and the Second World War.[11] It didn't simply disappear with liberation in 1944 and the French were deeply distrustful of Franklin D. Roosevelt's motives and methods when he called for the application of the Atlantic Charter and the granting of independence to Indochina on the model of the Philippines.

---

11. Jean-Baptiste Duroselle, *France and the Nazi Threat* (New York: Enigma Books, 2004), pp. 184-185.

2.

War, Defeat, and Resurgence
1940–1952

France Loses a Battle

By the summer of 1939, with war threatening in Europe, the Daladier government replaced the civilian governor general of Indochina with a military man, in this case General Georges Catroux,[1] who had solid colonial experience and an excellent military record. The idea was to send a signal to the Axis and the Japanese that France would stand and fight for its Asian possessions, indeed for all its colonies. Catroux took over in late August and in less than ten days had to deal with the repercussions of the European war declared by France and England on Nazi Germany on September 3. The need for military preparations in Indochina had been obvious as early as 1937 in light of the Japanese aggression in China. Georges Mandel, then minister of the colonies, spearheaded the effort in 1938 that even included a plan to build military aircraft in Tonkin within five years. Most of those

---

1. Georges Catroux (1877-1969) was a St Cyr graduate and a battalion commander in WWI. As a fellow POW he became close to Charles de Gaulle in 1916 in the Ingolstadt prison camp. Governor General of Indochina from August 1939 to July 1940 when he was forced to resign, he decided to join the Free French. Appointed governor general of Algeria (1943-1944), then ambassador to the USSR (1945-1948); he headed the commission of inquiry into the defeat at Dien Bien Phu in 1954. In 1956 Catroux was again appointed governor general of Algeria by the government of socialist Guy Mollet, but he was unable to take the post because of unrest by local French pied noir population.

projects came to nothing, given the quickened pace of hostilities. The military call up in Indochina affected 80,000 men, of which only 20,000 were actually drafted and sent to France. General Catroux strenuously objected to having his ranks depleted of his most vital elements. An immediate shortage of shipping further isolated Indochina from France, making it necessary to find new trading partners for rubber and other products of the colony mainly in Singapore and the Philippines while aircraft, trucks, and machinery were being purchased directly from the United States.

One of the Daladier government's most sweeping measures in August 1939 was to outlaw the French Communist Party because of its vociferous support of the German Soviet non-aggression pact. French communists were strongly supportive of the Soviet alliance with the Nazis and suddenly became militant pacifists. A small number of French communists left the party at this time, never to return. The party leadership was jailed or fled to Moscow. The PCI (Parti Communiste Indochinois) was therefore also outlawed by General Catroux and most of its leaders were imprisoned in harsh conditions, while the key elements managed to slip into southern China: Vo Nguyen Giap, Pham Van Dong, and others joined Nguyen Ai Quoc (Ho Chi Minh) in Kunming. After the defeat of Poland and the failure of various peripheral campaigns, notably in Norway during the period known as the "phony war," Nazi Germany began its offensive into France. The Battle of France lasted from May 10 to June 25, 1940, when the armistice was signed with Germany and Italy by the new government led by Marshal Philippe Pétain. As early as June 18 General Charles de Gaulle broadcast his first radio appeal from London demanding that France remain in the fight against Germany and the Axis and reject the armistice. Very few Frenchmen heard the general's appeal and the Free French were initially fewer than 3000 strong. A number of French military men in England at that time opted to return home rather than face an uncertain future in the Gaullist ranks.

The image of France, the great colonial power that held sway over one hundred million non-Europeans across the globe, unexpectedly defeated in six weeks by the Germans represented an incredible loss of face. It was also welcome news to all nationalists in the colonies hoping for radical change. The trauma of defeat was to have long term consequences at the time. The first major change came within days of the German victory and even before the armistice was formally signed. On June 19, 1940, Japan demanded that Governor General Catroux close the border between China and Tonkin to all shipping and stop the supplies provided by the United States to Chiang Kai-shek through the port of Haiphong. The demand amounted to an ultimatum and Catroux was painfully aware of the weakness of his forces. He couldn't counter an aggression from the Japanese army of Canton. An urgent request for help sent through the French ambassador to Washington received a disappointing reply:

> [France's] Ambassador Saint Quentin was informed as of June 19 by Sumner Welles that the United States wished to avoid any possible conflict with Japan.[2]

Privately Welles, with Cordell Hull's approval, suggested to the ambassador that the French should accommodate the Japanese requests and avoid a confrontation.[3] The United States was in no position to provide assistance and was bound by the strict language of the Neutrality Act. Catroux then sent a purchasing mission to buy aircraft and anti-aircraft guns to the United States and attempted to obtain supplies from the new French government in Bordeaux. But none of these initiatives could be implemented in time to make a difference. The British, on the other hand, didn't hesitate to bow to Japanese demands that they close the borders in Hong Kong and Burma to all supplies earmarked for the Chinese. Churchill, under pressure during the Battle of Britain and unable to confront Japan in Asia alone, agreed on July 18. Catroux followed suit and accepted Japanese border controls to avoid a clash.

But the Pétain government appointed on June 16, 1940, rejected Catroux's decisions and Albert Rivière, the new minister of the colonies, immediately dismissed the general for insubordination, replacing him with the more docile Admiral Jean Decoux. Catroux, refusing to comply, defied the minister's orders and continued negotia-

---

2. J.-B. Duroselle, *L'Abîme 1939-1944* (Paris: Imp. Nationale, 1986), p. 252.
3. Fredrik Logevall, *Embers of War* (New York: Random House, 2012), p. 29.

tions with General Nishihara of the Japanese army of Canton who offered a defensive alliance to the French in exchange for Japanese rights to transit through Tonkin and the use of its airfields for the Yunnan campaign. Japan in turn agreed to recognize French sovereignty in Indochina. However, without asking for instructions from Tokyo, Japanese commanders decided to land their planes in Tonkin anyway while imperial navy ships flying the battle flag of the Rising Sun were dropping anchor in Haiphong harbor. French Indochina was now completely at their mercy. Catroux departed for Singapore, where he joined de Gaulle's forces, while Admiral Decoux was left to deal with increasingly intrusive Japanese demands.

The United States reacted to the Japanese expansion into Southeast Asia by the Export Control Act of July 2, 1940, to "prohibit or curtail the export of basic war materials...licenses were refused for the export to Japan of aviation gasoline and most types of machine tools beginning in August 1940."[4]

On August 2, 1940, Japanese foreign minister Yosuke Matsuoka during a meeting with the French ambassador to Tokyo asked that France declare war on China. If the French refused to declare war, Matsuoka said that he at least expected the French governor general to grant a number of air bases and free passage to the Japanese army in northern Tonkin. After a series of ultimatums and a brutal surprise attack by Japanese forces against a French garrison, an agreement was reached whereby 25,000 Japanese troops would be stationed in Tonkin. Several airfields would also be made available to the Japanese air force. On September 22 the Japanese army, in a brutal show of force, suddenly attacked Lang Son on the Chinese border, leaving 800 French and Indochinese troops dead. At the same time Siam (Thailand), taking advantage of France's weakness, issued demands regarding the Thai populations in Indochina, located mostly on the border with Laos and Cambodia: a short war began that culminated in a successful French naval attack in early 1941. The Japanese quickly brokered a cease fire that was nevertheless favorable to Thailand.

The United States reacted to the aggressive Japanese expansion into Indochina, making a move that meant widening the war in Asia,

---

4. *Peace and War. U.S. Foreign Policy 1931–1941.* Department of State 1943 publication reprinted 1983, p. 97.

and on July 25, 1940, on the recommendation of Secretaries Henry Morgenthau and Henry Stimson, FDR signed a U.S. Treasury Department proclamation limiting the export of aviation fuel oil and scrap metal to Japan. This was a momentous event that placed the United States on a virtually unavoidable collision course with Japan.[5] It was also clear that an absence of reaction would be interpreted as acquiescence to further aggression that could cut off key sources of raw materials and signal a further American retreat from world affairs.

As Walter LaFeber commented:

> Japan's decision to change the status quo in Southeast Asia by invading Indochina was perhaps the crucial factor that caused war between the United States and Japan.[6]

On July 25, 1941, Roosevelt decided to freeze Japan's assets in the United States because the Japanese were making new demands for air bases and the right to station an additional 50,000 troops—this time in southern Indochina. This move was clearly in anticipation of Japan's military expansion into Southeast Asia, which the United States could not accept and viewed effectively as an act of war. It prompted a reaction at Vichy on July 19 on the part of U.S. ambassador Admiral Leahy, who told Marshal Pétain: "It was necessary to say bluntly that if Japan was the winner, the Japanese would take over Indochina and if the Allies won *we* would take it."[7] The French army in Indochina was weak, cut off from the homeland and without access to meaningful supplies or reinforcements; any attempted resistance would have been

---

5. Robert Dallek, *Franklin D. Roosevelt and American Foreign Policy 1933–1945* (New York: Oxford, 1979), p. 240.

6. Walter La Feber, "Roosevelt, Churchill and Indochina" in *American Historical Review*, December 1975, pp. 1277–1295. The issue of the reversal of FDR's policy by Harry Truman as he took office is also discussed in the article. Truman was committed to following FDR's policy that was undergoing momentous changes just before his death in light of new difficulties with Soviet Russia. In early March 1945 Stalin appeared to be breaking the agreements reached at Yalta in February. The aggressive Soviet attitude announced an imminent danger to Western Europe that could not be ignored and FDR chose to de-emphasize his views on colonialism in favor of European stability and security. Therefore it would appear that there was no discontinuity in the policy choices made by President Truman for Indochina and France from 1945 to the end of his term. See also Wilson Miscamble, *From Roosevelt to Truman: Potsdam, Hiroshima and the Cold War* (New York: Cambridge, 2006) for an analysis of Truman's efforts to ensure the continuity of FDR's foreign policy goals.

7. Adm. William Leahy, *I Was There* (New York: McGraw Hill, 1950), p. 44. Interestingly, in his memoirs Leahy italicized the "we," presumably meaning the Americans, which was anathema to the French in the long run even though they were forced to agree to the Japanese occupation..

suicidal. Admiral Decoux agreed to the new demands to avoid a major disaster and the possible massacre of the population, both French and Indochinese, by the Japanese army in the Tonkin region. The United States viewed this as an extremely threatening action on Japan's part, besides being one more example of abject collaborationism by defeatist Vichy French officers. However, there were no alternatives—a desperate attempt at resistance would have ended in a bloodbath.

As de Gaulle would later write in his war memoirs:

> Indochina then appeared to be a huge rudderless ship that I would not be able to rescue until I had all the elements required to salvage it.[8]

For four years Indochina would be administered sternly by Admiral Jean Decoux, who diligently followed the edicts and policies of the Vichy government, including the anti-Semitic laws, even though the tiny number of Jews in the colony made the persecution all the more absurd. He made sure to severely punish anyone seeking to join the Free French. At the same time in South China, Vietnamese dissidents and nationalists were attempting to play a role under the Japanese, such as the one-thousand-strong pro-Japanese followers of Prince Cuong De, the pro-Japanese Dai Viet party, and the VNQDD nationalists. Several insurrections by Vietnamese nationalists were repressed with extreme brutality by French forces in Saigon-Cholon and in the rice paddy country at Mytho. The number of Vietnamese killed was estimated as high as 5,000, with 8,000 arrests and 100 executions after trial. There were no objections or any interference on the part of the Japanese forces stationed in Vietnam.

During the spring of 1941 Nguyen Ai Quoc (Ho Chi Minh) returned to northern Tonkin for a secret Communist Party meeting. The Indochinese Communist Party was a tiny group of no more than 300 members in 1940-41, with Ho Chi Minh attempting to provide leadership from his exile in China. He realized that he had to build up his strength through alliances and reached an agreement to create a broad coalition called the League for the Independence of Vietnam, or Vietnam Doc Lap Dong Minh—abbreviated as "Viet Minh." The

---

8. Charles de Gaulle, *Mémoires*, vol. III.

objective was to prepare an insurrection and take advantage of every weakness in the adversaries in two phases: first, to "Overthrow the Japanese fascists and the French colonialists," and then to "Establish a communist revolutionary government."

Ho's methods were inspired by Mao Zedong and his principles of revolutionary warfare: "The most important thing is popular mobilization. The people must be a great ocean where the enemy will drown."[9] Ho, while still in Kunming, set up a base in northern Tonkin in and around Cao Bang, close to the Chinese border. Vo Nguyen Giap, Ho's main lieutenant, managed to enlist the support of a local bandit, Chu Van Tan, who had been fighting the French. That move opened up Tonkin to the Viet Minh. It was the pressing need for weapons that prompted Ho to seek Allied and Chinese support. However, in 1942 the Chinese suddenly imprisoned Ho and in his absence the Viet Minh was led by Pham Van Dong and Vo Nguyen Giap. But the group was too small to attract the attention of the Vichy French authorities and it had little difficulty in setting up the familiar cell networks throughout Tonkin.

Admiral Decoux was acutely aware of the need to maintain the loyalty of the bulk of the Indochinese population, and the Vichy administrators increased efforts to improve conditions at every level: education was improved, administrative jobs were opened to non-Europeans, and the number of Indochinese civil servants doubled. There were therefore tangible but still far too modest improvements throughout the colony in an attempt to ensure at least the cooperation of the Indochinese. The Japanese military government found it expedient to rely on the French to keep Indochina under control as a major asset to the war effort. But the conciliatory attitude of the higher Japanese officials didn't convince the more imperialistic and impatient younger officers, who provoked many incidents due to their often brutal arrogance. The feared secret police, the Kempetai, also played an increasingly important role after 1942. Among the sects the Cao Dai became strong supporters of the pro-Japanese league, while French

---

9. On Mao Zedong, see Jung Chang and Jon Halliday, *Mao: The Unknown Story* (New York: Knopf, 2005); Alexander Pantsov and Steven Levine, *Mao: The Real Story* (New York: Simon and Shuster, 2012). A controversy has surrounded both books: the former because of its firm anti-Mao positions and the latter for the less personal condemnation of the communist leader.

policemen were hunting them down as subversives. During the many raids on nationalists Ngo Dinh Diem managed to escape arrest and took refuge with the Japanese authorities, who viewed him as one of the best potential candidates to head a pro-Japanese government in the future.

By the end of August 1944, with the liberation of Paris and a new provisional French government headed by General de Gaulle, the Japanese occupiers were beginning to show signs of major concern. Some Gaullist agents attempted to infiltrate Indochina from China but were arrested by the Vichy police. Admiral Decoux was completely cut off from any regular communications with France once the Vichy government ceased to exist and he governed through a special law giving him full emergency powers to preserve French interests in the colony. After having been rebuffed by General de Gaulle in a failed attempt to change sides, Decoux pursued his policy of strict neutrality while still being considered nothing more than a Japanese collaborator. De Gaulle's plan was to liberate Indochina from Japanese occupation and reestablish French sovereignty, as he had written in a September 1943 memorandum addressed to Churchill, Roosevelt, and Stalin.

The American Position on Indochina

While a liberated France was celebrating the beginnings of renewal, President Roosevelt remained committed to ending colonialism. Parallel to winning the war, FDR also wanted to accelerate the opening of world markets to free trade, thereby helping American exports. A key issue debated with the British at the Atlantic Conference of August 1941 concerned the "Imperial Preference," or in its French equivalent, the "Colonial Pact," a form of protectionism that made it impossible for the United States to trade directly with individual countries that were part of the British or French Empires. FDR and Cordell Hull wanted to have economic access to those lucrative markets. With the Atlantic Charter Roosevelt wanted the colonial powers to remove all trade barriers and accept a trusteeship system that was to become the cornerstone of the future United Nations. The idea was to grant independence in orderly stages to all European overseas possessions and transition that process through the tutelage of either the UN or even carried out by the colonial power. It was an improved version of the League of Nations mandates which FDR thought had failed after the Treaty of Versailles and amounted to a new form of colonialism, mainly in Palestine, Lebanon, and Syria. In Roosevelt's view a gradual and progressive disengagement over several decades through the mechanism of UN "trusteeship" would succeed best.[10] Full independence was to be announced as the ultimate goal by the colonial powers, but FDR was realistic enough to understand that most colonies would need a long transition period to achieve full independence. What he didn't factor in were the high expectations created by many American statements, including the Atlantic Charter and the potential use of violence by extremists to take advantage of the expected freedom. The high expectations of the colonized populations did eventually turn to violence when they realized independence was not about to be granted, but it appears that FDR was perhaps too confident that those impulses would be preempted by his formula.

Anti-colonialism was a key component of the American position and it directly targeted Great Britain, still viewed as the quintessential colonial power that the young United States had heroically expelled during the War of Independence. It was almost an article of faith for Americans to decry the exploitation and oppression they saw in European imperialism, omitting some of the darker pages of American expansion in the Philippines, the wholesale forced importation of African slaves to the Americas, Indian removal in the American West, or the Chinese Exclusion Act of the 1890s. Those negative episodes in American history were set aside and explained away by the "exceptionalism" of the United States and its greater contribution to world freedom. Because of the pressing issues relating to the war effort in 1942 and 1943, the anti-colonial positions and their accompanying plans were progressively relegated to postwar far behind the urgent business of defeating the Axis. Several joint Anglo-American commissions examined the issues of trusteeship for the islands in the Pacific where the discussions focused on reconciling the trusteeship principle and

---

10. See Wm. Roger Louis, *Imperialism At Bay* (New York: Oxford, 1974).

eventual independence with the need to ensure the future military security of the United States.

While the British knew and understood the American position, they did all they could to undermine it, at times even openly. On November 10, 1942, just three days after the landings in Morocco and Algeria, Churchill made a famous speech published the next day in the *Times* where he declared:

> We mean to hold our own. I have not become the King's First Minister in order to preside over the liquidation of the British Empire.

The British statesman was responding to the Republican challenger in the 1940 United States presidential race, Wendell Willkie, who made a number of public statements, and published a report and a book about his trip around the world in 1942. The book, entitled *One World,* contained his impressions and a number of foreign policy ideas that matched FDR's, thus inaugurating a new liberal Republican internationalism. In a radio speech on October 26, 1942, Willkie stated: "…there is no more place for imperialism within our own society than in the society of nations."[11]

By 1944-45 the fervent American anti-imperial idealism of early 1942 had progressively been eroded by the harshness of the war on all fronts. General George Marshall, Secretary of War Henry Stimson, Secretary of the Navy Frank Knox, and later James Forrestal, were all critical of the trusteeship principles and demanded instead the outright annexation of large areas that included most of the Pacific islands to ensure that no hostile Asian power would again gain the strategic advantage of being able to directly threaten the United States mainland. In the early stages of the Second World War a Japanese attack on the West Coast was expected and feared by the U.S. military. Roosevelt understood the point made by the military leadership but refused to revise his anti-annexationist views, insisting on trusteeships instead, knowing that the time limits on such arrangements could be extended and that independence would be probably half a generation away.

---

11. Wm. Roger Louis, op. cit., p. 199.

FDR, the master of a particularly effective form of realpolitik wrapped in Wilsonian idealism, had clearly not foreseen the dismantling of the colonial system in the precipitous and violent manner it took after the war. He was convinced that a lot more time would be available to implement his policies, possibly up to 25 years. No one can tell how he would have reacted to the situations that developed in Asia and North Africa had he survived to the end of his term. For example, Roosevelt met with the Sultan of Morocco, then a French protectorate, and his son Prince Moulay Hassan (later King Hassan II), who later reminisced about that memorable dinner:

> The confidential talk between the Sultan and President Roosevelt was very important. They were able to speak freely. Had Roosevelt not died so soon he would have played a major role in the emancipation of Morocco and of the entire African continent.[12]

Yet the basic danger of doing nothing was obvious to him, and taking the long view, he was fearful of creating enemies among the vast numbers of the colonial peoples. "1,100,000 potential enemies are dangerous," he said. And later on he added, talking to his assistant for colonial matters, Charles Taussig, of the State Department in March 1945:

> …French Indo-China and New Caledonia should be taken from France and put under a trusteeship. The President hesitated a moment and then said—well if we can get the proper pledge from France to assume for herself the obligations of a trustee, then I would agree to France retaining these colonies with the proviso that independence was the ultimate goal. I asked the President if he would settle for self-government. He said no. I asked him if he would settle for dominion status. He said no—it must be independence. He said that is to be the policy and you can quote me in the State Department.[13]

The State Department, as FDR implied with a touch of sarcasm in his response, continued to maintain a pro-French colonial viewpoint

---

12. Georges Vaucher, *Sous les cèdres d'Ifrane* (Paris: Julliard, 1963), p. 118
13. *Major Problems in American Foreign Policy, Volume II: Since 1914*, 4th edition, edited by Thomas G. Paterson and Dennis Merrill (Lexington, MA: D.C. Heath and Company, 1995), p. 190.

for a number of reasons but mainly to ensure economic and social stability, prevent violence in the short term, and above all protect the relationship with France. The career diplomats always played a moderating role in interpreting Roosevelt's more aggressive positions about dismantling colonial empires, which they saw as rooted in Wilsonian principles and the League of Nations Covenant.

As the war in Europe was predictably moving toward its conclusion, Asia became the focus of attention just before the collapse of the Japanese Empire and its vaunted "Greater East Asia Co-Prosperity Sphere." That well-publicized policy had elicited an enthusiastic response among various nationalist groups—especially in India, Indonesia, and Burma—enough for Britain, France, and the Netherlands to be concerned about the future of their colonies once they were liberated from the Japanese. Clearly General de Gaulle's plans included reestablishing French sovereignty over the French Empire and most urgently in Indochina. He made many major statements to that effect throughout the war. At his rather cold and acrimonious meeting with Roosevelt during the Casablanca Conference in January 1943, de Gaulle was reassured to hear FDR say:

> The only course of action that would save France, said the President, was for all of her loyal sons to unite to defeat the enemy, and that when the war was ended, victorious France could once again assert her political sovereignty which it had over her homeland and her empire.[14]

But perhaps the best view of the Roosevelt-De Gaulle relationship was expressed by Walter LaFeber: "To FDR's mind De Gaulle was too close to Churchill, too impervious to American wishes, and too egocentric and intelligent to be manipulated."[15] The issue from the start was de Gaulle's usefulness to the Allied cause and Roosevelt's view of France and her prospects in the postwar world. As soon as the Germans occupied France, a number of French politicians, civil servants, journalists, and businessmen arrived as refugees in the United States. Among them was the former secretary general of the Quai

---

14. U.S. Dept. of State, *FRUS The Conferences at Washington 1941-1942 and Casablanca 1943* (FRUS, Washington D.C., 1968), p. 696.
15. Walter LaFeber, "Roosevelt, Churchill and Indochina," in *American Historical Review*, December 1975 pp. 1277-1295.

d'Orsay and fervent Anglophile Alexis Léger, who had been cashiered by the government of Paul Reynaud during the battle of France on May 19, 1940. After a meeting with de Gaulle in London Léger refused to commit himself to the Free French and left for the United States. With excellent connections in Washington, where he was given a job at the Library of Congress, he was often consulted by Sumner Welles and began warning about de Gaulle's authoritarian and possibly anti-democratic tendencies. Léger described the general as a "Boulangiste," meaning a potential nationalistic dictator and most likely an unreliable adventurer.[16] Those warnings were relayed to FDR, who conceived in any case a negative predisposition toward the leader of the Free French. Those exaggerated views remained and pursued de Gaulle all the way to 1958, when he made his bid to return to power in the wake of the revolt of May 13, 1958, in Algeria. At his press conference he was asked if he would take full powers and rule as a dictator, to which he indignantly replied that he had, in the past (in 1944), restored both the republic and democracy.[17]

Restoring France as a World Power

To bring France's world image, power, and prestige at liberation in 1944 back to what it was and better before the war remained de Gaulle's main objective: that policy of *grandeur* would always be his. Reestablishing sovereignty in the colonies was a necessary step in that direction even if the path to independence would later be accepted by France. Everyone in 1944-1945 was eager to erase the shame of collaboration and reassert France's position around the world. Every political party, including the communists, subscribed enthusiastically to such a policy at the time as a wind of proud nationalism swept up the French people at every level.

---

16. The dashing General Ernest Boulanger was the darling of the far right in France as a candidate to overthrow the Third Republic and restore the monarchy in 1889. The plot failed and Boulanger fled first to Brussels, then London. He later committed suicide in Brussels in 1891. The term "Boulangisme" refers to an authoritarian political movement led by a military officer intent on overthrowing the political regime in France.

17. Eric Roussel, *De Gaulle*, Vols. I and II (Paris: Gallimard, 2002); François Kersaudy, *De Gaulle et Roosevelt* (Paris: Perrin, 2006); Ted Morgan, *FDR* (New York: Simon and Shuster, 1986); Raoul Aglion, *Roosevelt and de Gaulle* (New York: Free Press, 1988); Georgette Elgey, *De Gaulle à Matignon 1958-1959* (Paris: Fayard, 2012).

To move ahead with plans to retake Indochina while fighting the Japanese, de Gaulle set up a military and covert operations mission at Kandy in Ceylon within Lord Mountbatten's Asia command. According to various accounts of what went on between the Free French and the Indochina Vichy officers, Admiral Decoux made several attempts to contact de Gaulle but never received a reply. When an emissary from de Gaulle was sent to Tonkin, contact was made with the head of the French army in Indochina, General Eugène Mordant. Finally, a fractious double-headed leadership consisting of Decoux and Mordant, whom de Gaulle had secretly appointed as his representative in Indochina, was supposed to come into being. The main objective was to counter the Japanese occupying army. French forces numbered 62,000, of which only 12,000 were Europeans, with indigenous troops being considered undertrained and possibly unreliable.

Beyond military operations de Gaulle was hoping, somewhat unrealistically, for a massive resistance to the Japanese by the Vietnamese and European populations joining together. The general had no experience of Indochina and knew little of the mindset of the local population toward the colonizer. Although the nationalists were already a force to be reckoned with, they remained splintered into small groups and parties. The Free French also sent Professor Paul Mus, a renowned scholar of Annamite culture and sociology, as an agent to organize the Vietnamese resistance, but his mission met with little success. The main actions were taken by small groups of Viet Minh guerrillas that attacked isolated French outposts. The French army had not yet identified those groups and only responded with modest mopping up operations.

A signal that changes in the Pacific war were in the offing came with the American victory in the Philippines in January 1945. At the same time British aircraft were bombing the Vietnamese coast on a regular basis and sank some forty Japanese ships near Saigon. Other key areas of Indochina were also subjected to bombing raids. The Japanese military concluded that these actions were the prelude to an invasion. In fact, Roosevelt and Churchill had agreed that there should be no distractions from the main objective of defeating the Japanese on the home islands. Indochina was to remain a sideshow. FDR summed up his worried perceptions about the French colonies while he was in Morocco right after the Casablanca Conference to American vice consul Kenneth Pendar: "The President's greatest concern was how in the future France, weakened by defeat, could possibly control her vast empire."[18]

The Japanese Coup of March 9, 1945

Japanese reinforcements were brought in from Burma and southern China to form the 38th Army. In February the military council in Tokyo decided to overthrow the surviving Vichy French administration. Japanese diplomats attending the meeting pleaded the case to keep the creation of independent states in Indochina in line with the pan-Asian policy. On March 9, 1945, the Japanese army issued an ultimatum and attacked all French garrisons and outposts. Many French soldiers were indiscriminately massacred throughout Indochina and in some cases managed to put up a stiff resistance before capitulating and being executed, often by decapitation. Captured French soldiers and officers were placed in concentration camps under awful conditions. Civilians were practically under house arrest and subjected to random brutality. The Japanese overthrow of the Vichy administration was a second deadly blow to France's prestige in Indochina and Asia, where loss of face is unpardonable and a sure sign of bad luck. Furthermore, the Japanese proclamation to the Indochinese people justified the action by appealing to Asian solidarity: "The Japanese government declares that it shall never cease, per the content of the Common Declaration of Greater East Asia, to fully support the aspirations to independence of the Indochinese people who have been oppressed for so long until today…"[19]

All three nominal rulers of Annam, Cambodia, and Laos declared the various treaties establishing the French protectorates to be null and void. Emperor Bao Dai then proclaimed the independence of Vietnam on March 11 and offered the premiership to Ngo Dinh Diem, who refused it. Trang Trong Kim then became prime minister with a cabinet of Dai Viet Party pro-Japanese ministers. Kim was a notable in

---

18. Kenneth Pendar, *Adventure in Diplomacy* (London: Cassell, 1966), p. 149.
19. Philippe Franchini, *Les Guerres d'Indochine*, vol. I (Paris: Pygmalion, 1988).

the old tradition and had belonged to the Hanoi Confucius Masonic Lodge, which included French and Vietnamese before the Vichy laws declared freemasonry illegal. The Kim government promptly dismissed all French administrators and imposed the "quoc ngu" script, replacing French as the official language. French nationals and mixed race Eurasians were forced to live in segregated areas, such as the Cité Hérault in Saigon, where they were unprotected and systematically terrorized and subjected to humiliation and beatings for months. On August 7, just before Japan's surrender, the Kim government resigned in the wake of the atomic bombing of Hiroshima the day before.

The various nationalist factions in Indochina attracted the attention of American OSS units operating in southern China under Generals Claire Chennault and Albert Wedemeyer, both outspoken about their anti-colonialist sentiments.[20] The OSS mission was to help Indochinese nationalists rise up and fight the Japanese forces, rescue allied flyers, prevent a French return and encourage independence. The confusion created by the Japanese army coup of March 9 prompted American commanders in China and OSS officers to step up those operations and prevent French colonial administrators and military forces from returning to the colony and resuming their previous positions. The initiatives of several low-level OSS officers, such as Lieutenant Colonel A. Peter Dewey in Saigon and Captain Archimedes Patti in Tonkin, were recommending American support for the Viet Minh and Ho Chi Minh in his quest for the immediate independence of Vietnam. The OSS was hoping to secure Viet Minh help for guerrilla actions against the Japanese.[21] Ho Chi Minh had already offered his services to the OSS in Kunming in February 1945 but any fighting the Viet Minh actually undertook against the Japanese was minimal and the tiny OSS missions in Saigon and Tonkin (the "Deer" group) accomplished very

---

20. See Albert Wedemeyer, *Wedemeyer Reports!* (New York: H. Holt, 1958), which gives a vivid account of his meeting with an exhausted FDR in March 1945, where the French Indochina issue was discussed in the context of anti-colonial policy, pp. 340-41.

21. D. R. Bartholomew-Feis, *The OSS and Ho Chi Minh, Unexpected Allies in the War Against Japan* (Lawrence: Kansas UP, 2006). "Many in the OSS believed they were acting on the wishes of President Franklin Roosevelt, who was on record as opposing French colonialism...," p. 7. The author fails to explain the vacillations of FDR's anti-colonialist policies in 1945 and the increasing hesitations, if not opposition of State Department personnel to counter a return of French rule. Patti and other OSS officers were favorably impressed by the fervor displayed by Ho Chi Minh and Vo Nguyen Giap believing that they were genuine nationalists seeking independence and eager to fight the Japanese rather than intent on creating a "pure" Marxist Leninist dictatorship.

little apart from obstructing the French return in the extremely short time they were operational and showing their support to Ho Chi Minh's declaration of independence.[22] Dewey arrived in Saigon with his team on September 4, 1945, and was almost immediately declared *persona non grata* by British general Douglas Gracey because of his activities and contacts with the Viet Minh. Ordered to leave Indochina, Dewey was killed—accidentally it appears—on September 26 in an ambush near Tan Son Nhut airport in Saigon as he was about to leave. The attack was apparently set up by Viet Minh guerrillas in the midst of the general chaos gripping the city. He was probably mistaken for a French officer because he didn't display the American flag on his Jeep and cried out in French to the Viet Minh guerrillas manning the roadblock. Press reports in the United States focused on Dewey because he was the son of a congressman and a distant relation to New York governor Thomas E. Dewey, rather than on the situation in Saigon and Indochina that was considered a backwater in the Pacific War.

FDR and Churchill had finally agreed to recognize the French Provisional Government in October 1944, thereby implying that they accepted the stated French goal of reestablishing its colonial empire in its entirety. Yet, as late as January 1, 1945, the president was adamant about avoiding any action that would encourage or help France return to Indochina but at the same time he also wanted to keep the whole issue at bay and postpone a definite policy:

> I still do not want to get mixed up in any Indochina decision. It is a matter for post-war. By the same token, I do not want to get mixed up in any military effort toward the liberation of Indochina from the Japanese… action at this time is premature.[23]

The Japanese coup forced a radical change in the American attitude and Roosevelt was compelled to adjust his own well-publicized policy of keeping the French out of Indochina. A meeting between

---

22. The Patti mission was also very limited, lasting about one month, since the objectives of rescuing American and British flyers and fighting a guerrilla war against the Japanese had become moot with the surrender. Keeping the French out of Indochina appeared to be a secondary objective having little to do with ending the war. See Richard Harris Smith, *OSS* (Guilford: Lyons Press, 2005), pp. 295-330.
23. U.S. Dept. of State, FRUS *Diplomatic papers, 1945. The British Commonwealth, the Far East, Volume VI (1945)* (FRUS, Washington D.C., 1968), p. 293.

U.S. ambassador Jefferson Caffrey and General de Gaulle on March 13, just four days after the Japanese action in Indochina, took a dramatic turn:

> As I told Mr. [Harry] Hopkins when he was here, we do not understand your policy.[24] What are you driving at! Do you want us to become, for example, one of the federated states under Russian aegis? The Russians are advancing apace as you well know. When Germany falls they will be upon us. If the public here comes to realize that you are against us in Indochina there will be terrific disappointment and nobody knows to what that will lead. We do not want to become Communist; we do not want to fall into the Russian orbit, but I hope that you do not push us into it.[25]

FDR read Caffrey's report on March 16, probably in the presence of Admiral Leahy, and was moved by de Gaulle's remarks because they clearly indicated a potentially catastrophic break in the French Provisional Government's policies toward the United States. Even though France was weak and devastated by four years of Nazi occupation, the entire Western alliance could be placed in serious jeopardy, gravely endangering the precarious balance that existed in Western Europe. Within two days FDR decided what amounted to a drastic change in his policy and ordered that help be provided to the beleaguered French troops stranded in the jungles of Indochina.[26]

---

24. Robert Sherwood, *Roosevelt and Hopkins. An Intimate History* (New York: Enigma Books, 2008). Reprint of the original edition 1948-1950; see p. 659. The meeting with de Gaulle took place on January 29, 1945, while the Yalta conference was being convened. France had been conspicuously excluded from that key meeting much to de Gaulle's disappointment. Also see U.S. Dept. of State Foreign Relations of the United States, *Diplomatic Papers, 1945. The British Commonwealth, the Far East, Volume VI (1945)* (FRUS, Washington D.C., 1968), p. 300.

25. U.S. Dept. of State Foreign Relations of the United States, *Diplomatic Papers, 1945. The British Commonwealth, the Far East, Volume VI (1945)* (FRUS, Washington, D.C., 1968), p. 300

26. As Admiral Leahy notes in his memoirs: "...we did attempt to give a helping hand to the French resistance groups in Indochina. Vice Admiral Fenard called me on March 18 to say that planes from our 14th Air Force in China were loaded with relief supplies for the underground but could not start without authority from Washington. I immediately contacted General Hardy and told him of the President's agreement that American aid to the Indochina resistance groups might be given provided it involved no interference with our operations against Japan." Admiral William D. Leahy, *I Was There* (New York: McGraw Hill, 1950) pp. 338-339. Leahy had convinced FDR to relent and authorize help for the French. Following Harry Hopkins' illness right after the Yalta Conference, Leahy was the closest advisor and confidant to the president, who was himself greatly diminished because of his health. See Charles Bohlen, *Witness to History 1929-1969* (New York: W. W. Norton, 1973) and Walter Borneman, *The Admirals* (Boston: Little, Brown, 2012), who states that Leahy was then the "unquestioned chief counselor and trusted confidant on *all* matters."

De Gaulle's exasperation about delays in parachuting supplies is palpable in a further meeting with Ambassador Caffrey on March 24:

> General de Gaulle said to me as we were leaving: "It seems clear now that your Government does not want to help our troops in Indochina. Nothing has yet been dropped to them by parachute." I spoke of the distances and he said: "No, that is not the question; the question is one of policy I assume.[27]

On that same day, March 24, the French provisional government issued a key declaration on Indochina, stating that it was France's objective to liberate the colony from Japanese occupation, include it in an association of federated states, and improve conditions for the Indochinese people within the French Union.[28] The declaration was mostly the work of Léon Pignon, a high-level colonial civil servant who would later be appointed high commissioner in Indochina.[29] His brief in compiling the document was to remain vague on the details of the key issues and offer a broadly defined "freedom" within the French Union without mentioning the word "independence." The declaration came as a disappointment to the Indochinese nationalists, who were expecting a firm commitment from France granting full independence. De Gaulle for his part was interpreting the ultra-nationalistic mood of the French people at the time in his attempt to reestablish sovereignty and French presence over the colonies.[30]

Roosevelt and Churchill were set on the strategy to end the war in Asia by concentrating all military efforts on the final push to defeat

---

27. FRUS, *Volume VI (1945) cit.,* p. 302.

28. The *Union Française* had been announced at the Brazzaville Conference on colonial issues in 1944 and was viewed as a major liberalization effort by de Gaulle of the French colonial empire, but didn't promise outright independence.

29. Léon Pignon (1908-1976), a graduate of the École Coloniale, had studied law and become a colonial administrator. He joined the Free French in Algiers where he was appointed director of the Indochina section of the ministry of the colonies and later joined the Sainteny mission to Hanoi. Pignon supported negotiations with Ho Chi Minh and was also close to Admiral d'Argenlieu. He was instrumental in setting up Emperor Bao Dai in 1948 as a counter to Ho Chi Minh and served as High Commissioner (1948-1950) until he was replaced by General de Lattre de Tassigny.

30. On May 8, 1945, the events in Sétif, a small town in eastern Algeria, where 147 French colons were killed in a nationalist uprising, prompted brutal and traumatic reprisals by the French army with an estimated 5000 to 15000 Algerians killed. De Gaulle commented during a cabinet meeting that this was no time "to let Algeria slip through our fingers." His thinking on colonial issues would change in the 1950s, especially in the wake of Dien Bien Phu. But in all instances de Gaulle remained closely in tune with French public opinion at large, modifying his position slowly. By temperament and experience, he only served very briefly in Syria: he was not a colonial army officer but oriented toward fighting Germany on France's eastern borders, as most St Cyr graduates of his generation.

Japan and avoid diverting forces to a secondary theater of operations, such as Indochina. While the concentration of Japanese forces was heavy—there were over 75,000 men in Cochinchina and the Saigon area alone and 130,000 in the whole colony—they remained at the periphery of the main Allied offensive against Japan and posed no direct threat to that campaign. However, FDR's comment that Indochina was a "matter for post-war" also confirms his longer term decision to prevent France from returning to its former colony. The reasons included the perceived strategic importance of Indochina to the United States for the future military and communications control of Southeast Asia, access to vital raw materials such as rubber and oil, and the role the U.S. expected to play in Asia after the war. Roosevelt's well publicized but suddenly de-emphasized anti-colonial policy was also a major factor.[31]

FDR approved minor tactical assistance to the beleaguered French army units through parachute drops following de Gaulle's threatening outbursts. In spite of many pre-war conversations FDR had with Sumner Welles and other foreign policy advisors where he regularly vented his frustrations about French parliamentary deadlocks that produced chronic governmental instability, he was counting on France to put up a strong fight in case of war with Germany and repeat its strong performance of the First World War. As most observers, Roosevelt was stunned at the sudden collapse of the French army in 1940. In his vision of post-war Europe France, because of her inherent weakness, was destined to play an important but minor role that entailed abandoning her colonial empire through the trusteeship formula. The idea of an independent Indochina appears so firmly anchored in Roosevelt's mind that many biographers and historians have speculated on its origins.[32] Perhaps the proposals voiced in 1920 after the First World War by former governor general and minister of the colonies Albert Sarraut to attract massive American investments to

---

31. FRUS, *Volume VI (1945)*, cit., p. 312.
32. Sumner Welles noted to his staff in the Postwar planning group at the State Department: "The truth concerning Indo-China is that in the hundred years the French have had it, very little has been done for the benefit of the dependent peoples in that area, and according to the present Chinese government the people there are far better fitted to obtain their independence that the people of any other protected area in the Far East." in Christopher D. O'Sullivan, *Sumner Welles, Postwar Planning and the Quest for a New Order, 1937-1943* (New York: Columbia, 2003), p. 163. The remark fits in almost to the word with FDR's thinking and his private statements seeking to make Indochina a "showcase" of decolonization in Asia.

build Indochina's infrastructure or to trade portions of colonial territory to erase the huge war debt to the United States had impressed FDR at the time and may have awakened his interest in the area.[33]

The pressure of events in Indochina and Europe, as well as the insistent recommendations of the State Department and possibly Admiral Leahy, had persuaded FDR to modify his policy, if not alter it. The change had started in 1944 with pressure coming from the diplomats against any immediate U.S. demands for decolonization.[34] In fact, when Roosevelt met with de Gaulle in Washington in July 1944 he agreed to not prevent France's return to Indochina.[35] In private conversations FDR would reiterate his misgivings about the French colonial situation but in fact he implicitly followed the State Department's "Europe first" position.

When Roosevelt died on April 12, 1945, modest assistance was finally reaching the French and the tension with de Gaulle subsided. Roosevelt's basic policies were still being officially promoted by the United States once Harry Truman took office and the new president's first statements promised to carry on the work done by his predecessor. This presumably included Indochina although the area was not given much emphasis compared to the other momentous issues facing the Allies and the United States. At the San Francisco United Nations conference the subject came up in conversation between French foreign minister Georges Bidault and Secretary of State Edward R. Stettinius:

> ...although the French Government interpreted Mr. Welles' statement of 1942 concerning the restoration of French sovereignty over the French Empire as including Indochina, the American press continued to imply that a special status will be reserved for this colonial area. The Secretary made it clear to Bidault that the record was entirely innocent of any official statement of this government questioning, even by implication, French sovereignty over Indochina but that certain elements of Ameri-

---

33. Franchini, op. cit., p. 123.

34. George Herring, *America's Longest War. The United States and Vietnam 1950–1975* (New York: McGraw-Hill, 2002).

35. "After his meeting with Roosevelt in July 1944 de Gaulle stated that Roosevelt would not bar the way to Indochina. When the United States officially recognized the provisional government of de Gaulle in October 1944 it signified among other things the waning of Roosevelt's hopes for international trusteeship in the French colonies." Wm. Roger Louis, *Imperialism at Bay* (New York: Oxford, 1974), p. 41.

can public opinion condemned French policies and practices in Indo-china.[36]

The use of the word "innocent" is curious in this context and could indicate a very defensive reaction on the part of Stettinius and the State Department to accusations of malicious neglect or even betrayal coming from the French provisional government. The main-stream American press, including all of Henry Luce's publications, remained adamant in its opposition to colonial possessions by the European powers.

Yet a broad consensus existed in France in 1945 to reclaim sovereignty over the colonial empire as a necessary step toward reversing the shame of the 1940 defeat and recapturing France's position as a world power. The French Communist Party, which was part of the French Provisional Government, was explicit regarding Indochina in its traditional mouthpiece, the daily *L'Humanité*:

> France must make an effort to dispatch forces to the Far East in order to collaborate with the Allies and the peoples of Indochina to free that territory for the greater good of Franco-Indochinese relations.[37]

Other statements from the same sources were even more explicit about keeping Indochina firmly within the French colonial posses-sions.

Japan Surrenders: August 15, 1945

The Japanese surrender elicited the following statement from General de Gaulle on August 24, 1945: "France's position is rather simple. France intends to reestablish its sovereignty over Indochina"—correctly reflecting the desire of French public opinion at the time.

Since March 9 Indochina was plunged into a vacuum: the Japanese had imprisoned almost all the old French colonial administrators and military in prison camps. The Viet Minh took advantage of the sudden

---

36. FRUS, *Volume VI (1945)*, cit., p. 312.

37. *L'Humanité*, April 13, 1945. See Philippe Franchini, *Les mensonges de la guerre d'Indochine* (Paris: Perrin, 2005). French communists would be firmly on the colonialist side in restoring order in Algeria during the Sétif revolt of May 8, 1945, and quickly blamed those troubles on stay-behind pro-Nazi Algerian nationalists.

disappearance of French police and civil servants to further terrorize the old mandarin administrators, pro-French Vietnamese middle class and Eurasians who were the object of special hatred. Assassinations and terror became routine while Europeans were being indiscriminately brutalized. In fact, the actions taken in Cochinchina by nationalist and Viet Minh groups amounted to a racially inspired insurrection with horrific murders and beatings by roving bands of all types, including gangsters posing as freedom fighters. The Viet Minh, however, had a plan and made several attempts to manipulate the situation to their advantage.

The Potsdam conference, to which France was not invited, causing further bitterness toward the United States, was held in Berlin from July 17 to August 2, 1945. A decision was reached to divide Indochina into two occupation zones along a line arbitrarily set at the sixteenth parallel, similar to the two Korean zones of occupation. Northern Laos and Tonkin would be occupied by the Chinese army while the British were to take over in southern Laos, Cambodia, southern Annam, and Cochinchina. All Japanese forces, 139,000 strong, were to surrender. The end of the war came much faster than expected as the two atomic bombs were dropped on Hiroshima and Nagasaki, followed by Emperor Hirohito's announcement on August 15 that Japan would lay down its arms.

The formal ceremony took place on September 2 on the deck of the USS *Missouri*. General Philippe Leclerc signed for France and was told by General Douglas MacArthur as they were standing side by side on the deck of the battleship that France should quickly dispatch as many troops as possible to Indochina.[38] On that same day Ho Chi Minh was proclaiming the independence of the Democratic Republic of Vietnam in Hanoi in the presence of a few American officers. The proclamation that Ho read was considered to be violently anti-French

---

38. Philippe de Hauteclocque, *aka* Leclerc (1902-1947), was a graduate of St Cyr, and came from a family with a long military tradition; he served in World War II and joined the Free French Forces of General de Gaulle. He took on the pseudonym "Leclerc" and fought in Chad, Tunisia, and then landed with the 2nd Armored Division in Normandy before entering Paris on August 25, 1944. De Gaulle appointed him as commander of the French Expeditionary Forces in the Far East. Leclerc signed the Japanese surrender on behalf of France on September 2, 1945, in Tokyo Bay. After routing the Viet Minh in Cochinchina he attempted negotiations with Ho Chi Minh, for which he was bitterly criticized by Adm. D'Argenlieu. Leclerc refused the appointment as High Commissioner to Indochina and was killed in a plane crash in Algeria. He was posthumously given the rank of Marshal of France.

and stated among other things: "We…declare that we no longer have any connection to imperialist France." He had also used words from the American Declaration of Independence that Capt. Archimedes Patti recited to him from memory and made sure the OSS officers in uniform were conspicuously visible to the crowds and the photo-journalists.

In Paris, the sudden end of the war in Europe and Asia carried the expected thirst for retribution after four years of German occupation. The trials of the major French collaborators were taking place in an angry atmosphere, including those of Marshal Pétain and Pierre Laval, while many lower level collaborators known to have been pro-German were being summarily executed. The need to return the country to peacetime normalcy and a wave of proud nationalism prompted de Gaulle to reassert French sovereignty everywhere in an attempt to erase the shame of defeat and collaboration. He appointed General Leclerc to head the army in Indochina with fresh troops outfitted with American equipment and weapons that were being painstakingly assembled at various points, including Madagascar. A dearth of shipping delayed the arrival of troops and supplies by weeks and months. Leclerc was to report to the civilian leader, the new High Commissioner Admiral Thierry d'Argenlieu, whose position was equivalent to the old governor general.[39] Both appointments indicated that de Gaulle attached the greatest importance to Indochina by selecting two of his earliest and most unconditionally faithful followers. With d'Argenlieu in particular de Gaulle knew that "…his liberal policy would be applied by a man who wouldn't compromise on maintaining French presence."[40]

In addition to those appointments de Gaulle also dispatched more representatives: Jean Cédile, a colonial administrator who was sent to Cochinchina; Pierre Messmer went to Tonkin, but was held prisoner

---

39. Georges Thierry d'Argenlieu (1889-1964) was a naval officer who had served in North Africa and Morocco under Lyautey in 1912 and later in the First World War. As a deeply devout Catholic he was ordained as a Carmelite monk under the name of Father Louis de la Trinité. Returning to the navy in 1939 he was among the first to join de Gaulle in 1940 and rose to the rank of admiral of the Free French navy. He entered Paris at de Gaulle's side on August 25, 1944. Arriving in Saigon in October 1945 he is often wrongly accused of starting the Indochina war by ordering the naval bombardment of Haiphong on November 25, 1946, when he was actually in France at the time. D'Argenlieu was determined nevertheless to wipe out the Viet Minh through military action. He was replaced by Emile Bollaert in 1947.
40. Yves Gras, *Histoire de la guerre d'Indochine* (Paris: Plon, 1979), p. 60

by the Viet Minh; and Jean Sainteny finally managed to reach Hanoi by accompanying the OSS Patti mission.

The Truman administration remained committed to Roosevelt's decolonization policy but the issue was at the bottom of the list of the problems facing the United States. The president and his administration were focused on urgent domestic problems, Europe's future and relations with the Soviet Union rather than on Indochina in 1945-1947. The most urgent matter was the massive demobilization of 12 million Americans in uniform and their seamless reintegration into civilian life without creating a severe recession. The administration, and mainly the War Department, were successful in fulfilling that task and avoided the economic nightmare that many were expecting. Truman's ambition was to be a domestic president who would faithfully carry out the New Deal and remained aware of his lack of experience in foreign affairs. Roosevelt conducted foreign policy in a very personal manner, relying on his immediate entourage, which was mostly external to the state department until 1944-45 while many of his original confidants were no longer close to the president.[41] During the 1944 campaign and later on, FDR didn't reveal the existence of the Manhattan Project and the potential destructive effect of the atomic bomb to his vice president. But, in fairness, as of April 12, 1945, no one could determine exactly when the bomb would be ready and whether or not it would work at all. The American military leadership reasonably expected to be at war against the Japanese for at least one more year and was ready to incur over one million casualties in any invasion of the Japanese home islands. The State Department had also been largely isolated from major policy decisions, particularly since the resignation of Sumner Welles in August 1943, which created a vacuum filled by professional diplomats, first with FDR and later under the new president. The professionals at State were focused on Western Europe, with most other areas remaining secondary, and Indochina, like Korea, ranking lower than Japan and China at that point.

De Gaulle had several options to reassert French presence in Indochina. One of them involved Prince Vinh San, the former emperor Duy Tan who had been deposed at age 16 during the First World War

---

41. See Frank Costigliola, *Roosevelt's Lost Alliances* (Princeton: Princeton UP, 2011).

by French colonial administrators and shipped off with his family into exile on the island of La Réunion near Madagascar. Contrary to his father, the former emperor Thanh Thai, Prince Vinh San had accepted French culture and had always refused to abdicate, which gave him a legitimate claim to the throne that had devolved to his cousin Bao Dai. As an enthusiastic ham radio operator, the prince was probably the only person in the Indian Ocean to have heard de Gaulle's June 18, 1940, appeal on the BBC. He immediately joined the Free French navy and was assigned as a radio operator on board ship. In August 1945 Vinh San broadcast a speech from Madagascar calling for the independence of Vietnam within the French Union in the spirit of de Gaulle's Brazzaville program.

The idea had already been made public in an article that Vinh San published in the daily *Combat* on July 16, 1945. But there was opposition on the part of functionaries at the ministry of the colonies and within the French army to any declaration of future independence. De Gaulle then appointed the prince to the staff of Admiral d'Argenlieu, who was about to take over as high commissioner in Indochina. In December 1945 Prince Vinh San met with General de Gaulle in Paris and agreed to reclaim the throne as Emperor of Annam. It was a scenario that could succeed since Bao Dai had acquiesced to the Japanese occupation and was still considered an Axis collaborator at that point. Prince Vinh San's legitimacy was unimpeachable and de Gaulle professed admiration and keen interest in the man. The prince told a friend that de Gaulle wanted to put him back on the throne and was planning to travel to Indochina in early March 1946 to sign formal agreements between France and Vietnam. Unfortunately Vinh San's plane crashed on December 26 in the jungle of Oubangui Chari while flying to Saigon, killing everyone on board. In his memoirs de Gaulle felt that this untimely loss was indeed a stroke of bad luck for Vietnam and for France.

The issue of de Gaulle's long term intentions for Indochina and the other colonies is subject to debate. While the Brazzaville declaration appeared liberal in granting a measure of autonomy and representation to the colonial empire, de Gaulle's main goal in 1944-45 was to first reestablish France's sovereignty over all the territories and place them firmly under French control. De Gaulle's subsequent move toward decolonization in Algeria in 1959-1962 represented a radical change from his previous position of restoring France's colonial power.[42] His view remained that independence was to be awarded by France, and not as a form of bounty that nationalists would be allowed to conquer through violence.

France's Return to Indochina

A dramatic turn of events at the start of 1946 was to change France's political picture: on January 20, General de Gaulle resigned abruptly as president of the French provisional government, rejecting the proposed draft of the new constitution being discussed because it would give too much importance to the political parties and create a weak executive branch. The general saw it as a carbon copy of the Third Republic, a party-dominated regime that proved ineffectual during the Second World War. In the wake of de Gaulle's resignation three provisional presidents would quickly follow one another: Felix Gouin, a socialist from January to June; then Foreign Minister and MRP leader Georges Bidault from June to December 1946; and finally Socialist party senior statesman Léon Blum, the former leader of the Popular Front of 1936, from December to January 1947, when the provisional government was replaced by the Fourth Republic. New elections on June 2 placed the MRP (Mouvement Républicain Populaire) party slightly ahead of the communists. A new constitutional vote approving the constitution of the Fourth Republic took place on October 27, 1946.

Bidault was one of the key political figures of the new regime, with his prestige as a leader of the resistance to the Nazis giving him a hold on the MRP party, especially on colonial and Indochinese policy.[43] The

---

42. In 1945 de Gaulle as president of the provisional government invited the Sultan of Morocco and the Bey of Tunis to Paris. He told the Sultan: "When at Anfa, President Roosevelt promised Your Majesty a marvelous and immediate independence. What was he offering other than dollars and a spot as one of his client states?" The Sultan politely concurred: "...my country's progress must take place with France's help." Charles De Gaulle, *Mémoires de Guerre, Le Salut Vol. III* (Paris: Plon, 1959) pp. 262-263.

43. Georges Bidault (1899-1983) was an *agrégé* (PhD) professor of history, active in Catholic youth organizations before World War II and a political columnist in the daily *L'Aube*. He was among a handful of editorial writers to oppose the Munich Agreements in October 1938. During the occupation he joined the resistance, rising to the top leadership when he was appointed to replace Jean Moulin, who had been executed by the Gestapo. An ardent anti-fascist and a sincere French patriot, he entered Paris with de Gaulle in August 1944 and was appointed foreign minister of the provisional government. Bidault was one

MRP was a centrist Christian Democratic Party that felt duty bound to protect the millions of Vietnamese Catholics threatened by the Viet Minh. For the entire period from 1946 to 1954 the politicians involved with Indochina were almost exclusively members of the MRP. Communist leader Maurice Thorez, who was serving as one of two vice presidents of the provisional government and who played an important role in the government during the brief pre-Cold War period, also displayed the same nationalist and colonialist ideals as his colleagues. Under orders from Stalin, Thorez would later switch positions once the communists left the government in May 1947. Between them the MRP and the Communist party had over fifty percent of the votes in the chamber of deputies at that time. Ho Chi Minh was understandably anxious to reach an agreement as quickly as possible, since his party comrade Thorez, whom he knew from his Moscow days at the Comintern, was still at the top of the Paris government pyramid.

In Saigon, where he arrived in October 1945, Admiral d'Argenlieu was immediately intent on seeking retribution against his fellow Frenchmen who had chosen to remain loyal to Admiral Decoux and Vichy. The mood in France was one of revenge, in particular during the trial Marshal Pétain and the execution of Pierre Laval, both of them the focus of public hatred for the Vichy policies. But in practical terms this narrow obsession to punish all collaborators deprived General Leclerc of 5,000 experienced French officers and soldiers held in prison camps where the Japanese had kept them and about to be returned to France to stand trial as traitors. Most of them would be acquitted a short time later. The obsession with punishment elicited Leclerc's remark that d'Argenlieu was a modern-day Torquemada, with his tendency to see every problem in Manichean terms. The two men did not get along. The Admiral's main shortcoming was that he had no

---

of the founders of the MRP and served as president of the provisional government in 1945, then as foreign minister almost continuously from 1944 to 1954 with a few interruptions, twice prime minister. He was also responsible for the creation of the French Union that he had personally included in the constitution of the Fourth Republic in 1946. More left of center in domestic affairs he was considered the architect of the new colonial policy and resisted the idea of independence, especially in the context of the Cold War. A fervent anti-communist, Bidault's career was irreparably damaged by the defeat at Dien Bien Phu, which signaled his last government position. He supported French Algeria and opposed de Gaulle's plans for decolonization, even joining the extreme wing of the anti-de Gaulle movement of the OAS in 1966. He went into exile in Brazil until he was pardoned and returned to France in 1968, but no longer played a significant role.

experience of Indochina and relied on his immediate staff for direction. He would also bitterly criticize Leclerc for attempting to reach an agreement with the Viet Minh and trusting Ho Chi Minh instead of making war on him, but as we shall see further, this was far from being a legitimate complaint.

The French divisions that Leclerc desperately needed were arriving piecemeal from various parts of the French empire, thus limiting his plans to reoccupy the colony. Cochinchina was the first area to be quickly retaken, using small units of motorized cavalry and paratroopers. The area outside Saigon was systematically cleared of Viet Minh elements, often after heavy fighting. After those initial battles the Viet Minh, led in the south by the fanatical and cruel Nguyen Binh, vanished by going underground and started a campaign of terror against its Vietnamese opponents and using hit-and-run guerrilla tactics against French troops.

Terrorism also surfaced in Tonkin in October 1945: the mandarin intellectuals and Catholic leaders were being systematically killed, including Ngo Dinh Khoi, a brother of Ngo Dinh Diem, and other non-communist nationalists. But those Maoist revolutionary tactics failed to produce the expected results, mainly because of the catastrophic economic situation created by Ho Chi Minh's government when it decided to abolish all taxation and was left without revenues. With massive flooding and a poor harvest the DRV regime was barely hanging on, mainly thanks to Ho's mysterious psychological hold on the population of Tonkin. His charisma came from his carefully etched image as a martyr of colonialism and a disinterested, incorruptible leader: a pure and simple man who had chosen revolution for the love of his people. Such claims resonated with the peasantry of Tonkin and his thorough knowledge of Marxist-Leninist dialectics impressed the intellectuals.

The Chinese army, 150,000 strong, occupied Tonkin above the 16th parallel in accordance with the Potsdam decision. It promptly subjected the area to a rough form of occupation that included wholesale looting, speculation on the exchange rates of the Indochinese piastre, and the brutal harassment of the 22,000 French nationals who had just been freed from Japanese rule. French citizens were considered as so many hostages by both the Chinese and the Viet Minh. Ho Chi Minh called for general elections on January 6, 1946, which his coalition won by a stunning 96 percent. The result angered the anticommunist nationalists, who suspected massive fraud, and fighting broke out among various factions.

On October 6, 1945, General Raoul Salan was ordered to reestablish French sovereignty over Tonkin and cleverly managed to ease the Chinese back over the border, officially replacing them as the occupying force. General Leclerc was seeking an accommodation with Ho Chi Minh in negotiations that were to include all the players on the French side: Sainteny, Pignon, and d'Argenlieu. Ho was then mistakenly assuming that he would have the support of Maurice Thorez, but the French communists were also riding the patriotic and nationalist wave. Thorez made several statements, including a significant one to the head of the Cochinchina delegation to the French assembly: "The Communist party in no way wishes to be seen as the liquidator of the French position in Indochina."[44] In the atmosphere of patriotic fervor, the communists were not about to risk losing the largest slice of the electorate.

On March 6, 1946, Ho Chi Minh and General Leclerc reached an agreement: France recognized the Republic of Vietnam as a free state within the Indochinese Federation and the French Union. The three parts of Vietnam would be joined together after a popular vote. The Viet Minh agreed that the French army would replace the Chinese army of occupation. Finally, French forces were to evacuate Vietnam within five to ten years, a promise the Vietnamese viewed as being equivalent to full independence. During those negotiations Ho Chi Minh was also issuing secret orders to resume guerrilla actions and terrorism. French military intelligence was reading his messages and informed an outraged French high command.

Admiral d'Argenlieu agreed to meet with Ho Chi Minh on March 24 at a preliminary conference at the Bay of Halong as a prelude to a more detailed negotiation that the Viet Minh insisted on having in Paris. Ho was convinced that he could get what he wanted if only he could meet face to face with the top leaders of the French provisional

---

44. Gras, op. cit., p. 134.

government. D'Argenlieu grudgingly approved the Leclerc-Ho Chi Minh agreement but refused to consider any further concessions. Leclerc blamed the admiral for the failure of his policy of seeking accommodation but he also acknowledged that dealing with Ho Chi Minh was not a simple matter. The issue with Ho was clear: France had no intention of giving up its original colonial possession of Cochinchina, which included the Mekong delta and the city of Saigon. The Viet Minh on the other hand were adamant about the territorial integrity of Vietnam. This disagreement became the main reason for the war that followed. A second conference was held at Dalat on April 17 and an agreement appeared possible on most issues, except the nature of the federation and the autonomy of each state within it. Both parties were far apart on Cochinchina: the French insisted on a referendum vote since it was a colony. The conference ended on May 13 with the recommendation that the main issues were to be resolved in Paris.

Ho Chi Minh and Vo Nguyen Giap left for France on May 31 with the Vietnamese delegation accompanied by General Raoul Salan. Their flight was delayed several times and they reached Biarritz on June 12. Foreign Minister Bidault asked for a further delay because the French government, headed by the socialist Felix Gouin, had just resigned. New elections had given the MRP the edge but a new cabinet had not yet been formed. As he waited, Ho Chi Minh was taken on various sightseeing tours which he cleverly used to engage in very effective public relations. The French press created the image of an amiable and exotic old gentleman: the legend of "Uncle Ho" was born and would have a positive effect in the future. Within days his Marxist-Leninist intransigence was forgotten as he was suddenly transformed into a reasonable, ordinary middle-aged man.

Admiral d'Argenlieu agreed and encouraged the proclamation of the Republic of Cochinchina on June 1 in Saigon, the day after Ho Chi Minh's departure. This was seen as a direct provocation by the Viet Minh, tantamount to a declaration of war.

In France meanwhile, negotiations finally began on July 6 at Fontainebleau. It was clear to those close to the talks that if the Viet Minh didn't show some flexibility the conference would fail. France

"...couldn't go beyond internal autonomy without running the risk of harming the entire structure of the French Union. The Communist Party also agreed with that policy."[45] That risk would consistently be the deciding factor in avoiding the granting of independence to the colonies: once one territory achieved independence, the floodgates would be open and everyone else would demand the same treatment. Foreign examples attested to that kind of reality: the Philippines, Syria, Lebanon, and India were all poised to become independent, putting pressure on France. Finally, on September 13, after long interruptions, the Vietnamese delegation decided to return home: with no agreement on Cochinchina the interminable conference had failed. Ho Chi Minh wanted to avoid returning to Hanoi empty handed, so at a hurried meeting a *modus vivendi* was signed at the last minute with French minister of the colonies Marius Moutet. The document stated that both parties would "end all hostile acts and violence in Cochinchina as of October 30 and negotiations would resume in January 1947." The trip and its disastrous aftermath were the result of major diplomatic and political miscalculations by both sides.

The French government, absent General de Gaulle, gave the impression of being hopelessly weak, an image that was to remain unchanged until the dramatic collapse of the Fourth Republic in 1958. France never developed a coherent colonial plan once the decision to return and reclaim Indochina was made, except for de Gaulle's aborted attempt with Prince Vinh San. Ho Chi Minh was counting on the confusion and political paralysis of the provisional government to obtain the independence of Vietnam with the Viet Minh in charge almost by default. But Ho also miscalculated: he was trying to succeed without a conflict, and refused to accept an accommodation bowing to the pressure from the extremist wing of the Viet Minh leadership that believed it could prevail through violence. The question remains, however, whether or not Ho Chi Minh wasn't actually the greatest extremist of all.

The Indochina war was declared informally at Fontainebleau as Ho Chi Minh stated in an interview as he was leaving Paris.[46]

---

45. Gras, op. cit., p. 119.
46. David Schoenbrun, *As France Goes* (New York: Harper, 1957), pp. 231-235. Ho Chi Minh told Schoenbrun: "We have a weapon every bit as powerful as the modern canon: nationalism. [...] It will be a war

The First Indochina War Begins

Phase I: The Colonial War (1946–1949)

The Viet Minh went to war over Cochinchina: Giap secretly raised an army of 60,000, which included 12,000 guerrillas in the south. French military intelligence found out that the Viet Minh was preparing to attack the French army. While outwardly the Viet Minh affected a cordial and even pleasant attitude as Ho Chi Minh had accomplished so successfully in France, the plans were drawn for a surprise attack. Incidents began to multiply and were clearly the result of detailed preparation. General Leclerc left Indochina on July 18, and noted in his end of mission report how the Viet Minh could be described: "Like Janus that government has two faces."[47] He also sent a personal letter to Maurice Schumann, president of the MRP and a fellow veteran of the Free French:

> Who is Ho Chi Minh? It is important to not forget that he is a great enemy of France and that the goals he and his party have been striving to achieve for six months are to purely and simply usher us out the door. The date has changed but the idea remains. We have in our hands all the documents and telegrams we intercepted to prove this. Furthermore, the extension of the civil war and the endless murders of pro-French Annamites, all of them wanted and ORDERED by him, is also the obvious proof.[48]

Some historians have minimized the importance of Leclerc's letter, attempting to show that the general's words were atypical at the time. The fact remains that he did write it in confidence to a comrade-in-arms of his Free French days, who was also a powerful politician and that, on the contrary, it probably reflects his innermost thoughts at the time.

Cambodia and Laos were the other kingdoms in the Indochinese Union where a major conflict had been averted and agreements had been reached with their traditional rulers: France would protect them

---

between an elephant and a tiger [...] slowly the elephant will bleed to death. That will be the war of Indochina."
47. Gras, op. cit., p. 130.
48. Georgette Elgey, *La République des Illusions 1945-1951* (Paris: Fayard, 1965), pp. 161-162.

against the encroachments of Thailand, China, and an aggressive Vietnam under Ho Chi Minh. Both kingdoms were to remain loyal to the French throughout the Indochina War, with the exception of smaller armed rebel bands inspired by the Viet Minh.

The Incidents at Haiphong and Hanoi

Out of office, General de Gaulle continued to project a long shadow over French politics and Indochina while he remained in favor of a full colonial reestablishment, as he wrote to Admiral d'Argenlieu: "Should things go in the direction of cowardice and surrender, then you obviously could not be the one to undertake such a policy."[49]

On November 13, 1946, d'Argenlieu went to Paris, leaving General Valluy, his military and intelligence chief, in charge in Saigon. The admiral strongly opposed the "modus vivendi" signed by Marius Moutet and Ho Chi Minh, convinced that it would lead to the loss of Indochina. The Viet Minh on the other hand feared a sudden French "coup" against them, similar to the one undertaken by the Japanese in 1945.

On November 20, off Haiphong, a French naval boat stopped a Chinese junk loaded with smuggled gasoline. Viet Minh troops opened fire from the docks at the French boat, causing a wild panic in the streets of the city where unarmed French troops and civilians were being suddenly attacked. Colonel Pierre Louis Debès, the French military commander, reestablished order but other incidents were reported, including the deaths of several French soldiers and the wounding of others. Debès occupied the European quarter, since the Viet Minh was shooting indiscriminately at all French troops and civilians. Similar incidents were taking place in other locations of Annam and Tonkin, in particular at Lang Son, an outpost close to the Chinese border.

General Valluy assumed overall command of operations from Saigon. He no longer trusted any form of negotiations with the Viet Minh. As he wrote: "The time has come to impart a harsh lesson on those who have attacked us so treacherously…" On November 23 Debès opened fire on Viet Minh positions. He only had 2,500 men to control a city of 100,000, yet the French successfully pushed the Viet

---

49. Jacques Dalloz, *Georges Bidault. Biographie Politique* (Paris: L'Harmattan, 1992), p. 146.

Minh out of Haiphong. In the end 23 French soldiers were killed and 86 wounded, while Vietnamese losses were estimated from 300 to 6,000, the latter number appearing to be unquestionably exaggerated.

The Viet Minh was encouraging the population to leave the city of Hanoi, while the French were attempting to negotiate. Jean Sainteny was dispatched back to Hanoi on December 2, where he held meetings with Ho Chi Minh and Vo Nguyen Giap; both sides said emphatically that they did not want war. However, the population was rife with ominous rumors of events about to unfold. Giap was preparing his men and felt he could strike a decisive blow with his army of 25 to 30,000 strong facing only 13,000 French troops. Ho was calling for peace while Viet Minh soldiers and workers were quickly exiting Hanoi.

On December 19, at 8:04 p.m., in a move that could have come out of Leon Trotsky's technique of the coup d'état, the Viet Minh blew up the Hanoi electric power plant, cutting off all electricity to the urban center and its environs. Intense fighting broke out and the Pont Doumer was repeatedly damaged but saved from destruction by a French unit. The Viet Minh seized several buildings where 43 French civilians were murdered and 200 others taken as hostages. Sainteny himself was seriously wounded. On January 14 Colonel Debès decided to launch a major operation to take the city center where the Viet Minh were holding out. By January 17 the Viet Minh and most of the population had fled, leaving the wounded behind. At the end of February most of the other towns had returned to normal, including Hué, after a siege lasting 46 days. The French Expeditionary Corps had gained the initiative across Indochina with the enemy taking refuge in the area known as the Viet Bac in the upper Tonkin, across from the Chinese border. Yet, while enjoying complete superiority and facing a guerrilla type enemy, French forces were still not large enough to attain decisive victory.

On December 20 Ho Chi Minh changed his position and issued an appeal for national resistance: "May everyone fight colonialism to save the homeland!" and further, "On December 19 at 2000 hours they attacked Hanoi the capital of Vietnam." That statement has been taken at face value by historians as proof that the French were simply out to re-conquer Tonkin and therefore unleashed their attack. The facts show that this is only partially true: the French did intend to retake Indochina, but they also wanted to destroy what they considered was a violent communist movement in the Viet Minh. The stated policy was not simply to reestablish the colonial empire but to negotiate a reasonable solution with the non-communist nationalists—something that Ho Chi Minh feared and sought to prevent.

French Political Issues

On November 28, 1946, Georges Bidault resigned as president of the provisional government and Léon Blum, the venerable leader of the Socialist party, became president. The new government was formed only on December 12, and, in a familiar pattern, for two crucial weeks France was left completely rudderless. It was obvious to the Blum government that Admiral d'Argenlieu could no longer be in charge if the ultimate goal was to seek a negotiated settlement in Vietnam. Addressing the national assembly on December 23, Léon Blum expressed the dilemma that would haunt every subsequent French government dealing with decolonization: "We have been faced with the need to respond to violence… We must continue the task that was interrupted: a free Vietnam in an Indochinese Union associated with France. But above all peaceful order must be reestablished." The difficulty of having negotiations with revolutionary groups engaged in often cruel and brutal fighting would remain a constant issue during France's long process of decolonization.

A fact-finding mission consisting of Marius Moutet and General Leclerc was quickly dispatched to Indochina with the two men reaching separate but identical conclusions. Leclerc confirmed what he had written in his July letter to Maurice Schumann and was offered the job of replacing Admiral d'Argenlieu as high commissioner. After consulting with General de Gaulle, now officially retired but still very influential and even thought to be preparing a comeback, Leclerc turned down the offer, suggesting that a civilian would be best suited for the position.

The wheels of political change were turning: on January 16, 1947, the socialist Vincent Auriol was elected as the first president of the

Fourth Republic and he appointed another socialist, Paul Ramadier, to head the government that still included Maurice Thorez and the communists. In his acceptance speech the new prime minister spoke at length about Indochina, echoing Léon Blum: "This war was imposed on us, we never wanted it and we don't want it. We did all we could and made all reasonable concessions. We know it will resolve nothing. We shall end it as soon as order and security have been reestablished."[50] He also stated, for the first time coming from a French government leader, that yes, Vietnam would have its independence, but this would still be *within* the French Union. Ramadier then tried to change Leclerc's mind about returning to Indochina, but when pressed by the general to define the government's political objectives the prime minister had little to add. Leclerc then rejected the offer for a second and final time. He would die in a plane crash in Algeria in November 1947.

It was clear to all observers that the main issue was the fundamental hostility of the Vietnamese population to French colonial presence or any foreign presence in the country. The solution French politicians came up with was to encourage a nationalist Vietnamese political force that would oppose the Viet Minh and still be rooted in traditional Annamite society and values while accepting the French Union. The new Vietnamese government would be in the front line opposing the communists. The architect of this plan was Léon Pignon, who was trying to avoid having French forces fighting a war where they might create collateral damage among the population and increase the existing hatred. Emperor Bao Dai, living in self-imposed exile in Hong Kong, was the logical candidate for the task. The emperor at first refused but would later change his mind.

The search for a high commissioner became even more urgent because of divisive French politics: the communists and many socialists were now pressing for negotiations with the Viet Minh but the MRP and the right wing remained vehemently opposed. Finally, they picked a resistance hero and radical-socialist councilor of the republic: Emile Bollaert.[51] General Leclerc advised him to "negotiate, negotiate

---

50. Gras, Ibid., p. 168.
51. Emile Bollaert (1890-1978) was a civil servant (prefect) who rejected Vichy and joined the resistance. He survived three concentration camps in Germany and was appointed commissioner of the republic in

at all costs…" But the conditions for talks set forth by General Valluy were equivalent to surrender, since no French military commander now trusted the Viet Minh. Yet French politicians sounded as though the war was over, that it had already been won by France. Bollaert agreed to negotiate not just with the Viet Minh but with all the nationalist parties. Major international changes in March 1947 suddenly made any negotiation virtually impossible.

The first indication came from Washington when President Harry Truman addressed Congress on March 12 and spelled out the content of what would become known as the Truman Doctrine.[52] The main thrust of his address was to send a signal to the USSR that it must not advance any further into Europe and that America would defend and provide economic and military aid to Greece and Turkey. This dramatic move had been preceded the year before by Winston Churchill's "Iron Curtain" speech in Fulton, Missouri, on March 5, 1946, prompted by the worry over Soviet Russia's reluctance to evacuate its occupation zone in northern Iran. Truman's policy of containment reflected U.S. concern with the large communist parties in France and Italy, which both appeared and acted belligerently at the time. It also announced an anti-communist turn in French politics that took a few months to set in until Prime Minister Ramadier decided to expel the communists from the government in May 1947. Their exit was just a matter of time, since the communists had plans of their own and expected to be part of a new coalition government, given the strength of their numbers in the chamber of deputies. But that was not to happen and, in fact, they were to be permanently shut out of all French government posts until the election of François Mitterrand in 1981.

French Military Strategy in Indochina 1947–1948

General Jean Etienne Valluy was in charge of running the war. His plan was to thoroughly defeat the Viet Minh and convince the population that the war was useless. He was counting on the fundamental

---

Strasbourg then high commissioner in Indochina from March 5, 1947 to October 21, 1948. He appointed General Raoul Salan as interim commander of the Far East expeditionary corps. Bollaert was not reelected to the senate and went into private business.

52. David McCullough, *Truman* (New York: Simon and Shuster, 1992), p. 547. See also Robert J. Donovan, *Conflict and Crisis. The Presidency of Harry S Truman 1945-1948* (New York: W. W. Norton, 1977).

opposition between the atheistic Viet Minh brand of Marxist-Leninism and the traditional Annamite Confucian world view. Until the fall of 1947 the bulk of the effort was to pacify Cochinchina and then move to Tonkin in the dry season. In the north the aim was to destroy enemy forces near Bac Kan. Valluy's conclusion was that if France became impatient "for the current xenophobic, racist Indochinese movement [to be defeated]…in favor of hurried negotiations, then *Indochina will be lost.*"

Cochinchina was pacified but the extreme mobility of the Viet Minh and their capacity to blend into the population made the task of fighting them that much more difficult. The campaign in the south would yield meager results. Nguyen Binh, the fanatical guerilla leader whose wanton brutality led the political-religious sects to join the French side as early as November 1946, would later be mysteriously assassinated and by some accounts that he was executed because of his unpredictable behavior.

The Fall Offensive and Operation Léa, 1947

In Annam and Tonkin the French were more successful during the first two years of the war. As French units began venturing into the countryside to clear the roads and seek out the enemy, they discovered that the bulk of Viet Minh forces had retreated into the mountains, leaving behind small militia units to harass French troops. By April most of the territory of Annam and Tonkin had been cleared of the Viet Minh, even though the French army was still not strong enough to occupy the whole country. General Valluy was preparing for the October offensive in Tonkin and drawing lessons from the failure in Cochinchina. His plan was to cut off the head of the pyramid in a single sweeping blow. The enemy was well organized and disciplined: the object was to separate the leadership from the rest of the troops and finish them off separately. The window of opportunity was very tight: a few months in the fall season after the monsoon rains. Responsibility for the fall offensive in Tonkin was given to General Raoul Salan.[53]

---

53. Raoul Salan (1899-1984) graduated from St. Cyr in time to serve in the First World War. He spent most of his career in the colonial army in Syria and Indochina for long periods 1924-1933 and 1934-1937.

Operation Léa took place in October and November 1947, concentrating on the village of Bac Kan, where intelligence reports placed the Viet Minh leadership. General Salan was convinced that he could wipe out the enemy in three weeks. A Battalion of 950 paratroopers reached the area only minutes after Ho Chi Minh and his top staff had managed to flee. In ten days Salan's ten-thousand-man army had taken most of Tonkin. After October 15 the Viet Minh began reacting but still avoided direct contact and melted away into the jungle. Military intelligence estimated total Viet Minh forces at 16,000 at that time. General Valluy ordered a new operation to complete the destruction of the enemy main force that was thought to be in the Thai Nguyen region, close to Hanoi. General Salan assembled 7,800 men for that operation. The objective was to use paratroopers and once again capture or kill the leadership in a surprise attack. The French were confident in their superior firepower and mobility. For the second time the surprise effect was lost and the leadership managed to elude the paratroopers. The fall offensive ended on December 20, 1947, without the results General Valluy was expecting yet Ho Chi Minh and Giap were forced to hide in the jungle and could no longer operate, which in a sense made the offensive a success. Viet Minh losses were estimated at 8,000 guerrillas killed and 1,600 taken prisoner.

A French officer pointed to the real problem as he saw it: "The entire country is held together by a powerful political network with a well-staffed security service devoted to the party and its cause. The villages are terrorized by the militias and the resistance committees."[54] General Salan was convinced that he needed one more month to reach

---

Salan became very much attached to Tonkin and fathered a boy with a Vietnamese woman. Later he was appointed to the ministry of the colonies under Georges Mandel, where he coordinated intelligence matters. He was sent on intelligence missions to Cairo and the Sudan; in World War II he distinguished himself during the battle of France in May-June 1940, and the liberation of France in 1944-1945. Appointed to Tonkin in 1945 as commander of French forces in northern Indochina, he was in charge of Operation Lea, which almost captured Ho Chi Minh. Salan served as deputy to General de Lattre de Tassigny, then replaced him as high commissioner and commander in chief in Indochina in 1951-1953. After Dien Bien Phu he returned in 1954 as General Paul Ely's deputy for a short time and left at the end of the year. In 1956 he was appointed to head French forces in Algeria and played a key role in the May 13, 1958, movement that engineered the return of Charles de Gaulle to power. Salan officially retired in 1960 and took part in the military "putsch" in Algeria in April 1961, went into hiding, and became one of the leaders of the OAS in 1961-1962, until he was captured. Sentenced to life in prison in 1962, he was freed in a general amnesty in June 1968 when he was reintegrated into the armed forces with his rank and pension. He published four volumes of memoirs.

54. Gras, op. cit., p. 207.

his objectives but High Commissioner Bollaert disagreed. The clock was ticking against the French because of their political agenda: from 115,000 men the expeditionary corps was to be reduced progressively to 90,000 in early 1948.

Pressured by the need to take action in Cochinchina, Valluy had to withdraw key units from northern Tonkin and therefore abandon the Route Coloniale 4 (RC4) that connected Hanoi to Lang Son and Cao Bang, a key point the Viet Minh was bound to attack in the near future.

Reducing troop strength was anathema to Valluy, who decided to resign and returned to France in February 1948. General Salan was appointed as interim commander. The pursuit of operations in Tonkin was made more difficult by the heavy shift of troops to the south. Upper Tonkin, known as Thai country, was populated by numerous minorities and offered opportunities for French counter guerrillas recruited within the ethnic and tribal groups. A population of 400,000, made up of Meo, Man, Lolo, and other tribes, had traditionally been hostile to the Annamites and now opposed the Viet Minh in a mountainous region isolated from the main roads and paths. The Muong tribe was recruited and given special autonomy by the French. The strategy in Tonkin was based on the idea that as long as the Viet Minh could fall back on rest areas eluding French control, the region would not be cleared of the enemy.

The Religious Sects in Cochinchina

In the south the main competition to the Viet Minh came from the political and religious sects that included more than one-fifth of the population. The sects would to remain active throughout the war and in some cases until the American exit in 1975.

The Hoa Hao originally came from a village by the same name in the Mekong River delta. The founder, Huynh Phu So, was born there in 1918 and proclaimed himself the reincarnation of Tran Nguyen, a prophet who in turn said he was the reincarnation of Tran Tinh, the reincarnation of Buddha. Huynh Phu So was well educated and probably psychotic. A hermit monk taught him how to preach and prophesy as he conceived his doctrine conserving essential Buddhist beliefs but rejecting monks and pagodas. The statue of Buddha was replaced by a wine-colored veil and the offerings could only be clear water, flowers, and incense. In 1939 Huynh Phu So announced France's defeat and the triumph of Japan's Greater East Asia Co-Prosperity Sphere, as well as the apocalypse for the living, except those who would follow his teachings—making them invulnerable. He also announced that a great king would "return" and many of his followers were convinced that he meant Prince Cuong De. By 1940 the Hoa Hao had 300,000 followers, but the French were wary of his ideas and the Japanese authorities found them strange. The prophet was packed off to a psychiatric hospital where he converted his psychiatrist and became a Japanese propagandist when he was released. The Hoa Hao became auxiliaries of the Japanese army and split up into covert cells. After Japan's surrender the sect joined the Viet Minh. By then they had over one million followers and Huynh Phu So allied himself with the nationalists, carrying out robberies and attacks in the Mekong delta. A conflict with the communists led to thousands of deaths and the Viet Minh was almost destroyed in the process in western Cochinchina. When Huynh Phu So in one of his poems ordered the Hoa Hao to join the French, he was murdered by Viet Minh chief Nguyen Binh in 1947. Eventually the military wing became part of the French army in Indochina under Tran Van Soai and they were loyal to Bao Dai. The Hoa Hao steadily reduced Viet Minh influence in the delta but were split up by Col. Edward Lansdale and then disbanded by President Diem in 1956. After 1975 the Viet Minh completed the destruction of the movement, although it continues to exist underground in Vietnam.

The Cao Dai movement was created in 1920 and expanded in 1926 under Le Van Trung, a minor government employee who formed the sect as a blend of all existing religions. Contrary to the Hoa Hao, who were viewed as anarchists and uneducated warriors, the Cao Dai boasted a pope and a college of cardinals. The bizarre ritual was a concoction of several religions, including Freemasonry: the Supreme Being was represented by an eye in a triangle. The prophets were Buddha, Confucius, Jesus Christ, Muhammad, Joan of Arc, Victor Hugo, Louis Pasteur, Sun Yat Sen, and Ernest Flammarion. In 1936 Proudhon and Jean Jaurès were added as well. By 1938 Pham Cong Tac announced that he was receiving divine messages, that the west was about to collapse and that Greater Asia would triumph. Japanese Kempetai secret policemen became very interested in the sect. The Cao Dai pope was sent to Madagascar in exile and by 1941 the sect had become a tool of the Japanese. They backed the March 9, 1945, Japanese coup then joined the Viet Minh until 1946 when they switched to the French side. At that time the Cao Dai were the best organized of the southern sects with some 500,000 followers from all walks of life. They had an army of 3,000 that fought against the Viet Minh and was very effective in pacification operations. They promised protection if the groups or villages converted to the Cao Dai faith and used brutal methods to enforce their objectives. President Diem disbanded them in 1955. They ended up being decimated like the Hoa Hao in reunited Vietnam after 1975.

The Binh Xuyen were Chinese gangster-pirates who appeared around 1925 in the village of Binh Xuyen and expanded from there to assert control of the Saigon-Cholon area. Their leader, Bay Vien, was a former inmate at the forced labor camp at Poulo-Condor. In 1941 they began collaborating with the Japanese, providing spies and hit men while pursuing their criminal activities. In September 1945 they joined the Viet Minh, but Bay Vien had a falling out with Nguyen Binh and by 1948 they were at war with one another. Nguyen Binh tried to murder Bay Vien, who asked for French help and in the process obtained the concession to police the Saigon city area. The Binh Xuyen were to increase from 900 to 3,500 by 1954 as Bay Vien effectively became the chief of police, raising taxes for Emperor Bao Dai from gambling, prostitution, opium, and various other rackets. After the 1954 Geneva Accords they joined the Hoa Hao and Cao Dai in a National Front financed by the CIA. Bay Vien, with French support, attempted to overthrow Diem in 1955, but failed and fled to France, while his followers joined the Viet Cong.

An operation to capture Nguyen Binh failed in early 1948. A major incident had far reaching political consequences in March 1948 when a convoy of 70 vehicles traveling from Saigon to Dalat was attacked by the Viet Minh. Some 82 French nationals were killed, including 11 soldiers, and 150 civilians were kidnapped and disappeared into the jungle. The incident made the front pages in the French press—a rare occurrence during the Indochina war.

The Tonkin Border with China

As nationalist China continued to lose battle after battle to Mao Zedong's Red Army, the civil war had spread to southern China. It was inescapable that the communists would reach the border by 1949 and General Salan felt the Viet Minh had to be defeated before that happened. But the French Expeditionary Corps had been reduced to 87,000 men, and about one hundred obsolete aircraft. Salan wanted more troops and better equipment very quickly and High Commissioner Bollaert forwarded those requests to the government in Paris. The hope that a new Vietnamese government might bring about the crumbling of the Viet Minh was an illusion shared by some French politicians but that had no currency in Vietnam. General Salan intended to destroy the Viet Minh, and insisted on making his demands for reinforcements known directly to Paris, to whom he openly complained about "the lack of direction and coordination of those responsible," i.e., the French government bureaucracy and the relevant ministries.

Such language didn't sit well with the leadership in Paris so Salan was quickly replaced by General Roger Blaizot on May 15, 1948. The new commander in chief increased Salan's requests, adding even more men, but in the end he obtained only 108,000 and not in the required time frame. Blaizot wanted to crush the Viet Minh in the upper Tonkin area but his campaign plans were limited and the promised reinforcements arrived far too slowly; nevertheless, he was determined to pursue his northern strategy. The new commander in Tonkin, General Alessandri, who had longstanding experience of the area, wanted to occupy the Red River delta. In the end, the 1948 fall campaign yielded meager results. On January 10, 1949, as the Red Army captured some 600,000 nationalist troops and Mao Zedong was about to take power in China, the French were bracing themselves across the border in Indochina, expecting major challenges from the Viet Minh and possibly from Mao's army itself.

The entire pacification dilemma in the south could be summed up in the words of a local leader in Cochinchina to General Pierre Boyer de la Tour: "The troops came here three years ago and municipal councils were elected. Then the troops left and the councilors had their throats slit. We have no intention of repeating that experience. You must decide, will you leave or will you stay?"[55] The eternal question of pacification and collaboration with the colonial power was constantly being asked by the Vietnamese and the response was becoming less and less convincing.

The Bao Dai Solution

On March 8, 1949, President Vincent Auriol and Emperor Bao Dai[56] signed an agreement at the Elysée Palace that once more proclaimed the independence of Vietnam within the French Union, with major limitations. For example, Vietnam was to have direct diplomatic representation only with India, Thailand, and the Vatican. Bao Dai was not pleased to remain under tight French control but he was ready to live with the situation out of expediency and in the hope for better times in the future. He was also realistic enough to understand the major threat represented by Mao's now inevitable victory in China.

The plan to bring back the emperor and attempt to have him rally the population in a nationalist and anti-communist Vietnam was the brainchild of Léon Pignon. It took over fifteen months to persuade the recalcitrant monarch—living in luxury in Cannes—to return on the throne. Finally, an agreement was reached but the key issue of adding Cochinchina to Annam and Tonkin to form a united Vietnam remained unresolved. The French dragged their feet but eventually agreed. The alternative to Bao Dai was thought to be General Xuan, a nationalist Vietnamese military man who had the support of the SFIO, the French socialist party. Bao Dai, at age 36, had considerable finan-

---

55. Gras, op. cit., p. 252.
56. Bao Dai, Emperor of Annam (1913-1997), was to be the last emperor of the Nguyen dynasty and ascended the throne in 1932. In March 1945, after the Japanese coup, he repudiated the French protectorate and proclaimed the independence of Vietnam, the new name given to Annam. With Japan's surrender he abdicated in August 1945 and departed Vietnam for Hong Kong, Cannes, and Paris, where he lived in splendid self imposed exile. In 1949 he agreed to return as head of state—after signing a treaty with France. In 1955 he was overthrown by Ngo Dinh Diem and returned to Cannes where he remained until his death.

cial needs, living as did in great opulence, with the need to support a large family, many mistresses, and just as many concubines, as well as having an addiction to high stakes casino gambling. France was well aware of the dangerous flaws in the monarch's character but eagerly satisfied all his requests no matter how outrageous.

Georges Bidault described Bao Dai:

> The last in a long line of mandarins to lead Annam. He had an above average intelligence and embodied the main characteristics of his people. In particular, the familiar resentment of all Westerners that one finds among most Asian elites. He was also a complete sybarite and given to long bouts of laziness and fatalistic inertia. He spent far too much time at the roulette tables in Monte Carlo and Cannes rather than in Hanoi and Saigon, among his people. Deep down, as many well-informed people told me, he just didn't have the "calling" to be a leader in such circumstances…well perhaps he just didn't have the "calling," period. But for France he represented a safe policy and had the strong nationalist credentials we needed. There was no doubt in anyone's mind that Vietnam would be independent very soon, the question was: under what kind of regime? Bao Dai was the best alternative to Ho Chi Minh in 1949.[57]

One of the first published postwar assessments of Indochina came from former U.S. ambassador William C. Bullitt, who had visited the colony at the request of the French government. He summarized his impressions in an article published in *Life* magazine on December 29, 1947, and came to a pessimistic conclusion that this was "…a war in which victory…can lead only to a replacement of the yoke of France by the terrible yoke of Stalin."[58] The worse disaster would be to surrender to Ho Chi Minh for the Indochinese, the French and the entire Western world. Bullitt was convinced that an understanding between the French and the Vietnamese nationalists was possible but these solutions were hampered by "ignorance of the situation in Vietnam almost as great in Paris as in Washington." In Bullitt's view Bao Dai was the best possible candidate and he paid the emperor a private

---

57. Interview of Georges Bidault by R. Miller, co-author, in Paris on November 7, 1968. Bidault's exact words in French were: "Il n'avait pas la vocation, un point c'est tout."

58. Will Brownell and Richard Billings, *So Close to Greatness. A Biography of William Bullitt* (New York: Macmillan, 1987), p. 313.

visit in Hong Kong, but found him reluctant and wary of both France and America. He met with him again in Europe, where at first the emperor shunned French offers then finally accepted, convinced— wrongly, as it turned out—that Bullitt had entrée to American policy- making for Indochina.[59] Bullitt was actually acting on his own and per- haps at the suggestion of French authorities. Nevertheless, with the Cold War casting its ominous shadows American support would rapidly increase after 1949 and Washington's recognition of the Bao Dai government.

The emperor steadfastly refused to reside in Saigon and opted for the mountain resort at Dalat, far removed from the politics of the capital. Although not a man of action, he was a wily political operator and used every opportunity to get his way, mostly through inertia. As a young man he ascended the throne at age 19 and attempted to modernize the Annamite Empire by demanding changes in the protec- torate agreement with France. French administrators in the 1930s turned a deaf ear to his suggestions and ignored his requests. He apparently lost heart at that point and became disinterested in politics. Returning to power in 1949 he appointed a government that included General Xuan and nationalists from the Dai Viet and VNQDD parties. Bao Dai began the negotiations with Léon Pignon by demanding far more than what he had just signed off on, so much in fact that Pignon had to suspend their talks.

The emperor was pursuing his own road to full independence and wanted to reach that goal ahead of Ho Chi Minh, who was also eager to negotiate with the French. The communist victory in China en- couraged the extremists within the Viet Minh leadership to demand all out war against France. With the appointment of hardliner Pham Van Dong as vice president and head of the superior council of national defense, a general counter offensive was agreed to with Vo Nguyen Giap. Responding to the sudden but expected turn of the Viet Minh toward the Soviet and Chinese Bloc, Bao Dai finally agreed to send his delegates to the Assembly of the French Union, but did little else, refusing to openly take France's side in the war. After four years of conflict France had lost the opportunity to achieve the military defeat

---

59. See Stanley Karnow, *Vietnam. A History* (New York: Penguin, 1997).

of the enemy. By dodging a greater effort at the beginning in 1947-
1948 the French government became compelled to do so under the
growing threat of Communist China, firmly installed on the borders of
Tonkin.

Phase II: The "Dirty War"

Saigon and the Piastres Traffic

Saigon, the capital of South Vietnam, was a major commercial
center for Southeast Asia. From 1947 to 1954 the city remained
vibrant, mysterious, and filled with all kinds of shady characters of
many nationalities, while French colonial elements and upper class
Vietnamese were living in privileged luxury. Despite widespread
terrorism the 30,000 Europeans living and working in the capital were
never in any real danger. It was in fact a place to relax, forget the war,
and indulge oneself in the many exotic pleasures of the Orient. They
would patronize the night clubs and casinos in the Chinese quarter of
Cholon, where the nightlife was filled with every form of entertain-
ment imaginable. The upper classes held elegant soirées in their palatial
villas, where they employed dozens of servants. The two million Vietnamese making up the bulk of the city's population were desperately
poor. Most of them had recently moved from their rural habitat out of
fear and in search of work. The war could be found in the rice paddies
and swamps a few dozen kilometers away, but the fighting rarely
reached the center of either Saigon or Cholon.

Business was brisk and fortunes could be made quickly, especially
by trafficking in the piastre, the currency created by France in the
1880s and given as a concession to the Banque de l'Indochine that had
the highly unusual authority to print money. Originally in the 1930s the
value of the piastre was fixed at a rate of 1 for 10 French francs. In
1945, following the Bretton Woods Agreement requiring a drastic
devaluation of the French franc and a fixed rate to the U.S. dollar, the
piastre was in serious jeopardy threatening the entire Indochinese
economy. In an effort to help the colonies that were exporting
agricultural products, minerals, and raw materials, France set up a
special currency value by arbitrarily fixing the rate between the colonial

currencies and the French franc.[60] In Indochina the 1945 rate for the piastre was set at one for 17 French francs. The problem that surfaced as of 1948 was that the market rate in Asia was actually at 10 French francs to the piastre and the French treasury agreed to make up the loss by reimbursing the difference of 8 to 8.50 French francs back to the commercial enterprise that was billing in piastres.

This turned quickly into a vast loophole allowing all kinds of fraudulent practices, such as false or inflated invoices, nonexistent companies and individuals, imaginary business deals that were impossible to trace. The objective was to cheat the OIC (Office Indochinois des Changes) that was unable or unwilling to conduct comprehensive investigations. The Viet Minh also benefited from the situation when weapons allegedly purchased for French troops ended up in the hands of Ho Chi Minh's men and were killing French and Vietnamese soldiers. A scandal surfaced in 1952 in articles and a book by journalist Jacques Despuech[61] that became a sensation and further turned the French public against the war and the colony itself. In 1953 the government of René Mayer lowered the rate to one piastre for 10 French francs, effectively ending the practice. Significantly, no legal proceedings were ever opened against any of the main suspects and the names tied to the traffic remain only rumors.

The Affair of the Generals

Disagreements among French generals on strategy prompted Prime Minister Henri Queuille to order a broad and updated review of the war. General Georges Marie Joseph Revers, chief of the general staff, was dispatched to Indochina to personally investigate the situation and produce a report in the shortest possible time.

Revers left for Saigon on May 13, 1949, accompanied by General Valluy and other officers. In the course of one month he produced a thick report that examined not only military issues but also political solutions, as well as strategic options and recommendations. Revers was very critical of the Bao Dai solution, given the atmosphere of

---

60. In French Africa, for example, the Franc CFA (originally standing for "Colonies françaises d'Afrique" and later "Communauté française d'Afrique") was set up at a rate of one CFA franc equal two French francs and that rate remained in effect beyond the independence of the African colonies in the 1960s.
61. Jacques Despuech, *Le trafic des piastres* (Paris: Les deux rives, 1953).

widespread corruption that he said he found in Saigon. Léon Pignon and Minister of the Associated States Paul Coste-Floret were being targeted. Both were associated with the MRP party, so the scandal appeared to have been engineered by the socialists for narrow political gain. General Revers' conclusion was that a major political and military personality that could be popular among the Vietnamese should be placed in charge of French policy in Indochina, combining both civilian and military functions and implementing a single strategy. But the true conclusion of the report was the idea that, given the communist victory in China, a military solution in Indochina had become impossible.

According to Revers France must seek negotiations from a position of relative military strength in Tonkin where a defensive line would be set up until the United States could come in and share in the effort. The threat of Chinese intervention would be seen by the United States as a prelude to World War III and that would be enough for the Americans to take on the commitment to help France in Indochina. In the context of 1949 and with the China Lobby in the U.S. loudly accusing the Truman administration of having "lost China," such a scenario appeared to be very plausible. Revers was seeking to extend the North Atlantic Treaty that had just been signed on April 4 to include Indochina, giving the French Expeditionary Corps the necessary supplies to conduct a far more vigorous campaign. Revers also agreed with General Blaizot that the upper Tonkin redoubt of the Viet Minh in Viet Bac had to be destroyed ahead of any other option. That strategy required some adjustments, such as the evacuation of Cao Bang on the Chinese border, a move that was vehemently opposed by General Marcel Alessandri. Blaizot overruled Alessandri and ordered the evacuation. In July 1949 the French army went into the Tonkin delta and the northern sector of the Red River.

Léon Pignon intervened and overruled General Blaizot, demanding a delay in the Cao Bang evacuation so that the useful areas of Tonkin could be pacified first. Alessandri was then dispatched to Tonkin and his strategic plan was accepted.

In August Viet Minh radio was suddenly broadcasting portions of the Revers report. Then in September, following an altercation at a

Paris bus stop near the Gare de Lyon between two Vietnamese students and a French Indochina veteran, portions of the Revers report were found in the briefcase of one of the two, named Do Dai, known to favor Ho Chi Minh. A vast intrigue followed involving Generals Revers and Charles Mast, the former Resident general in Tunisia who was angling for the job of military commander in Indochina. Mast was said to have passed on pages of the report to a shady character named Roger Peyré, who had contacts at the SDECE and had done prison time in the past. A Vietnamese delegation member, Hoang Van Co, provided Peyré with large amounts of money allegedly to be distributed to Generals Revers and Mast and even to the vice president of the National Assembly André Le Troquer, a socialist.[62] The Revers report was directed against Bao Dai, Pignon, and their entourage and favored those who were demanding negotiations with Ho Chi Minh—in other words mainly the socialists, who were adamantly opposed to the policies of the MRP. The scandal forced the resignation of the Queuille government, which was replaced by Georges Bidault. No criminal charges were ever filed in the case.

The Chinese Communist Factor

On October 1, 1949, Mao Zedong proclaimed the People's Republic of China in Beijing. The following day the new government was recognized by the USSR and all its satellites, while defeated Chinese nationalist troops were requesting passage to Haiphong to join Chiang Kai-shek in Formosa (Taiwan).

The communist takeover in China changed the scope of the Indochina War. "Ho began to receive masses of equipment [...] he formed his first infantry division in 1949; five more followed in 1950."[63] The strategic position of Vietnam, Laos, and Cambodia suddenly acquired far greater importance to British and American military leaders in this new context. American policy in early 1949 was just beginning to focus on the broader implications of the struggle in Indochina. Roving Ambassador Philip C. Jessup of the U.S. State Department visited

---

62. However, no tangible proof was ever produced that the two generals and A. Le Troquer actually received those or any payments. See Georgette Elgey, *Histoire de la IVème République: Vol. I La République des Illusions* (Paris: Fayard, 1965), p. 473.

63. Norman Friedman, *The Fifty Year War* (Annapolis: Naval Institute, 2000), p. 180.

Indochina from January 24 to 29 and had meetings with Bao Dai, bearing a friendly message from Dean Acheson. Jessup also promised significant aid from the United States to Vietnam. American help was predicated on a genuine French commitment to full independence for the colony.

On September 23, 1949, President Truman announced that the USSR had tested a nuclear device. The Cold War suddenly entered the nuclear fear phase, destined to linger until the collapse of the Soviet system in 1991.

Communist China immediately recognized the Democratic Republic of Vietnam as the "only legal government of all the Vietnamese people." With the signing on February 14, 1950, in Moscow of the Soviet-Chinese alliance treaty, the sudden broadening of the communist bloc turned into a global and very threatening reality to the Western democracies and their friends. Ho Chi Minh was also present at the end of those meetings: "Stalin told Ho that aid to Vietnam was China's responsibility—and cost."[64] Chinese supplies were already being provided to the Viet Minh. The centuries-old political antagonism between the Vietnamese and the Chinese was at least temporarily overcome by the new ideological solidarity between the two communist regimes. China's shadow would loom large over the Indochina and Vietnam wars after 1950. "It was having China as a secure rear and supply depot that made it possible for the Vietnamese to fight for twenty-five years and beat first the French and then the Americans."[65] The various Communist party lines around the world were being rewritten while the largest French union the CGT, began a campaign for "Peace in Vietnam" calling for the end of the "dirty war" and the sabotage of military supplies being shipped to the Far East. In April 1950 communist leader André Marty told the party congress: "The French proletariat has a stake in the fact that the Vietnamese people defeat the French imperialists, the colonialists and naturally their masters: the American imperialists." Cold War propaganda rhetoric was quickly reaching its most strident level.

---

64. Jung Chang, and Jon Halliday, *Mao. The Unknown Story* (New York: A. Knopf, 2005), p. 357.
65. Ibid., p. 357.

The United States began a broad assessment of the situation in the Far East and Southeast Asia with an ambassador's conference chaired by Philip Jessup in Bangkok on February 13. Ho Chi Minh's protest to the UN against American intentions prompted the first delivery of seven C-47 transport planes flying from California directly into Than Son Nhut airport in Saigon on June 30, 1950. The Korean War had just started five days before and the possibility that it could be the prelude to the third World War was on everyone's mind. In October, in the Christian democratic newspaper *L'Aube*, Georges Bidault recalled his efforts in 1946 to secure some kind of settlement with the Viet Minh: "We were really encouraged that we could reach an understanding with Ho Chi Minh. We tried, I have every reason to remember, but it all came to nothing, nothing at all."[66] The determination of the Viet Minh to gain maximum advantage now had the backing of Mao's China and to a lesser extent the Soviet Union, boosting the morale of both the guerrillas and the regular units.

Military Operations 1949-1950

In Cochinchina Viet Minh leader Nguyen Binh set up a special force of 15 battalions to attack French forces and to divert attention from Tonkin where Giap was preparing his own operations. In December 1949 Nguyen Binh ordered two attacks that were repulsed by the French in brutal fighting with many casualties on both sides. Lacking fire power the Viet Minh used human waves of fanatics in suicide attacks, as would the North Koreans and Chinese communists later on in Korea. Superior fire power prevailed and Nguyen Binh was forced to withdraw and call off his offensive by the end of April.

At the same time an urban terror campaign was launched within Saigon itself, with the assassination of notables and pro-French Vietnamese. Informants were scattered among the population, behaving as a parallel administration in what was referred to as the "pourrissement" or "rotting" of a particular area. Nguyen Binh infiltrated specially trained "death squad volunteers" to prepare terrorist attacks. The Vietnamese population became even more fearful and withdrawn at the possibility of retaliation by the Viet Minh. There were grenade

---

66. *L'Aube*, October 21, 1950, cited in Gras, op. cit., p. 343.

and mortar attacks on American officers and ships carrying military supplies. Bao Dai then decided to sack his prime minister and replace him with Tran Van Huu, the governor of South Vietnam, giving him full powers to reestablish order. But the key man in the government was Nguyen Van Tam, a former colonial official who enforced strict law and order throughout the city and quickly improved the situation, owing to his energetic and ruthless methods. In July and August the entire terror network had been dismantled and Saigon returned to normal. Nguyen Binh's offensive ended in defeat.

General Marcel Carpentier was under no illusions as to the timing and feasibility of the plan to beef up the Vietnamese army and he warned of the possibility that such an effort would fail. This could lead to the destruction of the entire administrative apparatus of the Bao Dai government and to the emperor's abdication and departure from Vietnam. The pessimistic Carpentier told French president Vincent Auriol, "Military victory is no longer possible, there can only be a political solution." The president replied impatiently: "We don't intend to be the ones who abandoned Indochina."[67]

General Alessandri was determined to use the forces now at his disposal to occupy and hold the Red River delta. French forces attacked those areas where the Viet Minh had been entrenched for four years and where the population was heavily indoctrinated and fervently participating in the war effort. He managed to break the Viet Minh's hold and reoccupy the delta. This success came four years too late, since Viet Minh forces could now count on the Chinese to back them up with their safe havens for supplies and weapons just across the border.

Signs that Giap's army was improving at every level were being regularly misread by the French command: this was no longer a guerrilla army but a regular force with heavy combat experience that was steadily improving with time. France was now facing a resurgent and aggressive Communist China that, together with the Soviet Union, provided support for Ho Chi Minh. There was virtually no hope, it seemed, that the French could hold on to Indochina in the longer term, even with American help while the Korean War was raging.

---

67. Gras, op. cit., p. 295.

Indochina in Korea's Shadow, 1950–1951

On June 25, 1950, the forces of communist leader Kim il Sung crossed the 38th parallel and invaded South Korea. President Truman decided to support the South and immediately dispatched U.S. troops to counter the invasion. North Korea had Stalin's backing and Chinese support on a far larger scale than Ho Chi Minh had ever obtained. Almost overnight the traditional American objections to France's "colonial" war were silenced when the U.S. was faced with potential worldwide communist aggression. This was the common perception at the time, with vivid examples of a global conspiracy orchestrated in Moscow and Beijing, creating a wave of fear throughout the American public. A few days before, on June 16, 1950, following the arrest of Soviet spy and courier Harry Gold in May, the FBI took David Greenglass into custody in New York City. A few weeks later, with the war in Korea just beginning and the entire peninsula about to be overwhelmed by the North Korean army, came the turn of Greenglass's brother-in-law, Julius Rosenberg, and then that of Julius' wife Ethel. They were charged, along with fugitive Morton Sobell, with conspiracy to commit espionage. The Korean War and the Soviet atomic bomb formed the deadly backdrop to the new challenge in Asia, along with a fear of subversion inside the United States that quickly terrified the nation. This new Red Scare was exploited by Senator Joseph R. McCarthy, a Wisconsin Republican, who earlier in the year had denounced the existence of "205 card-carrying communists in the State Department."

While France continued to fight to hold on to its empire, the United States and the United Nations were embarked on a crusade against communist aggression. French forces in 1950 were at an all time high of 180,000, but they were still far too thin to properly control the entire Indochinese peninsula. Vast portions of Vietnam remained under Viet Minh control since the war began. Ho Chi Minh was counting on the war weariness of the French population in France itself, backed by strong French Communist Party propaganda, while the Viet Minh never stopped mobilizing the Vietnamese people against the French inside Vietnam.

Some historians insist that the amiable "Uncle Ho" was merely a pure Vietnamese patriot, a nationalist; that he couldn't be an ally of Communist China because of the centuries' old antagonism between Vietnamese and Chinese; that the USSR was too far removed and not terribly interested in Indochina, and so on. The facts, however, show that he remained a diligent student of Marx, Lenin, and Stalin, as well as Mao, whose teachings he adapted to fit the Vietnamese mentality and cultural experience.[68] Once Vietnam fell into Mao's sphere of influence, Ho quickly adapted his extreme brand of communism to adopt the Chinese model and took every step to mold the Viet Minh to fit the harsh characteristics of the new ally to the north.

Culturally collectivization was not deeply repugnant to the population of Tonkin, the area of the country the Viet Minh controlled best: the village being a natural "collective" and the peasants of that densely populated area so poor that they welcomed the tough discipline and accepted the required sacrifices. Ho Chi Minh, behind his gentle and amiable façade, remained something of a ruthless fanatic in the image of history's great true believers in a utopian cause seeking to bend man and humanity to fit itself into a certain vision of destiny. Even when the path to the ideal society demanded blood and murder, Ho was ready to do whatever was necessary for the success of his revolution. But he also remained an astute realist: victory for the Viet Minh wouldn't come on the battlefield: "the key to the Indochinese situation was in internal French politics." French public opinion would eventually buckle as Ho liked to repeat to his visitors: "You will kill ten of us but we will kill one of yours and you will eventually grow tired." A vocal minority inside France, mostly the communists and their fellow travelers at first, clearly favored a Viet Minh victory, thus giving Ho a welcome advantage. Quickly center left politicians such as Pierre Mendès-France voiced doubts about the war and France's commitment in Indochina.

The practical result of the war in Korea was that in August 1950, following the C-47s that had arrived in June, three American cargo

---

68. Among the many biographies of Ho Chi Minh, the most complete study is William J. Duiker, *Ho Chi Minh* (New York: Hyperion, 2000), and innumerable earlier portraits that remain essential is Bernard B. Fall, *The Two Vietnams* (New York: Praeger, 1967).

ships filled with military supplies arrived in Saigon. They were the first of a long series to follow.

Phase III: General de Lattre de Tassigny as Commander

The Cao Bang Disaster and its Consequences

In Paris the new premier René Pleven—heading the tenth government since the start of the Fourth Republic in 1947—had the backing of the MRP and the socialists. The MRP wanted to pursue its strategy seeking military superiority before negotiating with a weakened enemy while the socialists wanted immediate negotiations with Ho Chi Minh. The French needed U.S. support to continue the war and the cooperation of the Bao Dai government to rally the population and oppose the communists. But Bao Dai was demanding full and complete independence viewing the French Union as a loose confederation of states. With Laos and Cambodia, Vietnam was demanding that Indochinese affairs be placed under the ministry of foreign affairs, and removed from the old ministry of the colonies that had been renamed for obvious reasons: ministry of overseas France.

Many Vietnamese non-communist nationalists, including Emperor Bao Dai, were hoping the United States would come in and take over from the French. In July 1950 American ambassador Donald Heath arrived in Saigon with a military mission—Military Assistance Advisory Group (MAAG)—sent to evaluate the Franco-Indochinese forces. The great fear throughout the Korean War and beyond was that Mao's China would suddenly invade Tonkin as it had done in Korea in 1950-51, when Kim il-Sung's forces were swept back to the Yalu River near the Chinese border by General MacArthur's offensive. But that fear was exaggerated in retrospect regarding Indochina: the Chinese had no plans for such a move and in turn feared a far more dangerous American response that might include nuclear bombardment. What China did provide was a rear base and training facility for the Viet Minh army, supplying it with large quantities of rifles, machine guns, and other military supplies that were smuggled into the Viet Bac area.

As early as the summer of 1950 the Viet Minh could field an army that was at least equal to the French in firepower.

In Hanoi General Alessandri, an experienced colonial officer known for his optimistic and offensive disposition, was convinced that with the right number of units and equipment he could permanently defeat the enemy. General Carpentier, on the other hand, who was more of a logistics planner than an offensive general, remained skeptical and cautious. Alessandri prepared a plan to attack the Viet Minh and destroy their supply bases and main forces in a repeat version of what General Salan had proposed in 1947.

Carpentier wanted to secure the delta instead and wait for the enemy to come down from the mountain ranges. Therefore, in such a scenario the strongholds along the Chinese border on either side of the RC 4 road would retain only minimal forces for their defense. The bulk of the French forces would then be withdrawn to defend the delta, including isolated posts on the border. This strategy gave the Viet Minh time to reorganize and prepare its attack.

The evacuation of Cao Bang, an isolated outpost very close to the Chinese border, had already been decided in 1949 but in August 1950 the French army was still holding the village. For political reasons High Commissioner Pignon and his staff wanted to keep a presence at Cao Bang to ensure the loyalty of the local population. Supplies from China to the Viet Minh could no longer be stopped should the border post be abandoned. General Alessandri was opposed to the evacuation of the outpost, which he said was the best fortified position in Tonkin; however, it was finally decided that several outposts, including Cao Bang, would have to be abandoned. The operation was very risky because of the heavy presence of the Viet Minh in the surrounding areas and the difficult mountainous jungle terrain with only two possible roads: the RC 3 and the perilous RC 4 with its blind bends and heavy forests that made any convoy easy prey to an ambush by the Viet Minh along the mountain roads. The alternative was to evacuate the garrison by air, but given the many Vietnamese and Chinese civilians and their families who had taken refuge in Cao Bang it would have been a long and equally dangerous move. The final decision was for the garrison to take the RC 4, since it was the shortest route to Hanoi.

At a meeting with Pignon and Alessandri on September 20, Carpentier announced that he would order the evacuation. Alessandri again reacted strongly against such a move but he had his orders and would be responsible for their execution. Carpentier was convinced that the Viet Minh would not attack and he therefore failed to consolidate his reserves and ended up by scattering his troops instead.

The Cao Bang garrison, led by Col. Pierre Charton, was to join up with Lt. Col. Lepage, so that both could march to the safety of Lang Son. But things didn't turn out as expected and the two columns found themselves facing a far larger enemy force. The problem was that Lepage was immediately encircled and could only hope for the arrival of Charton for relief. He was holed up in a deep valley and being pounded relentlessly by the Viet Minh without attempting a sortie. Once Charton arrived close enough, Lepage decided to break out by forcing his way. By then he was left with 560 men out of the original 2,500. Later, Charton also came under attack, was wounded and taken prisoner, while his unit was cut to shreds. Losses when totaled were of 4,800 men, a considerable disaster when measured against the usual low body count in Indochina. By October 9 the truth about the defeat hit the press and Pignon stood tragically contradicted in his optimistic statement to the press of two days before.

The high command in Saigon was surprised by the extent of their miscalculation: no one could conceive that the Viet Minh would be able to overwhelm seven battalions of the French army. Even with Chinese supplies it was gospel among French staff officers that the Vietnamese were not capable of being good soldiers, a conclusion that dated back to the earliest years of colonization and that was now being brutally challenged.

In the wake of Cao Bang came a second disaster on the RC 4 at That Khe, an outpost that had to be evacuated. Out of several thousand, only a handful survived. Lang Son was also precipitously evacuated before any threat from the Viet Minh even materialized amid contradictory orders from the high command in Saigon that appeared to be panicking. By October 10 the extent of the defeat was clear and the French government sent General Alphonse Juin, Minister of the Associated States Jean Letourneau, and General Valluy to Saigon with full powers to make the necessary decisions to ensure the security of Indochina.

An important debate in the chamber of deputies took place on October 19, 1950, where Pierre Mendès-France of the Radical Socialist party gave a speech critical of the Indochina policy. "We simply do not have in Indochina the means to impose the military solution we have been pursuing for such a long time, when it was far easier to achieve than it is today."[69] Mendès-France was not convinced by the attempt to create an alternative to the Viet Minh with Bao Dai and the Vietnamese nationalists who were opposed to communism. In 1950 the mood was in favor of containment and confrontation while the Korean War was raging. The Pleven government, mindful of the Korean and Cold Wars, opted for the military solution and the pursuit of its ongoing policies. Mendès-France would have his day four years later in the dramatic wake of the French defeat at Dien Bien Phu so that for the moment he sounded like Cassandra.

The solution that General Juin suggested was to "Vietnamize" the war effort, the alternatives being unacceptable: negotiate with Ho Chi Minh or hand over the problem to the United Nations. In both cases France would lose its prestige as a great power and the rest of the colonies would instantly demand immediate independence. Vietnamese units were being integrated into the expeditionary forces but French officers in Indochina were skeptical of the fighting spirit of the new units once they came under Vietnamese command. Bao Dai was requesting a Vietnamese army that would be truly autonomous and continued to request even more independence. The Dai Viet nationalist party was gaining support, particularly in Tonkin by being both anti-communist and anti-colonialist, hoping for the backing of the United States. It also wanted United Nations intervention in Indochina as in Korea. This pressured Prime Minister Tran Van Huu to step up his demands and prove that he was not a French puppet.

U.S. ambassador Donald Heath was having frequent meetings with Bao Dai and offered support for greater independence, a revision of

---

69. Jean Lacouture, *Pierre Mendès France* (Paris: Seuil, 1981), pp. 192-193.

the treaties with France and a new Vietnamese national army. Vietnamese nationalists were eager for greater American involvement causing irritation among the French. During the visit Letourneau and Pignon met with Bao Dai and agreed to create a 115,000-man Vietnamese national army in 1951, equipped and financed by the United States and trained by French officers. A military convention was signed on December 8, 1950, whereby France agreed to recognize the complete independence of the new Vietnamese army as a step toward full political independence.

Premier Pleven declared officially in the chamber of deputies that France recognized that the independence of the states of Indochina was its goal. All the attributes of sovereignty would be given to each one as well as an independent army for Vietnam. Negotiations with the United States would ensure the required material help in the event of a Chinese invasion. The implications of these declarations were that France would eventually withdraw from Vietnam, keeping only a few bases as an ally and protector for the duration of the Viet Minh threat. The colonial war had been transformed into a war of containment of Chinese-Viet Minh communism. On November 22, in the chamber of deputies, Mendès-France advocated that France should negotiate immediately with the enemy. "Don't get caught up any further into the Far Eastern quagmire. You can't fight a war in distant land—that is morally and materially ruinous and that leads nowhere." But Letourneau disagreed and his most convincing argument was "Our dereliction of duty would mean admitting that we are powerless on the international scene. It could harm the integrity of the French Union."[70] France was no longer playing a colonial role in Southeast Asia but doing its part in the struggle to protect the free world from communist totalitarianism and aggression. The best expression of the traditional French colonial position came from Admiral Jean Decoux, former Vichy governor general of Indochina, in his memoirs published in 1950:

> Should France ever resign herself to losing Indochina she would then be permanently swept out of Asia and therefore the Pacific and

---

70. Gras, op. cit., p. 359.

would risk losing her key positions in Africa. Our country would then have betrayed its mission and turned its back on its own history. France would cease to be a great power and would deserve its downfall.[71]

The de Lattre Experiment

After the Cao Bang and Lang Son debacle General Carpentier lost his nerve and ordered a further retreat from the RC 4 and the surrounding outposts, including the key villages of Lao Kai and Hoa Binh. French forces were far too thin to hold all those areas and Carpentier was even considering abandoning Hanoi and setting up a fortress in Haiphong. Letourneau was aghast at the defeatist mindset within the military leadership and wrote to the prime minister stating the problem. It was high time the military commanders in Indochina were replaced by men who would vigorously prosecute the war. General Juin refused the top job and recommended that the high command not be reshuffled too quickly to avoid hurting morale. He also thought the estimates of Viet Minh strength were exaggerated which turned out to be correct. Discussions between Giap and Ho Chi Minh prove that the Viet Minh was by no means assured of victory and they both correctly expected a strong French rebound.

President Vincent Auriol then suggested appointing General Jean de Lattre de Tassigny, who readily accepted the mission but demanded that he be given full military and civilian powers. The government agreed and on December 6 he was appointed high commissioner and commander in chief in Indochina.

In one month de Lattre, through the strength of his personality, was able to boost the morale of the officers and men of the expeditionary corps. He arrived on December 17, 1950, at Saigon airport and his presence in Indochina was immediately felt by all. He fired the officer in command of the welcoming company because of the less than military bearing of his men and went on to punish all those he found lacking. Later he would tour the bars of Saigon and Hanoi, telling officers that they either joined their units to fight or they'd be shipped back to France. The next change was to replace all the

---

71. Quoted in Philippe Héduy, *Histoire de l'Indochine* (Paris: A. Michel, 1998), p. 448.

commanders by the men he brought with him, including General Raoul Salan, who had valuable knowledge and experience of the country. The other key officers were Allard, Beaufre, and René Cogny, who had served under de Lattre in the French First Army during the 1944-1945 campaign to liberate France.

He ordered a grand military parade in Hanoi in the presence of Bao Dai but the emperor didn't wish to appear in the company of the new condottiere in his gleaming white uniform and he remained aloof in Dalat. In Hanoi de Lattre held a press conference after reviewing the troops and spoke to his officers in almost heroic terms reminiscent of Caesar and Napoleon, whipping up their enthusiasm and sense of purpose and making it clear that the goal in Indochina was freedom and independence: France's mission from now on was a "disinterested one." Then he castigated the supplies officer because the soldiers were dressed in rags. As General Salan commented: "The man is truly a magician! I saw it in the men's eyes, the general has transformed the expeditionary corps!"[72] B. Liddel Hart noted "He had more style than any other marshal since Turenne." But aside from the pros and cons of his personality de Lattre also had the qualities of an exceptional military commander: imagination, creative vision, remarkable intelligence and the art of going directly to heart of the matter in each situation. He was a terrible tyrant to his subordinates and their best friend at the same time. His son Bernard was also serving in Indochina, which created an additional aura for the commander in chief among the troops and the population.

The main point of the government's brief to the new high commissioner was "make the independence of the associated states as effective as possible...to defend Tonkin first and foremost...and Cochinchina where French interests are vitally important." The instructions left the general with very broad latitude as to their interpretation. The first point de Lattre was clear about was that the Tonkin delta must be held: if the area were abandoned it would be the signal for leaving all of Indochina. His first move was to appoint Salan as commander in Tonkin, replacing Boyer de la Tour and cancelling all previous pullback orders: enemy attacks in Tonkin would be countered

---

72. Raoul Salan, *Mémoires,* Vol. II (Paris: Presses de la Cité, 1971), p. 187.

every time. At the same time he managed to gain the confidence of the Vietnamese nationalists and government officials while Bao Dai remained somewhat remote. Then the general began giving interviews to noted journalists, such as Lucien Bodard of *France Soir,* and seeking as much public relations exposure as possible so that the Indochina War would become as important as Korea to obtain the needed funds and supplies from the United States. There was no doubt in de Lattre's mind that the war could and must be won.

Giap began his offensive in Tonkin on January 12 in what was called the battle of Vinh Yen. The best Viet Minh units, including the 308 Brigade, were attempting the encirclement of the outpost. De Lattre wanted to see for himself and took a small plane with General Salan that landed in the middle of the fighting. He understood that this was a major engagement. More units were sent in just as the Viet Minh was beginning its offensive to overwhelm Vinh Yen. All the attacks were repulsed and the Viet Minh took heavy casualties in the brutal assault. Finally Giap ordered a retreat, leaving 1,500 dead, 480 prisoners, and thousands of wounded behind. The Viet Minh had to revise their strategy and avoid a direct attack on the main French forces in the delta and rely far more on the Chinese for supplies and logistics.

In 1951 Ho Chi Minh adopted the political and ideological methods of Mao Zedong to align his struggle on the Chinese communist model. He decided to revive the formal Vietnamese Communist party that had been dissolved in November 1945 when it became necessary to appeal to the Vietnamese nationalists in forming the Viet Minh coalition. Now that he needed China, Ho was reverting to his ideological roots and announced the establishment of the Vietnam Dang Lao Dong, or Vietnamese Workers Party, generally known as the Lao Dong, that would be narrowly Marxist-Leninist, subjected to strict party discipline and intolerant of any deviation. The war effort became the top priority.

The de Lattre Plan

In de Lattre's plans Vietnamization was the cornerstone of a French military victory. This implied the rapid creation of the Vietnamese army with the help and cooperation of Bao Dai. De Lattre had to win over the emperor and was counting on his own charisma to bring that about. But Bao Dai remained aloof and reticent because he feared the domineering personality of the French general. De Lattre also wanted a strong Vietnamese government with a dynamic war minister to make up for Bao Dai's retiring attitude. It was urgent to implement the plan, since military intelligence was providing alarming information about Viet Minh preparations. De Lattre wanted to defend the Tonkin delta by building a concrete defense system that could repulse a Viet Minh or Chinese attack. But in anticipation he needed more troops and equipment and the buildup of the Vietnamese army. To speed things up Vietnamese recruits were being integrated into French battalions that would gradually become "Vietnamized," a process the French called "jaunissement" or "yellowing." France would provide the manpower required but most of the materiel had to come from the United States.

On December 24, 1950, Letourneau and Heath signed an agreement regarding the supplies the U.S. would provide to the associated states, and Pleven, in a meeting with Harry Truman, raised the issue of equipping the Vietnamese army. The response was positive but no timetable was provided. De Lattre couldn't get everything he needed as quickly as he wanted, yet he remained very optimistic: "We can win, I guarantee it," he told the government. Vast pacification operations were taking place in Cochinchina where 15,000 Viet Minh were being supplied through Laos in a preview of what would become the Ho Chi Minh trail of the Second Indochina War. Much of the Lao population was hostile to the Viet Minh and to the home grown guerrillas that were active in some provinces. In August 1950 Prince Souphanovong visited Ho Chi Minh's hideout in the Viet Bac and they agreed to create the Lao People's Liberation Front, also known as the Pathet Lao. The prince would be a useful fellow traveler for the Viet Minh later on. The same was taking place in Cambodia where a pro-Viet Minh group was created and signed an alliance with Viet Minh in 1951. Yet Tonkin remained the focal point for both de Lattre and Salan: it was in the north that the war would be decided.

De Lattre then traveled to Paris on March 17 to make his case for massive reinforcements but the government was divided on the issue due to the new NATO organization being created and its manpower needs. Yet Paris wanted to end the Indochinese war one way or another. De Lattre kept on meeting politicians and journalists, making statements and giving interviews. "As long as we hold on to Indochina we will remain a great power," he said. The new Viet Minh offensive forced him to return to Indochina sooner than he expected and it resulted in the battle of Dong Trieu, a victory for the French forces. The Viet Minh once again vanished into the highlands and the jungle and resumed guerilla warfare similar to Mao Zedong's long war of attrition strategy against the Chinese nationalists and the Japanese.

At the Singapore conference for the defense of Southeast Asia in May 1951, de Lattre made his point to the British and American generals. He contradicted U.S. admiral Arthur Struble, who wanted to abandon the area in case China entered the war. De Lattre disagreed: "Indochina was the lynchpin to the entire Southeast Asian structure." This was an early hint of the domino theory that was popularized later on. De Lattre knew that he must convince American public opinion and was preparing a major trip to the United States. A new Viet Minh offensive that combined guerilla and conventional warfare proved dangerous and deadly. De Lattre's son Bernard was killed in an engagement in Tonkin. The general flew back to France with his son's body on June 1, 1951, shattered by the loss. The battle raged in Tonkin in May and June 1951 and became another French success story under the command of General François Gonzalez de Linarès. The Viet Minh lost 1,159 killed to 107 French, but the main force managed to elude encirclement, using guerilla tactics as they were being overwhelmed.[73]

Despite these tactical victories the main problem for de Lattre was the authority, or lack thereof, of the Huu government that was having trouble securing the confidence and even the obedience of various groups like the Dai Viet and the Cao Dai. De Lattre was frustrated by the weakness of Prime Minister Huu and the indifference of the Vietnamese population. He was also aware of the armistice negotiations in

---

73. Gras, op. cit., p. 408.

Korea and the pressing demands from NATO, making the French effort in Indochina all the more pressing. It was made clear to the Bao Dai regime that France would not be able to pursue the effort against the Viet Minh indefinitely. Ho Chi Minh's army, after heavy losses, began using a form of conscription in Tonkin, giving far more urgency to the Vietnamization process for the French.

Korea suddenly appeared very threatening to Bao Dai and the nationalists, so the emperor finally decided to support de Lattre and agreed to sign mobilization orders for the Vietnamese to take part in the war. De Lattre made an appeal to the Vietnamese people that went to the heart of matter: "Be real men, which means that if you are communists you join the Viet Minh; there are some people there who are fighting well for a bad cause. But if you are patriots then fight for your country because this is your war. It no longer concerns France if only in the promises made to Vietnam... The Vietnamese national army is the very expression of Vietnam's independence."[74]

These statements had some positive effects and there was stirring among the Vietnamese population. De Lattre, using every public relations device he mastered so well, decided to give special meaning to the Bastille Day festivities in Hanoi in 1951. On July 14, in the presence of Bao Dai, 12,000 men marched past in front of an enthusiastic crowd of 120,000 in a grand ceremony that signaled the peak of the de Lattre experiment and its undeniable success. His problems now became personal after the death of his only son in battle and the first signs of the illness that would soon kill him appeared. But for the moment he remained vigorous and filled with passion and energy to find a solution to the war. The Korean negotiations—which would drag on for two-and-half years—were both a positive sign and a danger. Chinese troops could now be moved to the border with Tonkin and threaten Indochina. But there was also the possibility of an international conference to solve the problems in Asia that de Lattre was convinced would provide a solution for Vietnam and the Indochinese War. France would then need the full support of her Western allies to continue fighting communism in Southeast Asia, where the war would be long and costly for both sides.

---

74. Ibid., p. 412.

De Lattre's Visit to America and the End of His Mission

The general left for Paris on July 28, 1951, and sent his report to the government outlining what he had accomplished and the future prospects for Indochina. His proudest achievement was the creation of the Vietnamese national army and the spirit of independence accepted by Bao Dai and his government. Therefore any idea of negotiating with the Viet Minh would destroy what France and the West had achieved so far in the Indochina war. The morale and commitment of the Vietnamese anti-communists would be shattered. De Lattre was convinced that France could resolve the conflict with American help: he would make his case and enlist U.S. support in a fight against communism. The Americans, in the general's mind, were not truly committed to providing the French Expeditionary Corps with the supplies and weapons it needed. Why? Because the United States still felt that Indochina was a colonial war and didn't want to be associated with colonialism in spite of the progress the French had made in setting up Bao Dai. American suspicion that the French never really intended to leave Indochina would linger stubbornly until 1955.

De Lattre arrived in New York in early September and began a grueling round of meetings and interviews, pleading his cause with consummate skill. He met with Francis Cardinal Spellman, Dean Acheson, President Truman and the Joint Chiefs of Staff at the Pentagon, as well as the CIA. But his main objective was to seduce the American public and this he did by going on television programs, such as *Meet the Press*. Every time he countered the argument that France was fighting a colonial war by saying that, on the contrary, the Indochina war was a war against communist expansion. The second main idea was the strategic importance of Indochina: its loss would have disastrous consequences for Western defense, destabilizing the Middle East, North Africa, and Europe, which would be threatened on its southern flank. As long as the Viet Minh was the only enemy, then France could shoulder the burden with massive American help in the form of weapons and supplies. Should other powers, such as China, enter the war, then many more Western troops would become necessary.

The results of the trip were very promising: de Lattre made a great impression: he was immediately very popular and the press loved him. *Time* magazine gave him a cover and wrote about the second "miracle of the Marne." He returned to Indochina after stops in London for a similar campaign that was equally successful, and in Rome for a meeting in the Vatican with Pope Pius XII. They discussed the situation of the Vietnamese Catholics and the general wanted a commitment from the Holy See to the anti-communist cause and support for French efforts. The pope appointed Archbishop John Dooley as the Apostolic Delegate to Indochina and the Catholics became fervent supporters of the new effort by the Vietnamese government against Marxism. But in Paris de Lattre was diagnosed with cancer and was under no illusions knowing that his days were numbered and his mission accomplished.

Yet at the tail end of his Indochinese adventure de Lattre ordered a risky offensive outside the Tonkin delta. The reasons were as much political as they were military: it was necessary to pursue the victorious campaigns of 1950-1951 to persuade those in the chamber of deputies to vote larger funds for the war and encourage greater American help. The offensive would focus on Hoa Binh as General Salan was proposing. The intent was to attract the Viet Minh main force to take up the challenge in an area that would appear favorable to its kind of warfare: a mix of conventional attacks and guerrilla hit-and-run operations. Although Hoa Binh was located in difficult jungle terrain it was accessible by the Black River and close enough to the delta and Hanoi. This was to be the first phase of a vast operation to cut Viet Minh territory in two and then wipe out each part separately. That would require a massive U.S. weapons and supply effort that could be forthcoming with victory in the battlefield.

The Viet Minh refused to fight the advancing French troops and Hoa Binh was occupied without firing a shot. De Lattre in a press conference in Hanoi turned Hoa Binh into a great victory and a key strategic point. He was attempting to attract Giap and his forces into a set piece battle where the French forces could prevail. On November 19 de Lattre reviewed the troops at Hoa Binh for the last time and flew back to France, never to return. He was in terrible pain and had reached the end of his life, but he still kept it all secret, full of optimism that the war could be won with a real Vietnamese government that would rally the population around a national ideal. He was convinced that the war could end by May 1953 by breaking up the Viet Minh with a massive rallying of the population to Bao Dai. This was all predicated on the absence of Chinese intervention. De Lattre didn't survive surgery and died at the military hospital of Val de Grace in Paris on January 11, 1952. He was awarded the rank of Marshal of France and given a state funeral.

3.

Colonial Exit

Dien Bien Phu and the Geneva Conference 1953–1954

The Run Up to Dien Bien Phu, 1952–1953

With de Lattre gone Indochina had lost its miracle man. His natural charisma and sense of theatrics, combined with a keen grasp of strategy and tactics, made him a natural commander, more than just another general. He also knew how to pick his staff and his generals. The man left in charge of military operations was General Raoul Salan and for the next eighteen months he was to enjoy a long string of military successes. But after de Lattre no firm policy could be decided by the cascade of governments in Paris, mainly due to the growing problems in North Africa and obstruction and sabotage of the war by French communists. The government of Antoine Pinay decided to appoint Jean Letourneau, the minister of the associated states, as high commissioner in Indochina while General Salan became the military commander in chief. The political and the military leadership was once more split in two. In Vietnam the Huu government was replaced with a dynamic and energetic anti-communist politician, Nguyen Van Tam, whose policies differed very little from those of his predecessor.

The Battle of the Black River

Giap was preparing a bold move to infiltrate the entire Tonkin delta with his main force. At Hoa Binh, in a valley surrounded by high ground with an air strip resembling the tragically famous one at Dien Bien Phu, the French were holding a position on both sides of the Black River. Small firefights were taking place while two Viet Minh regiments were attempting to create a pincer movement. A plan found on the body of a dead Viet Minh officer alerted General Salan, who decided to preempt the move and be the first to attack. The attack was meant to break up the enemy forces and the Viet Minh suffered heavy casualties before retreating without having reached its objectives. The Viet Minh was able to stop traffic along the Black River so that all French units south of Hoa Binh had to be supplied by air. But each time French forces went on the offensive in greater numbers the Viet Minh would dissolve into the jungle. Salan knew that large Viet Minh forces were threatening the delta and decided to abandon the Black River and regroup.

At that point Giap was about to cut French communications on the RC 6 road in the hope of repeating the 1950 success on the RC 4 during the Cao Bang disaster. But the Viet Minh had no artillery at that time and used human wave assaults to submerge the enemy no matter the cost. French artillery was able to break the human waves and inflict considerable losses on the attackers. An attack on the outpost of Xom Pheo, a well-fortified position, demonstrated how field fortifications could work efficiently. The Viet Minh then changed tactics by trying to prevent supplies from landing. Viet Minh artillery was holding Hoa Binh in a state of siege: four planes were destroyed on the ground. Salan decided to break the siege while Giap was still expecting a replay of the RC 4. The task went to Colonel (later General) Jean Gilles.

Gilles used infantry only to mark enemy positions, then he would hit them continuously with artillery fire. Finally, the RC 6 road was cleared of enemy threats while Giap regrouped his forces around Hoa Binh ready to attack the moment the French began their planned evacuation.

The Tonkin Delta

The delta was the backbone of the French military network in northern Vietnam and the area where the Viet Minh also operated, especially to obtain its food supplies—particularly rice. Without the delta the Viet Minh was unable to sustain operations in the triangle, which included a population of 8 million scattered in 4,000 villages in a very tight space.[1] The French controlled the delta through fortified garrisons manned by about 100 men vulnerable to attack, especially at night, which was a Viet Minh specialty. During the day the Viet Minh could hide in the delta with the help of the peasants who were terrified by the ruthlessness of Ho Chi Minh's troops. Hundreds of villages with underground passages and storage facilities were set up with underground hiding places. It was a vast web of disconnected villages that made it impossible to clear the delta of the enemy in a single rapid operation. The Viet Minh could exist only with the cooperation of the peasants and the French could never be assured of their allegiance: what mattered most to them being the harvest and which side was going to win, as in all wars.

General Salan wanted to concentrate his efforts in the delta in early 1952 but because of the limited number of troops he had to disengage from Hoa Binh and shift them elsewhere. The problem was to withdraw from the fortified camp without getting cut off by the Viet Minh. Colonel Gilles organized the withdrawal in stages. Everything went like clockwork and even the Viet Minh would find out too late that many French units and Muong tribesmen had managed to slip away. Giap's forces suffered huge losses: 3,500 killed and 7,000 wounded and Salan could easily present the retreat as a success in terms of grinding down the enemy. Giap ordered his units to regroup and rebuild the decimated battalions.

The battles in the Tonkin delta continued relentlessly and manpower shortages forced the French to concentrate on Haiphong and move their forces to central Vietnam where the Viet Minh was active again. In 1952 the Expeditionary Corps had a total of 173,000 men; to these should be added the 128,000 men of the Vietnamese national

---

1. Gras, op. cit., p. 447.

army but not all those units were operational, yet they had come a long way from the original auxiliary units that were used before de Lattre. American supplies were shipped in from Korea and Japan in large quantities: 120,000 tons since 1950, without which the French could not carry on the war. The Viet Minh faced the same situation since their supplies came from China into the Viet Bac area in the northeastern border area. In 1953 French intelligence learned of a three-way agreement between the Viet Minh, China, and the USSR signed in 1951 for assistance of all kinds short of military intervention unless the very existence of the Viet Minh were to be threatened.

Upper Region Battles

In 1952-1953 Giap concluded that he would need far more troops than he could enlist to win in the Tonkin delta. He therefore decided to move the fighting to the Upper Region. French tactics in mountainous terrain were to set up small bases to serve as magnets for Viet Minh attacks and then inflict as many casualties as possible, since they invariably would use human waves of fanatics. The strategy was simple: attract the enemy into attacking, then hit them with heavy artillery and airborne bombing. The method worked at Hoa Binh and would be repeated again successfully by Salan. On October 19, 1952, the commander in chief decided to set up such a camp around the airstrip at Na San. General de Linarès was told to "force the enemy to fight on terrain favorable to us with an airfield allowing for regular supplies to the fighting units."[2] This same concept drove the planning for Dien Bien Phu with the caveat that while Na San was much closer to Hanoi, Dien Ben Phu was 400 kilometers away on the Laotian border, in Thai country—unreachable if not by air. Throughout the Indochina war the main problem was always to entice the enemy to stand and fight when and where he could be defeated. But the Viet Minh would shy away from doing battle unless they could overwhelm the French using unconventional tactics: attacking at night in small groups of hit-and-run teams, or when they were assured of having numerical superiority and could accept taking enormous losses.

---

2. Gras, op. cit., p. 477.

In Indochina the SDECE had created a commando unit known as GCMA to set up counter-guerrilla fighting units in Tonkin. These formations were run by Col. Roger Trinquier and Col. Edmond Grall. The objective was to arm and supply the Meo tribesmen who hated the Viet Minh. The plan was successful and the counter-guerrillas took over a large area near the Chinese frontier. Giap was forced to call in a Chinese unit across the border to defeat the Meo in August 1952. General Salan then dispatched Col. Grall to upper Laos, where the population was favorable to the French and feared the Viet Minh, to set up counter-guerrilla bases. The loss of Nghia Lo by the French revived the Indochina political debate in Paris, since the deputies in the assembly were fearful of another disaster similar to Cao Bang.

The Battle of Na San

The counter-guerrillas were supposed to draw Viet Minh forces away from armed camps such as Na San. Fortification works began reinforcing Na San with construction materials that were flown in. By November 23, 1952, the garrison numbered 12,000 men but the whole effort was predicated on the air force cutting corners on maintenance. Hanoi was located 200 kilometers to the east and accessible only by air. The French air force in Indochina then could count on 100 military C-47s plus a small number of civilian C-47s and Bristols.

As of October, French counter intelligence was able to crack Viet Minh military codes, showing how Giap's forces were approaching Na San without realizing the actual size and number of troops the camp contained. The Viet Minh commander-in-chief thought he was simply pursuing enemy troops retreating from the upper regions, that he would then catch in a vast ambush on the road near Dien Bien Phu. Finally, Giap concentrated his forces for the attack on Na San. But the fortified camp was too well-protected to be overwhelmed and its artillery barrage decimated the attacking forces. Giap had only mortars and no artillery, so he was forced to fall back. Finally, on December 3 he ordered a general retreat from Na San, which turned into another defensive victory for Salan. The French could have pursued the retreating Viet Minh, to draw them into a confrontation, but Salan preferred to stop the operation at that point and take no further risks. Caution had always been one of his trademarks and would in part be the cause for his dismissal in May 1953.

French signals intelligence was listening in on Giap's orders and planning that included an invasion of northern Laos. The Viet Minh was poised to attack with units that had been left behind. The war was now concentrated in the upper region known as Thai country, where in 1953 the French had tightened the alliance with the Meo tribesmen. A deal had been struck between General Salan and Meo leader Tuby Ly Fuong, whom he knew well, for the opium harvested by the Meo to be flown in French planes to Cholon where General Bay Vien and his men would handle distribution and sales. This source of revenue was essential to finance SDECE operations in Indochina.

Signals intelligence again picked up Viet Minh plans to extend the war into Laos, prompting the French command to set up more armed camps. Salan requested heavy transport planes from General Mark Clark, the UN commander in Korea: 6 C-119 transports with their crews—on top of the 21 C-47s already delivered in December 1952— were to fly into Hanoi.

Viet Minh Strategy

The strategy of the Viet Minh was explained in a military conference held in Beijing in October 1952: the idea was to attract as many French troops as possible into the upper region. Besides the military objectives the agenda was also to extend Viet Minh influence into all the countries of the Indochinese peninsula. Northern Laos was a step in that direction. But the Viet Minh encountered a serious logistics problem, since they were 250 kilometers from their home bases in difficult mountain terrain. One goal was to establish Pathet Lao leader Prince Souvanna Phouma as the sole legal government of Laos. By moving units into Laos, General Salan managed to discourage the Viet Minh attempt to take over the country at that time.

The government of René Mayer came under heavy pressure from the Eisenhower administration when the decision was reached in May 1953 to replace General Salan with General Henri Navarre. The reasons were many, among them the negative perception caused by the lack of progress made by the French Expeditionary Corps. Despite Salan's successes in waging a defensive war he was unable to deliver a plan that ensured the rapid resolution of the conflict that the Americans were urgently demanding in the wake of the Korean armistice talks. The French commander prepared a two-and-a-half-year plan that was tailored to the timing required for the Vietnamese national army to take over operations from the French. Breaking the Viet Minh would require an exceptionally large military effort, since Giap could count on vast supplies and bases conveniently located in sanctuaries across the border in China. France would be unable to raise an army of that size within the short time frame required by the United States.

The Eisenhower administration and the president himself were demanding a quick resolution to the war in Indochina and senior American officers viewed General Salan as being a major obstacle. He was considered too timid and unwilling to aggressively pursue a decisive victory that would bring about the total defeat of the enemy. His caution was informed by a long tour of duty in Indochina of more than twelve years since the 1930s, but he was also felt to be uncooperative and suspicious of American intentions—as were many French officers and indeed the French government itself. Salan was reluctant to share battlefield intelligence with the CIA, fearing damaging leaks to the enemy even in the form of press articles in U.S. newspapers. General John W. O'Daniel found him unyielding in his refusal to follow American suggestions and learn from the example of the Korean War that was based on an expected invasion of the south from the north using conventional forces.

The Pentagon was also demanding a far greater say in the conduct of operations in Indochina, feeling justified by the vast expenditures in materiel and funding originally meant for NATO's command in Europe. Eisenhower wanted a new French commander, hopefully possessing something of the charisma of a General de Lattre, who had fired up the imagination of the American public. Several candidates were being considered and Eisenhower suggested General Augustin Guillaume, whom he remembered as an aggressive fighter at Monte Cassino and who was serving as resident general in Morocco in 1953.

However, Premier René Mayer picked General Henri Navarre to replace Salan in May 1953.[3]

France would be unable to usefully end the war through negotiations from a position of strength without a major victory in the field. Letourneau refused to consider negotiations with Ho Chi Minh, which, he maintained, would send the wrong signal to all the nationalists in the French colonies who would immediately rise up and demand full independence. In Cambodia in April 1953 the king demanded complete independence to enable him to eliminate the opposition and expel the Viet Minh. The French government refused to listen and Prince Norodom Sihanouk published an aggressive statement in the *New York Times,* in which he threatened to join the Viet Minh if the French didn't grant his country far greater independence within a few months. The pressure was on and the French government was deeply affected by it.

On May 9 the Mayer government, responding to American pressure, also ordered the devaluation of the Indochinese piastre without consulting any of the three governments of the associated states. The piastre affair had become a public embarrassment. But the Vietnamese government of Bao Dai protested to Letourneau, demanding far greater reforms. Mayer resigned a few days later and all those issues were passed along to the next prime minister. The U.S. government wanted to bring the entire Indochinese issue to the United Nations in an attempt to solve the problem but Foreign Minister Georges Bidault strenuously opposed such a move, fearing once again the rapid dismantling of the French colonial empire as well as missing an opportunity for an early resolution to the war in Indochina. He argued that the UN would not give France the kind of solution she could live with.

The government crisis following Mayer's resignation lasted a record 35 days and saw the candidacy of Pierre Mendès-France fail by a mere 3 votes: a sure sign that the political class was desperate to end the Indochina war and was ready to accept direct negotiations with Ho Chi Minh. The new conservative government formed by Joseph Laniel, with Georges Bidault once again as foreign minister, openly stated its

---

3. Irwin Wall, *The United States and the Making of Postwar France 1945-1954* (New York: Cambridge, 1991), pp. 249-251.

desire to reach a negotiated settlement for the first time since the beginning of the war.

Dien Bien Phu (1953–1954)

By the summer of 1953 war weariness about Indochina had spread to every political party and to the French population at large: politicians, newsmen, and the general public—all were ready to end the war as quickly as possible. The government was divided on the issue of sovereignty: Bidault was firmly attached to the French Union formula which he had authored in 1946, while others, like Deputy Prime Minister Paul Reynaud, supported full independence for the associated states. The policy remained unclear and open to accusations of neo-colonialism. The ministry of the associated states was reduced to an under secretariat and Maurice Dejean, a former diplomatic aide to Paul Reynaud, was appointed as general commissioner in Indochina. The relationship with Laos and eventually Cambodia was quickly resolved in direct negotiations, with both countries taking over the basic administrative tasks the French were still performing. In May 1953 the Viet Minh moved into northern Laos with three divisions and appeared to be seeking to widen the conflict by threatening Thailand and Burma, apparently confirming what would later be called the "domino theory."

Reaching an agreement was far more difficult in Vietnam where Bao Dai and Prime Minister Tam were under intense pressure as they attempted to centralize the Vietnamese state and merge private armies into the new Vietnamese army. The main opposition was coming from the nationalists of the Cao Dai, while the Hoa Hao and Binh Xuyen remained favorable to Bao Dai. The emperor was also fearful that France would simply leave Vietnam high and dry and allow the Viet Minh to take over.

General Henri Navarre

Appointed on May 8, 1953, to take over from Raoul Salan, Henri Navarre was originally a cavalry officer who had later been involved in counter intelligence; contrary to his predecessor, he had never set foot in Southeast Asia. He was serving at NATO and tried to avoid the assignment, but to no avail. Prime Minister Mayer said quite candidly that France was seeking "an honorable exit" from Indochina but he gave no further details. Navarre had almost no time to prepare for his assignment and flew into Saigon to find that General Salan and almost all of the old de Lattre officers were packing their trunks, except for General René Cogny, who took command in Tonkin.

Navarre began by touring Indochina to analyze the situation of the expeditionary corps and reached a few basic conclusions: because of the need to hold so much territory French forces had to take a defensive position since they were not assured of adequate air and artillery cover. Units lacked cohesion because of too many rotations, except for the parachute regiments and the Foreign Legion, and were of mediocre quality. Training and morale needed to improve.

The commander in chief's mission statement closely followed what the recent strategy had been: "a complete military victory or at least a significant enough weakening of the enemy to induce negotiations favorable to us."[4] Navarre then took Salan's final plan, which called for a build-up of the associated states' forces (Vietnam, Cambodia, and Laos) to include a large mobile group. The goal was to inflict significant damage on the enemy to force him to negotiate in 1954-55. The strategy in 1953-1954 was defensive north of the eighteenth parallel, containing most of the Viet Minh forces to give French forces time to regroup and ensure the accelerated formation of the Vietnamese army. Until that was accomplished the bulk of French forces would be involved in a defensive battle in Tonkin, holding the delta for the balance of 1953. The French high command issued no written orders, appearing to agree to Navarre's demand for additional reinforcements. He also suggested that parts of the occupation forces stationed in Germany be sent to Indochina to reach the required troop strength.

Amazingly the Laniel government took six months to reply and offer any comments! In November Navarre was told to adjust his plan, using the troops at his disposal to convince the enemy that military victory was impossible. There would be no reinforcements coming his way. But that document didn't actually reach Navarre until December 4, when the valley of Dien Bien Phu had already been occupied by French forces and the armed camp was in the process of being set up.

---

4. Navarre quoted in Gras, op. cit., p. 512.

Total Viet Minh forces in the fall of 1953 numbered 350,000, including all regulars, guerrillas, and Chinese support troops. Should the Viet Minh concentrate most of its forces in the Tonkin delta in a general offensive the prospects for the French and Vietnamese forces would not have been good. The French Expeditionary Corps included 175,000 men in the regular army, 55,000 auxiliaries and 226,000 forces from the associated states. Only 54,000 were French, the rest were 19,000 Legionnaires (many of them of German origin), 29,500 North Africans, 18,000 Africans, and 53,000 Indochinese. The entire Expeditionary force was roughly fifty percent Indochinese. Motorized forces included 7 mobile groups and 8 paratrooper battalions. The air force had 336 fighter planes and the navy a small flotilla of river gunboats and deep water ships.

Navarre first had to take the initiative and convince his men that the defensive strategy was over. A paratrooper operation over Lang Son, an outpost the French had abandoned three years before after the battle of the RC 4, was spectacularly successful in July 1953. The objective was to destroy or capture enemy weapons stockpiles located nearby. The operation was a morale booster rather than a tactical move and the Viet Minh appeared indifferent about the outcome. Counter guerrilla forces operating in Thai country were the real danger to the Viet Minh, since its strategy included the progressive infiltration and control of upper Laos from Vietnam. Na San could no longer prevent the Viet Minh from using the road into Thai country. A new base had to be set up and General Cogny proposed to create another armed camp in the upper region, closer to Laos similar to Na San.

Dien Bien Phu was located high up in Thai country, overshadowing Luang Prabang, the endangered Laotian capital. Navarre was encouraged by those initial successes and felt that by October 1953 the Expeditionary Corps was ready to react quickly to Viet Minh attacks. The French commander was not aware that during that same month his plan had been stolen by Chinese spies and delivered to Ho Chi Minh by General Wei Guoqing, acting on orders from Mao Zedong. China agreed to provide the Viet Minh with massive military aid, enabling the victory over the French at Dien Bien Phu.[5]

---

5. Jung Chang, and Jon Halliday, *Mao. The Unknown Story* (New York: A. Knopf, 2005), p. 573.

Northern Laos and Thai Country

The base at Dien Bien Phu originated with the plan to retain control of the Thai country, located in the northeastern corner of Tonkin and the key to northern Laos. The Kingdom of Laos, one of the associated states, had just signed a defensive military agreement with France and both Maurice Dejean and General Navarre felt duty bound to ensure that country's defenses. The establishment of the armed camp at Dien Bien Phu began on November 14, 1953, in an operation dubbed "Castor" but officers on Navarre's staff had some misgivings. General Cogny, after having proposed the site, was now far less convinced, preferring to defend the delta rather than the Thai country, and he would soon get into a terrible row with his commanding general. The air force was uncomfortable about the flying distance of 175 miles from Hanoi—a very long round trip at that time—for supply runs with the aircraft available. General Jean Gilles, in charge of the paratroopers, voiced his opposition to the operation during the final briefing but was overruled by Navarre, who insisted that it was necessary to establish the armed camp at Dien Bien Phu as an offensive base to cover upper Laos from Thai country.

On November 20 Gilles' paratroopers landed and took over the valley in a massive operation requiring 67 C-47s to fly in 4,500 men and a battalion of engineers to prepare the landing strip. The true purpose of Dien Bien Phu remained unclear: was it a defensive and offensive armed camp or a base for operations into the mountainous jungle territory of northern Laos? Military intelligence signaled that the Viet Minh was moving large units into Thai country and even depleting units from the delta. But this information didn't change Navarre's mind or compel him to modify his plan even though he knew that the government in Paris would not provide the reinforcements he had requested. The government was wondering whether this was not the right time to seek a cease fire with the enemy. Navarre remained unshakably optimistic and wanted to wait for the results of the coming winter campaign.

General Cogny warned of the need for a defensive battle against the enemy as he was moving out of the delta and heading north. Navarre again overruled him, since he couldn't believe that Dien Bien

Phu would be facing the bulk of the Viet Minh main forces. On December 3 Navarre made the fateful decision that "the defense of the air and land base at Dien Bien Phu must be held at all costs."[6] The armed camp was a device to draw the enemy into attacking a base able to withstand the onslaught and destroy large numbers of Viet Minh forces. The Na San precedent provided the model for Dien Bien Phu but only up to a point: Na San was quickly evacuated once it had served its purpose. Salan was mindful that the fortified lines of the 1930s—the Maginot Line, Siegfried Line, Gustav Line, and Gothic Line—as history showed, had never worked.

Navarre was also reassured by his intelligence units, which he had greatly expanded, that the Viet Minh wouldn't be able to move more than two divisions with 20,000 coolies into the rugged terrain through the jungle. That assessment would prove to be tragically flawed. In another twist of fate Navarre was convinced that Dien Bien Phu was not the main battle of the war and that the most important effort was to be expected in central Vietnam instead. On December 8 General Gilles was rotated back to France and replaced by Colonel Christian de Castries, a cavalry officer trained to take the offensive. After reading the French press and Viet Minh intelligence reports, Vo Nguyen Giap decided to give battle at Dien Bien Phu. French officers, and even Cogny, were openly telling journalists that Dien Bien Phu was going to be "another Na San." Far too many details about the armed camp were being published in the French press, giving Giap a fairly accurate picture of the overall plan the French were putting in place.

The Viet Minh commander in chief overcame opposition in the central committee of the Lao Dong (Communist Party) to his decision to attack Dien Bien Phu. He feared that the steady increase of the Vietnamese army trained by the French could tip the balance against him in a relatively short time. But at Dien Bien Phu the isolation of the armed camp had real advantages for Giap's forces. The main problem was one of logistics and the central committee decided to mobilize the party and the people to ensure success. The Viet Minh would move four divisions into Thai country, use 75,000 coolies, and provide enough support for a 56-day battle. All this was thought to be im-

6. Gras, op. cit., p. 524.

possible by General Navarre. French intelligence found out that by the end of December Giap had a set up his forward headquarters at Tuan Giao and that several units were moving in that direction: a total of 22 battalions. The Viet Minh were getting ready to attack the armed camp. By mid-December French patrols were getting into serious firefights just 16 km beyond the perimeter with major Viet Minh units—the pressure was being turned on.

In spite of excellent intelligence Navarre still could not believe that Giap was mounting an all-out attack on Dien Bien Phu: signals intelligence and decryption were pinpointing the movements of almost every Viet Minh unit in real time. Navarre's lack of experience of war in Southeast Asia was suddenly working against him because at that point, when the entire armed camp could have still been easily evacuated by air, he remained rigidly wedded to his plan. The land route to northern Laos was extremely difficult, making an evacuation in that direction virtually impossible. The crack Viet Minh Division 308 reached the heights around the camp and closed the circle just before New Year's Day. For five more days Navarre could still have pulled out the 12,000 men of the Expeditionary Force but that window was allowed to pass. The French commander in chief was convinced that in any case he would have the upper hand and superior firepower. Perhaps the superiority complex of the Western military professional facing an Asian guerrilla army was at play once more in the fateful decision to accept the battle at that point. The French camp was brimming with confidence about the outcome of the coming test.

Press observers were also convinced that Dien Bien Phu would be the decisive battle of the war as Robert Guillain, the correspondent of the prestigious Paris daily *Le Monde* wrote: "They want this fight. To get the Viet [Minh] down into the valley is the dream of Col. de Castries and his entire staff. If he comes down he'll belong to us. [...] Finally, we'll have what we have been missing: a tightly concentrated target that we can clobber."[7] Cogny told the United Press: "I welcome the clash at Dien Bien Phu." The most chilling aspect was that no one had any second thoughts or dared express them if they did: only General Pierre Fay, the head of the air force, and General Clément

---

7. Quoted by Gras, op.cit. p. 529. (Our translation. Editor's Note.)

Blanc, army chief of staff, feared the rainy season and its effect on the dirt landing strip. British and American generals fell in line with the prevailing optimism and neither British commissioner for Southeast Asia Malcolm MacDonald, U.S. general John W. O'Daniel (head of MAAG), and Major-General Thomas Trapnell, Sir Edward Spears, or Commander in Chief of Far East Land Forces General Sir Charles Loewen ever expressed second thoughts: they all approved what Navarre was doing. In his memoirs Eisenhower commented on the Navarre Plan: "It was difficult to understand…why the French decided to send ten thousand crack troops into this position, strong as it was, whose only means of resupply was by air."[8] Later on Ike would have words of regret about the battle and the French defeat. However, authoritative American and British military observers had seen and approved the position and the strategy at Dien Bien Phu and they didn't appear to be confused about what was going on.

By early January, given his intelligence reports, Navarre began to consider negative outcomes and fall back positions. Chilling second thoughts began to cross his mind and he expressed them in his notes to various other officers: "What if the enemy…" His fatal weakness was in air cover, transport planes, B-26s, and fighter bombers. He asked the government for more air power. The 370 planes available in Indochina were not enough. The range of aircraft at the time didn't allow for the necessary offensive power against the attacking forces. The solution of attacking the Viet Minh forces from the rear by coming in from the delta, which had the advantage of using the air force and artillery closer to their bases, was rejected by General Navarre. He didn't think he had enough manpower to set up such an operation that would have required concentrating far more troops in Tonkin by depleting other areas of Indochina and particularly in central Vietnam (Annam). In a letter to the French government dated January 1, 1954, Navarre had already accepted the possibility that Dien Bien Phu could be lost but even in such a scenario it would have served the purpose of "[working] as an abscess and avoiding a general battle in the delta."

---

8. Dwight D. Eisenhower, *Mandate for Change 1953-1956* (New York: Doubleday, 1963), p. 339.

Navarre's true objective was Operation "Atlante" in central Vietnam, where the pacification effort would be the responsibility of Vietnamese authorities. He was later bitterly criticized for withholding troops from Dien Bien Phu that perhaps could have made a difference. He played into Giap's strategy by scattering the French forces while Giap was pushing French counter guerrilla units in Laos as far away as possible from Dien Bien Phu. Logistics remained the Viet Minh's main problem, since they had 80,000 men 600 km removed from their bases and needed far greater supplies for a longer period than usual. The road had to be cleared through jungle all the way up to Dien Bien Phu, something French commanders were convinced would be impossible. If bombed the coolies would quickly build deviations and continue to carry the supplies while the main road was being repaired. At no time during the battle was road traffic significantly interrupted—much like the Ho Chi Minh trail later on.

Giap accelerated his time table when it was announced on February 18, 1954, that the four major powers—the United States, the USSR, Great Britain, and France—had decided to convene a conference at Geneva at the end of April to discuss peace in Korea and Indochina. Navarre blamed that announcement, among other things, for the defeat at Dien Bien Phu. The Viet Minh now had a precise political calendar and they knew they must win by the end of April. Navarre still had a major option open to him: bring his forces up from the delta and attack Giap from behind to divert the Viet Minh from Dien Bien Phu and possibly even win the battle itself. Amazingly enough he made no such attempt and showed none of the flexibility of his predecessor, Raoul Salan.

By early March 51,000 Viet Minh had encircled 11,000 French and Vietnamese troops. Finally, on March 13, Col. de Castries was informed that the attack would begin at 1700 hours; he was convinced that victory would be his.

The Assault, Defense, and Fall of Dien Bien Phu

The battle itself lasted from March 13 to May 7, 1954, a total of 54 days. The armed camp had not been set up as a defensive base able to withstand a long siege but rather as a land and air base that could beat back an attack by one Viet Minh division. Dien Bien Phu was in a valley about 16 km long by 9 km wide, just a few kilometers shorter and narrower than the island of Manhattan (19 km by 11 km at its widest point). All the planners, including General Cogny, thought it impossible for the Viet Minh to haul 105 mm guns and anti-aircraft artillery up to the heights surrounding the valley and even if they did the air force and the artillery in the camp would quickly pick them off.

The main function of the armed camp was to keep the landing strip—the only access to the valley—open and to receive supplies and reinforcements. Dien Bien Phu had an asymmetrical shape in the form of eight strongholds, the largest being Isabelle at the southern end which was too far removed to cover the others: Claudine, Huguette, and Anne Marie in the west; Eliane and Dominique in the east; Gabrielle and Beatrice were in the center to guard the airfield using small mounds. The airstrip became immediately vulnerable at several points even before the onslaught. De Castries had dug a network of trenches around each position that was reinforced but was still unable to withstand anything like a barrage of 105 mm guns. There was also a conspicuous absence of any camouflage to cover the terrain that had been radically uprooted of all trees and vegetation and dug up so that all troop movements would be easily visible to the defenders.

Giap's first objective was to interrupt all traffic on the landing strip through continuous artillery bombardment. Viet Minh artillery went into action on March 11 hitting the airstrip repeatedly and destroying six Bearcat fighter planes. All air supplies and reinforcements had to fly in from the bases at Gia Lam (Hanoi) or Do Son and Cat Bi, near Haiphong. Viet Minh heavy artillery was located in limestone caves dug into the side of the mountain and protected by heavy foliage and narrow openings. Any attempt to obliterate the 105 mm guns had to hit the mountain directly at those openings. The Viet Minh had only twenty-four 105s and fifteen 75mm guns while the infantry could move up close with heavy mortars and 81 mm cannon. French artillery was visible and vulnerable while it remained unable to silence the larger enemy guns.

The Beatrice position held by 450 Legionaries was assaulted and taken on March 13 after a six-hour fight. The attack began with a 105 shell hitting the command post and killing the battalion commander and his staff. The second in command was also killed a few moments later. Col. de Castries made no attempt to counter attack even though the Viet Minh failed to hold the position and withdrew; instead he requested a temporary cease fire to evacuate the dead and wounded. The second position, Gabrielle, came under attack on March 14 and the previous scenario was about to be repeated: a lucky artillery shot knocked out the command post, killing all the officers and leaving the Algerian "tirailleurs" (fusiliers) leaderless. They resisted all night until the survivors retreated to the south when they realized that no serious counter attack was going to materialize.

On March 16 a paratrooper battalion led by Col. Marcel Bigeard landed on the base to make up for the losses. But no effort was made to take back Beatrice and Gabrielle. At Na San Col. Gilles had saved the day by reacting forcefully and quickly to any loss of a key defensive position. No such reaction came from Col. de Castries who was quickly mired in pessimism that spread like a diseased among officers and men. Lt. Col. Charles Piroth, in charge of artillery, blamed himself for the disaster and committed suicide. Two companies panicked and fled into the mountains. Neither General Navarre nor General Cogny went to Dien Bien Phu in the heat of battle to see for themselves and encourage the officers and men trapped in the pocket. De Lattre had not hesitated to go to the Vinh Yen airstrip, exposing himself to extreme danger. De Castries appointed Lt. Col. Pierre Langlais as head of operations while he, de Castries, was handling communications with Hanoi and logistics in what appeared to be an incomprehensible withdrawal from the action. Langlais showed far more character and took the initiative in leading the garrison in a last ditch resistance. By March 17 Giap had managed to stop the traffic on the airstrip and could now lay siege to Dien Bien Phu in a classic form of set-piece battle. By then the French forces were virtually defeated.

Giap took two weeks to rotate his troops that were severely depleted by heavy casualties. Bigeard became Langlais' deputy commander as the French also reorganized. The main problem was to replenish the supplies and ammunition while the airstrip remained under Viet Minh fire. Planes could no longer land or take off, so they had to resort to parachute drops. But with Langlais and Bigeard defensive operations became far more aggressive and effective with tough counter attacks against the Viet Minh. On March 30 a new general offensive began targeting all five hills. Giap was directing the battle himself and 12,000 Viet Minh went on the offensive against 2,000 defenders. Only French artillery firing at point blank range managed to stop the waves of attackers. By the next day three of the five hills were in Viet Minh hands. Giap immediately decided to go for an all out offensive while Bigeard retook two of the three hills but then had to retreat once more under Viet Minh pressure and in the absence of reinforcements from Hanoi.

Yet according to Nikita Khrushchev, as late as April 4, 1954, Zhou Enlai told Molotov during a meeting in Moscow: "Comrade Ho told me that the situation is desperate. If they don't get a cease fire very quickly they can't hold off the French army."[9] The Chinese were unable or unwilling to provide additional forces to the Viet Minh, particularly after their staggering losses in Korea but also because they feared a massive intervention by the United States.

Giap cancelled his order for a broad offensive after spirited French counter attacks. He then moved to the hill, Huguette, defending the far side of the airstrip; from April 1 to 5 intense fighting took place between French paratroopers and the Viet Minh, who had to withdraw in the face of heavy casualties. Giap now needed more men to replenish his losses. He finally opted to bring in most of the forces available in Tonkin and changed his tactics to a slow strangulation of the armed camp. By April 6 the situation became very difficult inside the perimeter, which had progressively shrunk in size. The Viet Minh, advancing relentlessly for three weeks, were preventing the dropping of supplies and reinforcements. The French and Vietnamese nationalist paratroopers took back Eliane, singing the *Marseillaise*. By the end of April Giap had reorganized his army of 15,000 men and went on the attack on May 1. After intense fighting by May 7 the entire camp was under Viet Minh control. The Ho Chi Minh government hadn't expected such a quick collapse of Dien Bien Phu. The French garrison surrendered and the Viet Minh marched some 9,000 prisoners off on

---

9. Céline Marangé, *Le Communisme Vietnamien (1919-1991)* (Paris: SciencesPo Les Presses, 2012), pp. 213-214.

foot to POW camps near the Chinese border, with many prisoners dying along the way.

Rescue Plans

On March 25 in Washington French chief of staff General Paul Ely and Admiral Arthur Radford discussed the possibility of using American long-range bombers to relieve Dien Bien Phu. General Navarre agreed and on April 4 the French government made an official request. The Pentagon prepared plans for Operation Vulture: a single bombing raid by 98 B-29 bombers flying round trip from Manila and Okinawa to drop 1400 tons of bombs on Viet Minh positions.[10] Congressional approval was predicated on British participation and the agreement of friendly Southeast Asian countries: Thailand, Burma, and the Philippines. The answer given by the United States on April 8 was tantamount to a refusal. But the U.S. Air Force went ahead with the planning and Generals Earle Partridge and Joseph Caldara flew into Saigon with Caldara taking a reconnaissance flight over Dien Bien Phu. But Generals Matthew Ridgeway and James Gavin were not convinced and feared that a land war in Southeast Asia would inevitably follow involving the Chinese. Eisenhower was also skeptical that a single bombing raid could be successful. Operation Vulture was therefore shelved on April 29. A few days before Bidault had written to Secretary of State John Foster Dulles: "A massive raid by American air forces could still save the garrison [...] the Viet Minh has concentrated a vast number of troops, weapons and most of its manpower." However, General Caldara's conclusions were not optimistic for technical reasons: a massive bombing raid would have necessarily killed many French troops along with the Viet Minh since the two armies were positioned at such close range of one another and the targets were not clearly marked. But in 1966 Caldara stated that a raid "could have destroyed the entire enemy force surrounding Dien Bien Phu."[11]

---

10. John Prados, *Operation Vulture* (New York: IBooks, 2002), updated edition, previously published as *The Sky Would Fall* in 1983. The most thorough account of the plans by the U.S. to save the French garrison at Dien Bien Phu.

11. Ted Morgan, *Valley of Death* (New York: Random House, 2010), pp. 450-452. Morgan's book is the most complete account of the battle of Dien Bien Phu and its aftermath at the Geneva conference.

American intervention was difficult to organize and didn't have Congressional or Pentagon support. Korea was too fresh in the public mind for a second military action in Asia. However, Vice President Richard Nixon, in an aggressive speech on April 16, threatened U.S. military intervention to relieve the French in Indochina. In later accounts of this unsettled moment Nixon would be held up as the bellicose hawk of the whole affair. Yet knowing how tightly Eisenhower held his cabinet it is more likely that Nixon was blowing up one of Ike's trial balloons aimed at Congress, the British, and the Chinese, who quickly reacted by proposing an armistice. U.S. requirements for intervention included British participation or, more likely, approval of an action. The UK however had a paramount interest in pursuing good relations with China: to protect the crown colony of Hong Kong. Indochina was expendable in Anthony Eden's view and the war was complicating the Asian picture at the time: the British foreign office wanted above all a settlement that would be as satisfactory and as complete as possible. Eden felt that "it would be folly to try and save Indochina by force of arms."[12]

On April 24, 1954, John Foster Dulles took one of his many trips to Paris to discuss the Indochinese situation. At the Quai d'Orsay he had a meeting with Bidault and in the course of the conversation off handedly offered France two atomic bombs to clear Dien Bien Phu.[13] But the French foreign minister refused the offer and promised that France would keep on fighting until the Geneva conference was scheduled to begin. With Eisenhower's backing Dulles had used the nuclear threat effectively before—during the Korean truce negotiations at Panmunjom in 1953. The Chinese were informed discreetly through India that the United States had atomic weapons in place in Korea to underscore the pressing need to come to terms in the cease fire talks. The Korean armistice was signed one month later in July. Dulles made no such move in Geneva because the United States was not officially attending the conference and sent Under Secretary of State Walter

---

12. Morgan, *ibid.* p. 476.
13. The offer made of the two atomic bombs has been often discussed and doubted by many historians. During the November 7, 1968, interview with Georges Bidault, the former French foreign minister confirmed the Dulles offer. Bidault declined saying that the bombs would also kill the entire French garrison he was seeking to save and therefore was unacceptable.

Bedell Smith as an observer. Nevertheless, Dulles later claimed that he had again gone to the brink at Geneva.

Military Situation in Indochina

With the fall of Dien Bien Phu France had actually lost only 5 percent of its fighting forces in Indochina. Large portions of territory—the two deltas of the Mekong and Red River in Tonkin, and most of central Annam—remained under French control. But the psychological effect of the defeat was far more devastating and in many ways a reflection of France's collapse of May-June 1940, albeit on a much smaller scale. The distance and the dramatic accounts of the fighting as reported in the press and media, its desperate nature, the sacrifice and heroism of individual men and women in uniform were all brought home to the French people on a daily basis. The "dirty war" was no longer filed away in the back pages of the major dailies. The French public was repulsed by the scale of the catastrophe as it was depicted and no voices could be heard demanding that the war should continue. France wanted to end the ordeal as quickly as possible. However, it remained conceivable that the war could drag on and that danger was on everyone's mind during the negotiations that had started long before the Geneva conference formally opened.

In terms of losses it may be said that the First Indochina War had actually started in June 1940 with the fall of France and ended in August 1954 with the cease fire, although the French army left Indochina permanently in 1956. According to rough estimates the conflict up to that point claimed from 500,000 to 2 million dead among Vietnamese noncombatants, including 100 to 150,000 assassinations by nationalists and communists, mostly of Vietnamese civilians and officials considered too pro-French. Military deaths among Viet Minh forces are estimated between 175,000 and 250,000, while French Union forces had about 90,000 killed and 65,000 wounded in nine years of actual fighting.

The Geneva Conference

The prelude to Geneva came in Berlin when the idea of a conference was accepted by Soviet foreign minister Vyacheslav Molotov in February 1954. The objective was to discuss Korea and Indochina, thereby reaching an accommodation in Asia. The United States, still refusing to recognize Communist China, was persuaded to accept the negotiations at the insistence of British foreign secretary Anthony Eden and by Georges Bidault. France saw Geneva as the only possible diplomatic solution since it couldn't make the necessary military commitment to remain in Indochina. What none of the Western countries and the Viet Minh knew was that Mao Zedong had already decided that he must have a settlement at the negotiating table. Zhou Enlai therefore appeared very accommodating, acting under specific instructions from Mao, including the partition of Vietnam, which neither the Viet Minh nor the State of Vietnam were prepared to accept.

The conference opened on April 26, 1954, as the battle of Dien Bien Phu was still raging. The French government was represented by Georges Bidault until June 19, when Pierre Mendès-France became prime minister and foreign minister with a mandate to resolve the war in Indochina within thirty days or resign. He had set that challenge for himself before parliament could force him to agree to almost any kind of deal he could get. On the other hand, it also made clear to the Viet Minh and the Chinese that the alternative could very well mean the resumption of war with massive U.S. intervention and the threat that nuclear weapons could be used.

The participants at Geneva were: the USSR (Vyacheslav Molotov); the People's Republic of China (Zhou Enlai); the Viet Minh (Pham Van Dong); the United Kingdom (Anthony Eden); France (Georges Bidault, then Pierre Mendès-France); and the Associated States (the State of Vietnam, the Kingdoms of Laos and Cambodia); and the United States (Walter Bedell Smith), acting as an observer when the object of negotiations switched from Korea to Indochina. Bao Dai and the government of Prince Buu Loc were under pressure from the ultra nationalists of the National Union Movement of Ngo Dinh Nhu, the brother of Ngo Dinh Diem, which was demanding full and immediate independence from France. Bao Dai refused to participate in discussions with the Viet Minh and rejected any partition of the country. But the battle quickly took on a dramatic turn with most issues and any semblance of posturing becoming moot. On the French side Jean Chauvel, the main diplomatic advisor to Georges Bidault, attempted to keep the demands of all sides to realistic and acceptable terms. But France had very little leverage, since Dien Bien Phu was clearly a major disaster. On April 25 Great Britain confirmed its opposition to the American proposal contained in Operation Vulture to bomb the heights around Dien Bien Phu. Both the USSR and Communist China feared that such a raid would force them to take a position that could lead to another conflict. The Eisenhower administration, reading the mood of U.S. public opinion, was emphatically opposed to a second war in Southeast Asia and dropped the plan. Some historians now feel that the United States came far closer to intervention than was previously believed.[14]

Once the Korean talks reached their conclusion John Foster Dulles left Geneva on May 3 after newsreels showed him turning his back on Zhou Enlai to avoid having to shake hands. Dulles wanted France to hold out in Indochina for two more years to give the U.S. time to build up support to take over the war and occupy the Indochinese peninsula in a "rollback" operation. But this was wishful thinking, since the president was adamantly opposed to any such scenario. French officials were suddenly making pessimistic statements to the press. Finally, on May 7 the armed camp was overrun by the Viet Minh, leaving French diplomacy with nothing to bargain with. Pham Van Dong, the Viet Minh representative and an old revolutionary comrade of Ho Chi Minh, spelled out a list of demands. He was well aware of the limits of the victory at Dien Bien Phu in the agendas of the great powers and at times had to face a lack of support from the Soviet Union. The Bao Dai regime made a few attempts to put forth its demands and legitimacy, begrudged by almost all the other participants. The South Vietnamese foreign minister stated bitterly: "Was it necessary in order to end colonial rule to introduce communism into our country, since it is

---

14. See Logevall, *Embers,* cit.

the most perfect form of imperialism…?" He then went on to denounce the crimes of the Viet Minh.[15]

The final disposition accepted by Pham Van Dong and the other delegates on May 25 was a temporary partition of Vietnam at the 17th parallel, with elections on unification within two years. France would evacuate the north and only maintain a token presence. But at that point there was still the possibility that the conference could fail and Bidault was hoping that the United States would be compelled to step in militarily. General Valluy was sent to Washington to make the case but his trip was not successful. The Laniel government dispatched reinforcements to Indochina and replaced General Navarre with General Ely on June 12. That same day the government lost the confidence of the assembly and resigned; on June 18 Pierre Mendès-France formed his government after a nearly unanimous vote by the chamber of deputies and confirmed what was called his "wager" of one month to reach an agreement or hand in his resignation.

Fearful of American intervention the Viet Minh agreed to most of the compromises offered by the British and French: the 17th parallel was finally accepted as a temporary dividing line. France would keep a garrison of 75,000 men in the south; there would be population exchanges and free elections for reunification under UN supervision within two years. The South Vietnamese delegate went on record to voice Vietnam's opposition to the agreements and on July 2 the newly appointed Premier Ngo Dinh Diem denied that the agreements signed at Geneva had any legal value. The United States "took note" of the agreements but also didn't sign them, in effect siding with Diem.

The State of Vietnam was still formally headed by Emperor Bao Dai, who had appointed Ngo Dinh Diem as prime minister on June 26, 1954. Both the French and Bao Dai disliked Diem, considering him too much of a "fanatic," but the new prime minister enjoyed firm U.S. backing and managed to remain in power. The new government of Vietnam (South Vietnam) rejected the accords in their entirety, including the clause calling for free elections, for fear of a Viet Minh victory. In spite of what many historians, critical of the Diem regime, have written, the elections also did not receive the support of the

---

15. Philippe Franchini, *Les Guerres d'Indochine*, Vol. II, op. cit., p. 131.

North as well since there was by 1956 fear of massive dissent by the peasantry against Ho Chi Minh and his police state. The other main objection was the partition of the country at the 18th, then finally at the 17th parallel. Diem was a staunch Catholic and he made sure that about one million Catholics from Tonkin were able to move south in a continuous migration that lasted until the end of 1955. One of the diplomatic and military consequences of the Korean and Indochinese wars was the creation of the SEATO pact signed in Manila on September 8, 1954, which was portrayed as the Asian version of NATO. The participants were the United States, France, the Associated States (Vietnam, Laos, and Cambodia) Great Britain, Australia, New Zealand, the Philippines, Pakistan, and Thailand. The defense of SEATO was to be a major reason offered for the massive intervention of the United States in Vietnam after 1964.

Unquestionably the French ended their role in the Indochina War full of bitterness toward America and to a lesser degree Great Britain.

> The United States interfered too much and helped too little. [...] it was not interested in supporting the empire which made European strength possible.[16]

The statement summed up the French view and set the stage for the final decolonization of French Africa and the Algerian War.

---

16. Friedman, op. cit., p. 183.

Part II

Cold War Vietnam

1.

North and South Vietnam

Ngo Dinh Diem

News of the Geneva Conference came as a shock to the population of Tonkin, since most people expected the war to go on and for the French to try and retain control of their colony at almost any cost. A general panic, encouraged by CIA agents, took hold of large groups of the population and the Catholics in particular as they were attempting to move south of the 17th parallel. The last French units left Hanoi in October while over 120,000 Viet Minh and pro-communist civilians in the south moved to the north. These exchanges, including the French and Vietnamese prisoner swaps, were part of a long and painful process. Many French and Associated States prisoners of the Viet Minh in the wake of Dien Bien Phu were near death and had suffered torture and starvation, besides the tropical diseases and dehydration common in the jungle.

The man who would leave his mark on South Vietnam and attempt to carve a nation out of half of his country was Ngo Dinh Diem. Born in 1901 in Hue into an old Catholic and Mandarin family, his father was a high official at the king's court and would hold a lifelong grudge against the French colonial presence. Diem had impeccable nationalist with anti-communist credentials. When French administrators decided to depose King Than Thai in 1907, Diem's father, Ngo Dinh Kha, resigned in protest and remained a dissident all his life. An amazingly diligent and successful student, Diem graduated at the top of his class in 1921, entered government service, and was quickly promoted into the upper Mandarin ranks.[1] In the 1930s he became an administrator in Annam and realized how deeply communist ideas had spread in the provinces where he was attempting to expose and fight the early Marxist-Leninist militants. This earned him wide respect among French administrators and a promotion by Emperor Bao Dai. Diem kept in contact with key Vietnamese monarchist dissidents Phan Boi Chau and Prince Cuong De, as well as other Asian nationalists who later became pro-Japanese—Sukarno of Indonesia and Subhas Chandra Bose of India, among others. More than anyone and like his lifelong opponent Ho Chi Minh, Diem understood that France's defeat in 1940 meant that colonialism was over in Southeast Asia. The issue of independence was only one of timing.

In the guerrilla and terrorist attacks that followed the Japanese coup of March 1945, one of Diem's brothers, Ngo Dinh Khoi, was murdered by the Viet Minh. Diem would never forgive Ho Chi Minh for that assassination. In 1946, during a dramatic confrontation while Diem was being held prisoner by the Viet Minh recovering from wounds he had received, he hurled insults at Ho Chi Minh and called him a murderer. Ho had shrugged off the death of Diem's brother as something that happens in a revolution, the familiar "you can't make an omelet without breaking the eggs" argument. Diem swore to seek both revenge and to pursue lifelong opposition.

In 1949 Diem also rejected offers from Bao Dai to join the new Vietnamese government and kept equally distant from the French and the communists. In June 1954, when Bao Dai called on Diem once more to form a government, the prime minister designate was virtually unknown outside a small circle in Vietnam and the United States. Through his uncle Ngo Dinh Thuc, a Catholic bishop, Diem had entrée to the Vatican and to New York's Francis Cardinal Spellman.

---

1. Seth Jacobs, *Cold War Mandarin* (Lanham: Rowman-Littlefield, 2006), p. 19.

The future president of South Vietnam was a devout Catholic and a layman of the Church; he spent several years in meditation at Catholic Maryknoll monasteries in New Jersey and Ossining, New York, as a guest of Cardinal Spellman. While in America Diem gave lectures on Vietnam at several universities, including Michigan State, and made important contacts with various U.S. political leaders that included Senators Mike Mansfield and John F. Kennedy. A powerful association the American Friends of Vietnam (AFV) was created with many important political and military leaders joining in and operating as a virtual Vietnam lobby.

Almost as important to Diem's ascent to power was his younger brother Ngo Dinh Nhu, a Westernized intellectual who had studied Latin and Greek in Paris at the prestigious École des Chartes and was influenced by French philosophers, principally Emmanuel Mounier. Personalism, according to Mounier, was a mix of Catholic theology and individual freedom within an organized society that some thought could have been a variant of fascism.[2] Nhu had married Tran Le Xuan, a very energetic South Vietnamese beauty, who was also a zealous convert to Catholicism and whose fame was closely related to the 1963 Buddhist crisis. Operating almost in secret in Vietnam, Nhu created the National Movement for Unity, an ultranationalist party that opposed the various governments and ministers appointed by Bao Dai prior to Diem. He also controlled another semi-secret political organization called the Can Lao, a revolutionary and "personalist" party destined to become the main political organization of the Diem regime. Can Lao was organized on the communist cell model and had successfully penetrated the army and government administration. The long process of influence and recruitment was to bear fruit in a few years' time when the Can Lao became the most effective political organization in South Vietnam capable of countering the Viet Cong.

Following the Geneva Conference, Bao Dai's absence from South Vietnam created a vacuum. The emperor was strongly criticized in the French press for his gambling nights in the casinos at Cannes and Nice instead of shouldering the rigors of being a head of state. Those

---

2. Personalism was criticized by several political scientists and historians as having potentially fascist tendencies according to historian Zeev Sternhell in his analysis of Emanuel Mounier. However, Personalism was also credited with having influenced Pope John Paul II and Rev. Martin Luther King, Jr., as well.

articles didn't help his already tarnished image. His appointment of Diem brought more heavy criticism from the French, who considered the new premier unfit to be a popular leader. Maurice Dejean described Diem as "too narrow, too rigid, [and] too unworldly...to have any chance of creating an effective government."[3] Diem was not the only candidate but the United States felt he would provide the strongest appeal to the nationalists who remained both anti-communist and anti-French.

Immediately following the Geneva Conference in July 1954, the Mendès-France government had to face new trouble spots in French North Africa: Tunisia and Morocco were agitating for independence and Algeria was ready to explode. Terrorism made its spectacular debut in Casablanca and Tunis as early as 1952 and on November 1, 1954, the Algerian rebellion started. The French were in a hurry to disengage from Southeast Asia and concentrate on saving their position in North Africa. France was both relieved and bitter about the United States taking a hand in Vietnam with their handpicked leader. A first attempt to overthrow Diem came in September 1954 when General Nguyen Van Hinh, the army chief of staff with strong ties to the French, tried his hand at conspiracy. Joint American and French intervention decided by General Paul Ely, the last commissioner in Indochina, ended the rebellion. France's aim was to keep a small expeditionary corps in South Vietnam after the cease fire. But that policy would be short lived and by 1956 any official French presence had disappeared. In fact, in September 1954 France secretly agreed to allow direct American aid to flow to the Diem government. thereby tacitly ending the Bao Dai "solution."

Deeply xenophobic, Diem felt uneasy with foreigners, yet he understood where his real interests lay and found in Major Edward G. Lansdale, the head of the Saigon Military Mission (SMM), his most fervent American supporter. Lansdale, whose résumé included a successful mission to the Philippines against communist-backed guerrillas, arrived in Vietnam right after Dien Bien Phu. He was working with former OSS Major Lucien "Lou" Conein, who had experience in Tonkin with anti-Japanese guerrillas in 1945. One of Lansdale's major

---

3. Jacobs, op. cit., p. 39.

successes in Vietnam was Operation Passage to Freedom, the transfer of close to a million Catholics from Tonkin to the south where by 1956 they became one of the most influential minorities. On the public relations side the story that emerged from the plight of the Catholics came as a book by U.S. Navy doctor Tom Dooley, entitled *Deliver Us from Evil,* excerpted in the *Reader's Digest* to a worldwide readership of over 12 million. Dooley painted a terrifying picture of communist persecution at the hands of the Viet Minh which in the context of the Cold War was both poignant and eminently credible, even though his claims were later found to be exaggerated. Much like *I Chose Freedom* by Victor Kravchenko in 1946, Dooley's book was also immensely successful, selling in the millions of copies. The perceived threat of Soviet and Chinese communist aggression also magnified the book's message to a fearful and receptive public.

Seeking a broader military base of support, Diem entered into an alliance with Cao Dai dissident leader General Trinh Minh Thé and his 3,000-man forces that were anti-Viet Minh, anti-French, and a CIA asset. It is very likely that Diem was able to finance General The's loyalty with additional CIA funding from Lansdale's war chest. Another potential threat to Diem, coming from General Hinh, ended with the general's resignation and exile to France. In December 1954 General J. Lawton Collins signed an agreement with General Ely transferring the training of the South Vietnamese army to the United States Military Assistance Advisory Group (MAAG) by February 1955. Diem's regime remained very shaky during this early period and he could really only rely on Major (later Colonel) Lansdale for effective support, apart from a few public relations opportunities such as Cardinal Spellman's visit to Saigon in January 1955 with its accompanying favorable press reports in the United States. Diem was then being called the new anti-Communist crusader of Southeast Asia. Yet just a few miles south of Saigon, the countryside was filled with Viet Minh and the other regions in the fertile Mekong delta were controlled by the Cao Dai and Hoa Hao sects, while the Binh Xuyen gangster army remained in charge of Cholon, the Chinese sector of Saigon.

In April 1955 Diem was faced with a new threat from the various sects, including the Cao Dai and Binh Xuyen, which retained ties to

French intelligence officers of the SDECE in Saigon. Troops loyal to Bao Dai attempted to overthrow Diem and failed after bitter street fighting. The various sects were then cleansed of anti-Diem elements like Bay Vien, the leader of the Binh Xuyen gang who was forced to flee to France, never to return. The remnants of the French expeditionary corps were removed by the French government at Diem's request in 1956. Yet France would continue to retain a strong cultural presence with some 15,000 French nationals living in South Vietnam, many of them mixed race and ethnic Vietnamese. One of the Diem regime's greatest mistakes that would come back to haunt it in 1963 was in the political and economic advantages extended to the northern Catholic refugees who also obtained a disproportionate number of government positions and other patronage jobs. That, plus the insensitive treatment of the Buddhist majority would ultimately lead to Diem's demise.

In the summer of 1955 Diem would face the crisis of the reunification elections that North Vietnam, with the support of the USSR and the People's Republic of China, was requesting in application of the Geneva agreements. South Vietnam—known as the State of Vietnam—having refused, together with the United States, to sign the accords restated its opposition to the elections. In the end both China and the Soviet Union (the latter seeking a thaw in the Cold War) agreed to suspend elections, thereby recognizing the partition of the country and the legitimacy of South Vietnam as a permanent fact.[4] In a referendum on October 23, 1955, a staggering and quite suspicious 98.1 percent of the vote approved of Diem as chief of state in replacement of Bao Dai. The Republic of Vietnam was proclaimed on October 26, 1955, with Ngo Dinh Diem as its president. The constitution gave the president, elected directly by the people, almost full power with a parliament that could not directly oppose the executive branch. It was an authoritarian regime of a dogmatic nature whose mix of Confucian and Catholic thinking was translated into a paternalistic kind of dictatorship.

---

4. The issue of the elections and reunification planned for 1956 has long been a factor in the critique of the American position on South Vietnam. While it was clear that the pro-communist factions would have the upper hand in such a contest it was also a fact that no truly free elections could be held in North Vietnam which was one of Diem's points in refusing to abide by that clause in the Geneva accords of 1954.

The Diem regime was often out of touch and removed from the realities of the country. Two examples will suffice to illustrate the decisions it made by decree that rankled the population: the 1958 Family Law decided that children born of "second wives" were automatically declared illegitimate. In Vietnam this would mean denying legitimacy to large numbers of women and children, something that didn't sit well with the majority of the non-Catholic population.[5] And in 1959, after a spate of terrorist attacks by the Viet Cong, Diem reinstituted the hated guillotine of the French colonial era that was greatly resented by the population.

General J. Lawton Collins was sent by Eisenhower, who valued his performance since World War II, as U.S. Special Representative to South Vietnam in November 1954, following the Geneva Conference. Collins would remain until mid-1955 and quickly concluded that Diem was the wrong man to run the country. The general made repeated recommendations to have the South Vietnamese leader removed and replaced by a more qualified and reliable politician. Collins viewed Diem as remote and removed from the people, clannish and too wedded to the Catholic Church in a country with a Buddhist majority. Another complaint was that Diem, the traditional mandarin had no idea of time management discipline and would get easily caught up in minute detail for inordinately long periods of time.

Back in the U.S. Senate, Gen. Collins found a worthy opponent in Senator Mike Mansfield, who was Diem's main supporter and had the reputation among his peers as an Asia specialist. After carefully observing Diem operating as head of South Vietnam's government, Collins found his approach counterproductive, since the Vietnamese president insisted on attending personally to every infinitesimal detail of every matter that crossed his desk, often losing track of the big picture. Although he spent an enormous amount of time on administrative matters, Diem's methods were not to General Collins' liking. For anyone familiar with Eisenhower's reputation for efficiency it would follow that Collins was in his former supreme commander's mold. Finally, the general rested his case, stating flatly, "No solution in Viet-

5. Franchini, op. cit., Vol. II, p. 167.

nam is possible as long as Diem remains in office."[6] But to the well-heeled pro-Diem lobby at the American Friends of Vietnam that now boasted an impressive roster of backers, including Senators Mike Mansfield, John F. Kennedy, and William Knowland, as well as Tom Dooley, and Henry Luce, Collins' advice was not at all welcome. Nevertheless, when Collins made his recommendation that the United States consider replacing Diem with a better politician—Phan Huy Quat—he faced serious political opposition from Congress and John Foster Dulles. During his visit to South Vietnam in February 1955 the secretary of state publicly voiced his support for the Diem regime to the press and in the presence of General Collins, who could only remain silent.

Thinking that he could count on Dulles' support Diem moved quickly to take on his enemies in the south, namely the sects that were a major threat and had the backing of the strong French military presence. The main opponents were the Binh Xuyen that Diem had to break to consolidate his regime. The showdown came when Diem sought to revoke the concessions of the Binh Xuyen in the city of Saigon-Cholon that had been granted by Emperor Bao Dai. The sects coalesced into a united front against Diem and a pitched battle began inside Saigon on March 30. The situation was confusing enough and reflected the contradictory information given to Eisenhower, who wanted to believe Gen. Collins but also had to listen to the pro-Diem senators such as Mike Mansfield. Congressional pressure from the Democrats was strong, so the administration summoned Collins to make his case for the removal of Diem. After many sessions he was able to sway the secretary of state even though the Congressional committees remained opposed to sacking the chief of state.

After Dulles had dispatched vital cables to Saigon on April 27 to the effect that the U.S. was withdrawing support from Diem, news came through that fighting had erupted in the South Vietnamese capital. Diem was able to crush the Binh Xuyen and reverse the situation. Dulles cancelled his previous communications and Diem's regime was saved, while General Collins had to leave South Vietnam since he

6. Jacobs, op. cit., p. 74.

no longer had the confidence of the prime minister and had caused friction in Washington.

The Diem regime was actually a patchwork of many different Southeast Asian traditions and realities indigenous to Vietnam with added Western features. While constantly keeping an equal distance from the hated French colonial past and the communist north, the contradictions were readily apparent. Most official communications were in the French language and the Vietnamese elites remained under the cultural influence of the long colonial presence. Diem himself and his entourage spoke mostly French rather than English as a foreign language and while he was grateful for American help he remained wary and deeply xenophobic toward all foreigners, even when they were allies. For example, he ruled that top government officials and diplomats should wear the traditional mandarin robe, creating a strange looking class of functionaries for a modern country. The personality cult that was created around him, with his oversize portraits everywhere, was uncomfortably close to that of the communist countries during the same period. His regime was certainly far from being a democracy, but at least in its early years it was accepted by the population as a lesser evil, especially when compared to the harsh police state in North Vietnam.

While Diem was known and admired for his ascetic virtue and personal honesty, the same cannot be said for his entourage, which for one reason or another was considered either thoroughly corrupt or too eager to profit from their powerful connections. His brothers, Ngo Dinh Can, a local potentate in the central province where he had organized a ruthless private police force, and Catholic Archbishop Ngo Dinh Thuc with his many real estate speculations and other financial operations that officially benefited the Catholic Church, were both intensely disliked by the population at large. Also, the northern and mostly Catholic refugees were by far Diem's staunchest supporters and benefited the most from his patronage. Ironically the northerners of the regime also made it remote from the mass of native South Vietnamese. The foreign ideas espoused by his younger brother Ngo Dinh Nhu were not easily understood by the population and were usually shunned by the elites. Yet Nhu was also a very effective political operator and intriguer, totally dedicated to his brother and to the state they had both created. Finally, Madame Nhu, a controversial figure within Vietnam long before she came to the attention of the Western press in 1962-63,[7] exhibited what were considered controversial "feminist" attitudes, disapproved of by traditional society. Yet Tran Le Xuan was always outspoken and politically on the far right of every issue confronting her country.[8]

Diem also had to deal with other attempts to overthrow his regime or at least force him to dismiss his entourage and enact reforms. He managed to beat back all such attacks coming from the anti-communist military or their allies. The CIA lent a helping hand in the repression of dissidents on the right. But against the Viet Cong Diem would face a far greater challenge. At first the regime managed to effectively counter the Viet Cong guerillas: between 1956 and 1960 the communists lost about 80 percent of their networks in South Vietnam. Diem had successfully cut off the peasant masses from the communist cadre and their propaganda machine. Agricultural reform was the main weapon he used to permanently win over the peasants. Mistakes were made with reforms, however, and the peasants were disappointed and often angry at the government when it failed to deliver on its promises. In 1960 the government ended the agricultural reforms it had promised opting for a security campaign that wasn't effective. The reason for the change was the beginning of a brutal terror campaign by the Viet Cong that had been decided in Hanoi to destabilize the Diem regime that was successfully decimating the stay-behind communist cadre in the south.

---

7. Born Tran Le Xuan known as Madame Nhu (1924-2011) was married to Ngo Dinh Nhu the brother of President Diem. Since Diem was a bachelor she was in fact the First Lady of South Vietnam during the Diem years. From a wealthy and important family in Hanoi, her father Tran Van Chuong was a lawyer and diplomat while her mother was a cousin of Emperor Bao Dai. Tran Le Xuan converted to Catholicism to marry Ngo Dinh Nhu, who was fourteen years her senior. Early on she advocated a strict form of morality and pushed for laws banning abortion, adultery, divorce, contraception, public dancing, beauty pageant, brothels, and opium dens. She had the reputation as an intriguer, as Robert McNamara wrote: "…diabolical and scheming—a true sorceress." (*In Retrospect*, p. 42.) When Diem and Nhu were assassinated, her comment was, "Whoever has the Americans as allies does not need enemies." (Howard Jones, *Death of a Generation*, p. 407.) Madame Nhu dictated her memoirs in French but no date of publication has been announced since she passed away in Rome in 2011.

8. The fascinating story of an attempt to communicate with the elusive Madame Nhu after the fall of Diem has recently been published by Monique Brinson Demery, *Finding the Dragon Lady. The Mystery of Vietnam's Madame Nhu* (New York: Public Affairs, 2013).

The Lao Dong (Communist party) central committee at a meeting in Hanoi in January 1959 adopted a resolution introduced by Le Duan to liberate South Vietnam by force. The infiltration of South Vietnam by way of the jungles and mountains of Laos over what would become the "Ho Chi Minh Trail" began in 1960. The former Viet Minh guerrillas who had taken refuge in the north after the Geneva Conference were now being secretly sent back south to start the war against Diem. Among the many weaknesses of the Vietnamese army that Diem had created was his attempt to enforce a form of conscription in 1957 that became instantly unpopular. Under the French the army had always been a volunteer force, but with the awakening of guerrilla activity more troops were needed. The draft didn't work well and there were massive desertions and failures to enlist. One of the reasons at the officer level was the political nature of promotions—based on loyalty, real or perceived, to the president and the regime.[9]

On November 11, 1960, ARVN (South Vietnamese Army) paratroopers launched a military putsch against Diem. Growing dissatisfaction in the army prompted two officers to attempt an uprising to force Diem to get rid of his hated entourage, mainly his brother Nhu and his wife. Saigon radio in the hands of the rebels, broadcast proclamations from the "Revolutionary Council" and it looked as if Diem was not going to survive. He was saved by two regiments that had remained loyal and attacked the rebellious troops. He beat back the plot and vented his rage at U.S. ambassador Elbridge Durbrow, who had been critical of the regime. Edward Lansdale at the Pentagon supported Diem, as did the head of MAAG, General Lionel McGarr, so the South Vietnamese leader remained in power with even stronger U.S. support than before.

An ominous new threat appeared with the founding on December 20, 1960, of the National Liberation Front (NLF) that claimed to be a local South Vietnamese communist group dedicated to Diem's overthrow and to "ridding South Vietnam of U.S. imperialists," as Le Duan, the Secretary General of the Lao Dong, put it. On paper the NLF, like the Viet Minh during the war against the French, presented

---

9. Brig. General J. Lawton Collins, "The Development and Training of the South Vietnamese Army 1950–1972," Department of the Army, Washington, D.C., 1991.

itself as not exclusively communist even though that claim didn't hold up to scrutiny for very long. At the same time Diem made the incredible error of imposing the "agrovilles," or new defensive villages, on the peasantry as a way of depriving the Viet Cong of new recruits. The main problem was separating the peasants from their ancestral lands and, in particular, the burial places of their ancestors—an essential component of Vietnamese Buddhist culture. The program had to be suspended and Diem's image was further tarnished by that failure. The Viet Cong began their terror campaign in 1961 by murdering over 500 local officials and civilians, as well as 1,500 ARVN soldiers. The repression that followed was just as bloody, with roving mobile courts and no possibility of appeal. The Diem regime's unpopularity grew exponentially.

In the early days of the Kennedy administration it appeared that Diem and his government had been given a new lease on life. JFK was an outspoken cold warrior and an early member of the AFV. The fact that he was also a Roman Catholic could only make the task appear that much easier to Ngo Dinh Diem, who is often portrayed with some exaggeration as lacking imagination and being withdrawn and sour toward all foreigners, as well as to his fellow Vietnamese. Diem was capable of normal human contact and even showing a degree of bonhomie in private, only these traits were not apparent to the journalists reporting from South Vietnam at the time. The question was whether the Vietnamese president was flexible and creative enough to seize the opportunity in the early 1960s.

Ho Chi Minh

The enigmatic founder of the Indochinese Communist Party (Parti Communiste Indochinois—PCI) was born on May 10, 1890, in the central Vietnam province of Nghe An, not far from Vinh in Annam. In the course of his life as a political agitator and subversive he used many different names—over one hundred it appears—but the one he was known by until the end of the Second World War was Nguyen Ai Quoc. Even though his father was a well-read classical Vietnamese intellectual and a fervent nationalist, Ho Chi Minh was mostly self taught after a difficult and poor childhood. However, his father, Nguyen Sinh Sac, did have some important friendships, for example with nationalist leader Phan Boi Chau, who came from the same area and who inspired Sac with his brand of uncompromising anti-French nationalism. As a teenager Ho would listen to the conversations between the two men and was impressed with Chau's ideas, which were fundamentally monarchist, seeking to replace the reigning and ineffective dynasty with a new constitutional ruler.

Ho was expelled from school for his behavior and identified by the colonial police as being subversive. In 1911 he decided to travel the world, working at odd jobs to support himself along the way. He was a keen observer of the places he visited, often drawing parallels to the conditions of the Vietnamese under the colonial regime. He had an engaging, poetic, and adventurous spirit and seems to have made friends easily. Soon after arriving in Marseille in the summer of 1911 he wrote a letter to the president of France requesting permission to attend the École Coloniale where twenty scholarships were made available every year to Vietnamese nationals. Those who graduated became part of the colonial administration with the coveted status of government functionaries. His application was rejected and it is impossible to assess whether or not this setback had an impact on his growing bitterness toward France.

Once again Ho traveled and became a jack-of-all trades, working as a steward, gardener, street cleaner, photo retoucher, assistant pastry chef, and bottle washer, unencumbered by any family or romantic attachments. With his meager earnings by working on ships as an assistant cook he was able to visit Marseille, Paris, London, New York, and Boston, the coast of Africa and South America—all before the First World War. In his memoirs he also recalls working in the kitchen of the Carlton Hotel in London under the famous chef Escoffier, who promoted him to pastry apprentice.

Ho returned to Paris in 1917 and decided that he would learn French well enough to write short articles published in well-known socialist dailies such as *L'Humanité* and *Le Populaire*. He made his mark during the Paris Peace Conference in 1919 when he addressed a petition to Woodrow Wilson entitled "Demands of the Annamite People," signed by Nguyen Ai Quoc, asking for basic freedoms and amnesty for political prisoners, among other things. Disappointed by the lack of any response he became disillusioned with Western democracy. However, the French police did read his letter and forwarded the document to the offices of former governor general of Indochina Albert Sarraut, who was about to become minister of the colonies. Ho was summoned to the ministry where he was secretly photographed by police agents and his movements would be tracked by the authorities in France and Indochina. Rather than meeting with Sarraut he was interviewed by a former colonial detective who was impressed by Ho's intelligence. He had instantly become what is today described as a "person of interest."

Ho was a delegate at the Socialist Party Congress held at Tours in 1920 where the French Communist Party was formed after a split among the socialists. He read Lenin's "Theses on the National and Colonial Questions," which changed his worldview and he became a lifelong communist. Ho gave an impassioned speech to the delegates, stating among other things: "In Indochina the colonialists find all ways and means to force us to smoke opium and drink alcohol, to poison and beset us."[10] That puritan streak would also remain part of Ho's character to the end of his life, something he shared with his arch rival Ngo Dinh Diem: purity of body, asceticism, celibacy, all qualities seen as admirable virtues by the Vietnamese people that gave an aura of superiority to those who practiced them. Of course, while the celibate Diem was also dour, often aloof and uncommunicative, Ho was the exact opposite: a man of the people, a baby-kissing politician and someone you would gladly share time with for good conversation. His natural bonhomie, whether sincere or artificial, came across as genuine and people who met him usually liked him even though they might not agree with his more radical ideas.

By 1920 Ho had been identified by the French police as the "dangerous agitator" Nguyen Tat Thanh, known to the colonial police in Tonkin since 1908.[11] In 1921 he published a pamphlet *Le Procès de la colonisation française* and was kept under close watch by detectives but not arrested.[12] In 1922 Albert Sarraut summoned Ho to a meeting at

---

10. William J. Duiker, *Ho Chi Minh* (New York: Hyperion, 2000), p. 14.
11. Duiker, op. cit., p. 70.
12. *French Colonization on Trial* (author's translation).

the ministry of the colonies where the police threatened him because he was a Bolshevik. But he was also told that he could also receive generous help if he were to cooperate. According to Ho's memoirs he responded: "The main thing in my life and what I need most of all is freedom for my compatriots."[13]

He traveled to Moscow in 1923 after being invited by Dmitry Maniulsky, who had heard him speak at the founding of the French Communist Party and was impressed by his determination. Along with other foreign comrades Ho was living in the Hotel Lux and attended the famous Stalin School where revolutionary agitators were being instructed while they were learning Russian. In November 1924 Maniulsky sent him to Canton to work for the Comintern with the understanding that his long-term goal was the creation of an Indochinese Communist party. Using yet another assumed name he reported to Mikhail Borodin, the main Comintern representative in China at the time. Ho founded the Vietnamese Revolutionary Youth League that quickly became a magnet for young expatriates and attracted the attention of the Chinese police in Canton. His apartment was raided the day after his departure in 1927.

Ho went to Hong Kong and Vladivostok where he met Jacques Doriot, the French communist leader who proposed that he first go to Paris and then to Siam to rebuild the communist organization there. Back in Canton in February 1930 Ho was the main mover in the founding of the Vietnamese Communist Party, the fulfillment of his lifelong dream. The French colonial police were now after him and the British arrested him in Hong Kong in 1931. He was released after a trial and an appeal held in London where the lawyers agreed that it was best for charges to be dropped and for Ho leave the colony.

The ease of his release gave rise to rumors that he had been recruited by British intelligence. Those indications, whether they were true or not, may have been sufficient to motivate Stalin's suspicion and lack of enthusiasm for Ho later on. Back in Moscow via Vladivostok in 1934, he spent several years giving lessons and mentoring Vietnamese students at the Stalin School. He managed to avoid the purges but there are indications that he may have stood trial in secret because of

---

13. Duiker, op. cit., p. 83.

his associations with several purged communists like Mikhail Borodin. Finally, after four quiet years in Moscow translating theoretical works, he was allowed to return to China in 1938. Ho resumed his revolutionary mission to Vietnam from Kunming in southern China where he was based. On May 10, 1941, the Indochinese Communist Party held a secret meeting in a cave at Pac Bo, near the Chinese border. Using the name Ho Chi Minh for the first time and emerging as the party leader even though he didn't take the post of general secretary, he set the stage for what would be the uprising and declaration of independence of Vietnam in 1945. The Communist party in its resolutions called for a temporary postponement of the class struggle in favor of the more urgent goal of national liberation that could include all moderate nationalists. The new group would be called the Viet Minh, short for the League for the Independence of Vietnam (Vietnam Doc Lap Dong Minh). Ho was arrested once more in China in 1942 and would remain in prison for one year. In the fall of 1943 he was released and returned to Pac Bo in Tonkin once the Chinese decided to allow Vietnamese nationalists organize guerrilla actions against the Japanese forces.

In November 1944 Ho and his longtime followers, which included Pham Van Dong and Vo Nguyen Giap, first encountered OSS officers stationed in China. An OSS pilot, Rudolph Shaw, crash landed his single engine reconnaissance plane and was taken to Ho, who provided help in getting the American officer safely back into China. The one favor he requested was a meeting with General Clair Chennault in southern China, describing himself as a nationalist ready to fight the Japanese. The meeting with General Chennault did take place and Ho requested and was promptly given a signed photograph of the general and some encouragement, but little else. In April 1945 OSS Captain Archimedes Patti arrived in Kunming on an intelligence gathering mission of Japanese military forces in Indochina and welcomed contacts with the Viet Minh. Patti, like many other OSS officers and General Albert Wedemeyer, shared the well-publicized official disdain for French colonialism and had been briefed to prevent the French from returning to their former colony. Patti also knew from Ambassador Patrick Hurley that both the French and the Nationalist Chinese were opposed to Ho and his group.

Ho Chi Minh understood the urgency of the situation as he commented, according to Vo Nguyen Giap: "We must at all costs seize independence. We must be ready for any sacrifice..."[14] The atomic bombs dropped on Hiroshima and Nagasaki on August 6 and 9 were a clear indication that the war would end in a matter of days. Ho called a meeting of the Viet Minh leadership to plan for a national uprising. After Japan's formal surrender of August 15, 1945, speed would be of the essence for the Viet Minh—given the Potsdam conference decision to divide Indochina into British and Chinese occupation zones and French attempts to reestablish sovereignty. The insurrection flared up all over Vietnam and many innocent people were to die at the hands of the Viet Minh. Ngo Dinh Diem's own brother was buried alive during that revolt and many other anti-communist Vietnamese were similarly tortured and killed. Such matters didn't faze Ho Chi Minh, who would always remain true to the pattern of Lenin and Stalin's ruthless brand of leadership.

In Hanoi on September 2, 1945, Ho Chi Minh proclaimed the independence of Vietnam as a Democratic republic even though the monarchy had not been formally abolished. A few days later the Chinese army of occupation entered the city while the British contingent took over in Saigon, which was being rocked by episodes of violence, mainly against Europeans and Eurasians. Capt. Patti was very much aware of the French presence and of the intentions of the Free French in southern China. Jean Sainteny, de Gaulle's representative, had traveled with Patti on the flight to Hanoi, having been appointed delegate of the Free French to Tonkin. Ambassador Hurley ordered Patti not to interfere in the negotiations that were underway between the French and the Viet Minh. Ho knew that his forces were very weak compared to the combined British, Chinese, and French units that were pouring in. It was best therefore to show all the many foreign invaders that the Viet Minh was seeking to be accommodating. Patti left Tonkin on September 30, 1945, and Truman permanently disbanded the OSS a few weeks later. A tragic fate was in store for OSS

---

14. Duiker, op. cit., p. 302.

Capt. Peter Dewey, who, having been declared persona non grata by General Gracey in Saigon, was killed at a check point by the Viet Minh. He had been mistaken for a French officer while he was driving in his Jeep on his way to the airport. Dewey's death less than one month after arriving in Vietnam caused a sensation in the U.S., mainly because he was the son of a congressman and a distant relation of Governor Thomas E. Dewey of New York.

Ho Chi Minh then began a long process of failed negotiations with France, leading to the Indochina war by December 1946. He successfully portrayed himself as moderate patriot and a nationalist rather than a Marxist-Leninist ideologue, a masquerade that worked for a time until the realities of terrorism and guerrilla war were held against him. Yet many who approached him were often mesmerized by his personality, his intelligence, and his supposed moderation. Others who had seen his uncompromising side knew better.

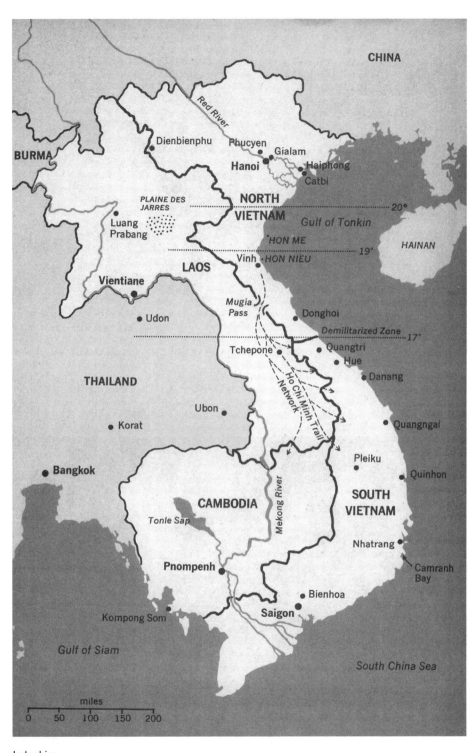

Indochina

Japanese forces enter Tonkin in the summer of 1940.

General Charles de Gaulle *(left)* and General Georges Catroux,
former governor general of Indochina.

Ho Chi Minh in 1946.

Enthusiastic welcome by French citizens for Free French forces
arriving in Saigon in 1945.

OSS Major Archimedes Patti with Vo Nguyen Giap
in August 1945.

Prince Vinh San in Free French army
uniform in 1945.

Vo Nguyen Giap *(left)* and Ho Chi Minh in 1945.

Admiral Thierry d'Argenlieu *(right)* welcomes General Philippe Leclerc on his arrival in Saigon in 1946.

French and Vietnamese troops fighting in the rice paddies.

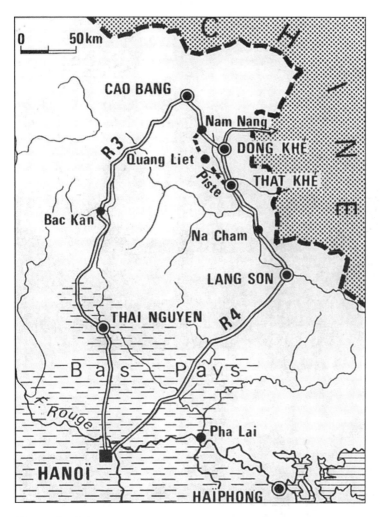

Chinese Tonkin border in 1950 and the
outposts of Cao Bang and Lang Son.

Bay Vien, head of the police in Cholon, was
forced into exile by Ngo Dinh Diem in 1955.

General de Lattre de Tassigny *(far left)* arrives on December 19, 1950, at Saigon airport to take over as military and civilian head in Indochina. At his left are Léon Pignon, Jean Letourneau, State of Vietnam Prime Minister Tran Van Huu, and General Carpentier.

General Raoul Salan, commander in chief in 1952-1953.

Emperor Bao Dai *(far left)* General Salan and Jean Letourneau in 1952.

The Indochinese piaster currency was at the center of a major trafficking scandal.

American General G. Lawton Collins *(second from left)* visited General de Lattre in 1951 with a U.S. congressional delegation that included John F. Kennedy *(hatless in back row)*.

General Mark Clark *(center)* flew from Korea to Hanoi to meet General Salan *(right)* in 1953.

The U.S. foreign policy team in 1949: *(from the left)* Ambassador Philip C. Jessup, Secretary of State Dean Acheson, advisor John Foster Dulles and Ambassador Charles Bohlen.

Meo tribesmen engaged in guerrilla warfare in Tonkin.

Dien Bien Phu: General Jean Gilles *(left)* and Colonel de Castries.

French Defense Minister René Pleven with General Henri Navarre, appointed commander in chief, 1953-1954.

Viet Minh victory at Dien Bien Phu, May 7, 1954.

Colonel Edward Lansdale
in Saigon, 1954.

2.

The Eisenhower Approach
1953–1961

The 1952 presidential campaign featured a major foreign policy issue that had plagued Harry Truman and the Democrats for two years: how to end the war in Korea? Negotiations at Pan Mun Jom were heading nowhere while the war dragged on. The issue was tailor-made for five-star General Dwight D. Eisenhower, the Republican candidate and World War II hero who was universally revered. Ike promised that upon being elected he would immediately travel to Korea and return with a solution to unblock the talks and end the war. It was a brilliant and eminently credible move for an America exhausted by the intense fighting and the heavy casualties since the June 1950 North Korean invasion, and because American foreign policy and the military establishment were concentrating on Korea, Indochina had a far lower priority. Since 1945 U.S. diplomats had been divided about the region: the Asia specialists, like John Carter Vincent, argued for an anti-French, pro-independence position by the United States that would ensure the takeover of Vietnam by the Viet Minh. Most of the "Asia hands," as they were called, were deeply embroiled in the China Lobby's "Who lost China?" controversy of the early 1950s and had either been fired or even prosecuted as pro-Communist subversives.[1] The State Department "Europeantists," such as H. Freeman Matthews, who were in the majority, were concerned with the cohesion and survival of Western Europe, and argued forcefully for a pro-French policy based on expediency regarding the colonies: the United States was better off supporting the French while encouraging them to grant independence and give more autonomy to the Vietnamese. There was never any question that the United States could follow a different course at that time given the extreme tensions of the Cold War.

On March 5, 1953, five weeks after Eisenhower's inauguration, Stalin suddenly died of a stroke at his dacha near Moscow. Many Western leaders were hopeful that the Cold War would end at last and perhaps even that Soviet communism might crumble. Two weeks later, on March 26, 1953, while the Korean War negotiations were slowly inching to the July armistice, President Eisenhower received a delegation of the French government. He was accompanied by Secretary of State John Foster Dulles, U.N. ambassador Henry Cabot Lodge, and a number of State Department officials working on European and French affairs, including Matthews. Premier René Mayer, Foreign Minister Georges Bidault, and the Minister for the Associated States (Indochina) Jean Letourneau were the main French officials. The most significant meeting took place in the morning aboard the presidential yacht, the USS *Williamsburg*. Eisenhower said, according to the official record:

> The United States is very sympathetic and has tried to help. Indeed we recognize that it [the war in Indochina] is part of the general struggle against Communism and that it is not merely a French colonial effort.[2]

The United States was therefore committed to pursuing the Truman policy of supporting France in the Indochina war. A few days later Eisenhower also met with Irving Brown, the AFL-CIO international labor representative in France who had successfully set up

---

1. John Carter Vincent was dismissed from the Foreign Service by John Foster Dulles in 1953. He had been accused of being a communist by Sen. Joseph R. McCarthy in 1952 and had the support of Dean Acheson at the time.
2. *FRUS 1952-1954 Indochina, Vol. XIII, Part 1*, pp. 429-432.

anti-communist labor unions and was involved in providing encouragement and support to the nationalist movements in French North Africa. Ike told Brown: "I just can't challenge the French on colonial policy… I can't lecture them about what to do about their colonies. That would be very counterproductive."[3]

As Dien Bien Phu began to sour by early March 1954, French and American officers drew up the so-called "Vulture Plan," as we have seen previously, aimed at breaking the siege by the strategic bombing of the hills surrounding the French base and sending relief columns from Laos. An intense debate took place within the Eisenhower administration in March and April 1954 on both the bombing issue and providing relief to the base: Admiral Arthur Radford, Chairman of the Joint Chiefs, Air Force Chief of Staff General Nathan Twining, and Vice President Richard Nixon were all supportive of a bombing mission, while Army Chief of Staff General Matthew Ridgeway was opposed, fearing that the involvement of American ground forces would inevitably follow.

Politically such a development would have been unacceptable less than one year after the end of hostilities in Korea. Furthermore, Eisenhower placed a number of requirements prior to any action: the British had to agree to participate and Congress was expected to approve, but both these preliminary hurdles were certain to fail. Churchill, who was prime minister for the last time, and Foreign Secretary Anthony Eden refused to be drawn in, citing the high risk of Chinese Communist and Soviet intervention and possible action against vulnerable British interests in Asia. Congress remained highly sensitive to public opinion and was reluctant to send U.S. ground forces into Indochina.

Eisenhower had the last word on June 1, 1954, when he told his National Security Council aide Robert Cutler (as quoted in the Pentagon Papers):

---

3. Chad L. Fitzloff, *The Limits of American Labor's Influence on the Cold War Free Labor Movement: A Case Study of Irving Brown and the International Confederation of Free Trade Unions in Tunisia and Algeria* (MA Thesis, Kansas State University 2010). Brown was basically an agent of Jay Lovestone, who was the head of the international section of the AFL-CIO and credited with creating anti-communist labor movements in postwar Europe. See also: Ted Morgan, *A Covert Life: Jay Lovestone, Communist, Anti-communist and Spymaster* (New York: Random House, 1999).

The United States should in no event undertake alone to support French colonialism. Unilateral action by the United States in cases of this kind would destroy us.[4]

Yet American intervention was being seriously contemplated, given the plans and studies prepared by the Air Force to bomb the high ground surrounding Dien Bien Phu using B-29 bombers from the Philippines and Okinawa, as it would during the Vietnam War. Fredrik Logevall has shown in his book, *Embers of War*, that there was no shortage of statements by Eisenhower and his administration regarding the importance of Indochina and the need to defend the Western position in Southeast Asia to prevent the countries in the region from collapsing like a set of "dominoes."[5] It appears from the full record now available that the United States did come very close to entering the Indochina war in March 1954. Major steps had been taken to make that possible but the preconditions that Eisenhower insisted upon did not materialize. The issue of Eisenhower's true intentions remains subject to interpretation: did he really want to intervene or was he placing enough obstacles on the path to avoid doing so even as he was getting ready? Was this an instance of what a recent study calls "Ike's Bluff"?[6] The question remains unanswered but it appears that the United States came far closer to entering the Vietnam War sooner than under Kennedy and Johnson.

Eisenhower's position had been forceful in his support of the French; he had even stated privately that Indochina was more important than Korea because of its strategic position as the lynchpin to Southeast Asia. The hope was that with a decisive push and U.S. equipment and supplies the French could finally defeat the Viet Minh. Yet in spite of the American supply effort the critical elements that the French needed most could not be delivered, namely massive airpower and helicopters. It remains difficult to understand why the United States after all the encouragement, inspections, and support still didn't object to the French creating a trap for their forces in a remote area

---

4. John Prados, *The Sky Would Fall* (New York: Dial Press, 1983), pp. 188-189. Also in the new edition *Operation Vulture*, cit.
5. Fredrik Logevall, *Embers of War* (New York: Random House, 2012), pp. 353-366.
6. Evan Thomas, *Ike's Bluff: President Eisenhower's Secret Battle to Save the World* (Boston: Little Brown, 2012).

with very weak air cover and no escape route. That tragic mistake gave Ho Chi Minh and Mao Zedong a major victory.

Beyond the Geneva Conference Eisenhower and John Foster Dulles had found their man in Vietnam in the person of Ngo Dinh Diem. After 1955, when Diem managed to overcome the threat from the right and the various sects that had residual French support, until 1960, the positive evolution of South Vietnam was proceeding at a steady pace. The North Vietnamese communists with their apparatus were busy tightening their regime and weeding out any potential opposition while South Vietnam was becoming more fearful of the North and relying increasingly on generous American aid and military advisors.

Under Eisenhower, however, the number of military advisors never went beyond 800. The larger problem, as reported by observers at the time, was Diem's inability to tolerate any kind of loyal opposition and his systematic use of extremely repressive measures. In the face of mounting criticism U.S. ambassador Elbridge Durbrow would come to Diem's defense, insisting that his critics didn't realize the kind of pressure the South Vietnamese president was up against. The Eisenhower administration was worried as communist influence in the countryside continued to grow in 1959-60. Several experiments intended to create greater stability in the provinces where the Viet Cong were beginning to take hold were the "agroville" and later the "strategic hamlet" programs that were Ngo Dinh Nhu's brainchild. Under Eisenhower, however, budgetary constraints remained tight and the U.S. continued to spend as little as possible on Vietnam.

The Diem crackdown on all dissent and on real or suspected communist terror was having its effect: thousands of communists and their sympathizers were being jailed and many secretly executed, thereby decimating the remaining structure of the Viet Cong cells in South Vietnam. In the north there were increasing calls for stronger support for the southern communists. While Ho Chi Minh was given only reluctant backing by Mao Zedong, the Soviet Union remained adamantly opposed to any insurrection that might draw the Americans into a new Indochina war and force Russia to get further involved.

Le Duan, Ho Chi Minh's hard line second in command of the Lao Dong, was calling for intervention and encouraging the Viet Cong to undertake more aggressive action in the south. At the January 1959 party congress Le Duan called for revolutionary war against the Diem regime, while Ho Chi Minh stressed caution. Both the Soviets and Chinese communists feared massive American intervention that could upset their gains in Southeast Asia even though the North Vietnamese were impatient to reunite the country under the communist banner. In July 1959 two American military advisers were killed in the first attack by Viet Cong guerrillas at the military base at Bien Hoa, a few miles outside Saigon. They were the first American casualties in the Second Indochina War.

During a visit to Paris in September 1959 Eisenhower received some cautionary advice from de Gaulle, with whom he had always entertained excellent relations. The French president encouraged the United States to withdraw the few hundred advisors that were in South Vietnam at the time: "You shall find yourselves in a spiraling process that you will not be able to get out of otherwise." But Ike didn't take the advice and de Gaulle deplored American involvement in what he predicted would become a quagmire, similar to the one France had experienced in Indochina.[7]

Eisenhower had concluded at the time that Laos—rather than Vietnam—was the main flashpoint in 1959-60 and his reaction was almost identical to the French experience in 1953-54 when Viet Minh inroads into northern Laos created the impetus for the establishment of the offensive air base at Dien Bien Phu. As Ike famously noted in his memoirs:

> For the fall of Laos to Communism could mean the subsequent fall—like a tumbling row of dominoes—of its still-free neighbors, Cambodia and South Vietnam and, in all probability, Thailand and Burma. Such a chain of events would open the way to Communist seizure of all Southeast Asia.[8]

---

7. Pierre Journoud, *De Gaulle et le Vietnam 1945-1969* (Paris: Tallandier, 2011), p. 93.
8. Dwight D. Eisenhower, *Waging Peace 1957-1961* (New York: Doubleday, 1965), p. 607.

Intelligence was reaching Washington about the confused struggle between Communists and Neutralists and other factions in Laos. The most urgent threat being a potential invasion by a North Vietnamese army that could cut the country in two and threaten Thailand, something Eisenhower had vowed to prevent. In handing over the executive branch to the new Kennedy administration, Eisenhower summarized his view of the situation: "We cannot let Laos fall to the Communists even if we have to fight with our allies or without them."[9] That was the message John F. Kennedy heard from the outgoing president about the most pressing problem in Southeast Asia. JFK later complained that Ike never mentioned Vietnam during the transition briefings.

---

9. Eisenhower, ibid. p. 610.

3.

Kennedy and the Crisis of 1963

In the opening days of his administration, Kennedy was handed a long report of a fact-finding mission by General Edward Lansdale regarding the situation in Vietnam. Walt W. Rostow had to insist that the president read the report and JFK's reaction was one of surprise: "This is the worse yet. You know Ike never briefed me about Vietnam."[1] The report described a very precarious situation and recommended much stronger support for the Diem government. But Kennedy was focused on Laos, which Eisenhower thought to be in imminent danger of being overrun by the North Vietnamese, thus neglecting South Vietnam during the transition briefings. Vietnam instantly became an explosive issue that would remain in the forefront of the Kennedy administration until the president's assassination. It should be noted that JFK took office without the kind of extensive command and staff experience that Eisenhower had after many years of military planning. The new administration quickly appeared to deemphasize the National Security Council and the kind of extensive background preparation in examining issues that Ike insisted upon in

---

1. Arthur Schlesinger, Jr., *A Thousand Days* (Boston: Houghton Mifflin, 1965), p. 320.

favor of a more ad hoc approach, limiting the debate to the inner circle around the president that was composed of men he knew and trusted but who were often just as inexperienced as he was.[2]

On May 31, 1961, President Kennedy met with Charles de Gaulle at the Élysée Palace where Vietnam was also briefly discussed. "France was present in Indochina for a long time. You may recall how she decided to leave. [...] the United States thought they would replace France: the result has not been a happy one."[3] De Gaulle was attempting to warn the president as he had done with Eisenhower two years before about deeper involvement in Vietnam, but JFK replied that the prestige of the United States was at stake in the area, thereby ending any discussion of the issue. JFK came to the presidency with excellent anti-colonialist credentials: he had visited Vietnam twice as a congressman and senator, was a charter member of AFV (American Friends of Vietnam) and had also made a well-publicized speech in 1957 on the floor of the Senate in favor of independence for Algeria that had turned him into the American beacon for the nationalists in Asia and Africa.[4]

In order to understand what was happening in South Vietnam Kennedy would dispatch a number of fact-finding missions, but first he decided on a new ambassador to replace Elbridge Durbrow. The choice fell on Frederick Nolting, a career diplomat who spoke fluent French and could therefore best communicate with President Diem and his entourage. The new ambassador arrived in Saigon in May 1961, quickly followed by Vice President Lyndon Johnson, who paid an official visit to bolster Diem and reassure him regarding the American commitment to South Vietnam. But LBJ was under no illusions about Diem and his regime as he remarked to Stanley Karnow, who was pointing out the problems facing the country: "Shit, man, he's the only boy we got out there."[5] The commitment Johnson promised Diem was practically open ended, with few strings attached—at least at the

2. Norman Friedman, *The Fifty Year War. Conflict and Strategy in the Cold War* (Annapolis: Naval Institute, 2000), p. 253. Interestingly the same point is made by Gordon M. Goldstein, *Lessons in Disaster. McGeorge Bundy and the Path to War in Vietnam* (New York: Holt, 2008). Bundy's expertise was as dean of faculty at Harvard University, which may not have been the best forum to sharpen the skills of advising the chief executive on matters of war and peace.

3. Vincent Nouzille, *Des secrets bien gardés* (Paris: Fayard, 2009), p. 70.

4. David Halberstam, *The Best and the Brightest* (New York: Ballantine, 1993), p. 119.

5. Jacobs, op. cit., p. 125.

beginning. LBJ would remain favorable to Diem at the National Security Council meeting of August 31, 1963, when he voiced his firm opposition to a military coup to overthrow the regime. He later deplored the course of action taken by Kennedy and his advisors when the time came to approve the coup to overthrow the Diem regime. Later as president, Johnson would not change the Kennedy Vietnam team and relied as heavily on Robert McNamara as did his predecessor.

Another important mission that visited Vietnam in November 1961 was led by General Maxwell Taylor and Walt Rostow, who recommended vastly increased assistance and 8,000 U.S. combat troops. The troop part was rejected by the administration but everything else would be enacted. The military mission MAAG changed its name to MACV in 1962 with expanded responsibilities and a hefty increase in personnel, including military advisers that quickly reached 9,000. General Paul Harkins, the commander of MACV, was an unrepentant optimist about success in Vietnam and in 1962 he went so far as to assure Secretary of Defense Robert McNamara that the insurgency would be over "by Christmas." That was, of course, the kind of assurance the White House wanted to hear.

The approach to military doctrine changed radically with the new administration and one of the decisions made was to turn the defensive posture away from massive retaliation and to prepare for counterinsurgency operations and fighting local wars of subversion. This led to the Kennedy directive to initiate CIA covert action against North Vietnam as early as January 1961. The task was shifted to the Pentagon one year later and resulted in the creation of the Studies and Observation Group (SOG) under MACV after 1964. JFK was a strong believer in guerrilla and counterinsurgency warfare and found in General Maxwell Taylor a military advisor and leader who thought along the same lines and was instrumental with Robert McNamara in increasing the scope and size of Special Forces. Soon the CIA was playing a secondary role within the covert warfare group and probably as a consequence of the Bay of Pigs fiasco. SOG operations took time to organize and were to begin only under the Johnson administration.[6]

---

6. Richard H. Shultz, Jr., *The Secret War Against Hanoi* (New York: HarperCollins, 1999).

The Kennedy administration's commitment to "special warfare" came in a presidential decision on January 18, 1962, to set up the Special Group—CI (Counterinsurgency) under General Taylor with the participation of Robert F. Kennedy, who was playing an increasingly important role as the president's personal representative on many different committees, going well beyond his duties at the Department of Justice.[7] Among the many programs thought up to defeat the Viet Cong and the North Vietnamese initiated around this time was the growing herbicide effort that was used to clear the foliage and deny the safety of camouflage to the enemy.[8] Known as Operation "Ranch Hand," it was carried out by the U.S. Air Force and reached its peak in 1967-1968, before being terminated in 1971 because of concerns tied to civilian casualties and environmental damage. Its effectiveness remains doubtful.

It became quickly apparent that the Diem regime's efforts to create peasant-led self-defense centers in the villages, known as the "strategic hamlets," were not working. Similar initiatives had been successful in Malaya under the British but could not be duplicated in Vietnam where the constraints imposed on the villagers further increased the government's unpopularity. In February 1962 two South Vietnamese air force jets bombed and dropped napalm over the presidential palace while Diem was inside working; he miraculously escaped unscathed while portions of the palace were destroyed and many killed or injured. Madame Nhu and her children were miraculously spared. It was a wakeup call of sorts and should have served as a warning to the South Vietnamese president that there was dangerous restlessness among elite military officers, a sure sign of trouble ahead. In fact, Diem was very sensitive about the dangers of a military uprising and kept a close watch on promotions and military doctrine. This practice prompted criticism on the part of a number of American military advisors who discussed these matters with journalists.

An interview given by Nhu to the *Washington Post* in May 1963 included the extraordinary suggestion that half of the American advisory forces, by then estimated at 13,000, should leave South Vietnam—his

---

7. William J. Rust, *Kennedy in Vietnam* (New York: Scribner, 1985), p. 64.
8. Edwin A. Martini, "Hearts, Minds and Herbicides: The Politics of Chemical War in Vietnam," *Diplomatic History*, vol. 37, No. 1 (2013), pp. 58-84.

reasoning being that large military operations didn't work and that the "strategic hamlets," once in place, were better suited to destroy the Viet Cong in smaller operations. U.S. congressional reaction was intense: could the U.S. begin pulling out its advisers and let the ARVN do the job on its own? Suddenly the administration saw that there was a real danger of being stampeded into withdrawal, something it wanted to avoid. Roger Hilsman protested to Ambassador Nolting that this kind of statement might cause extraordinary pressure toward a "premature withdrawal."[9] It also increased suspicion and irritation against Nhu.[10]

Diem was taking increasing offense at the growing negative reporting coming from the new breed of American correspondents in Saigon, who were far more critical and intolerant of the regime's autocratic methods. The articles by David Halberstam, Neil Sheehan, Malcolm Browne, and Peter Arnett ultimately set the tone for the increasingly harsh stories coming out of South Vietnam in the most influential American and European publications. In November 1962, as the crisis was beginning to build up around the Diem regime, Kennedy dispatched yet another fact-finding mission headed by the Congressional expert on Asia, Mike Mansfield, Democrat from Montana. During meetings with Diem Mansfield and his Congressional party had to endure hours of numbing monolog by the Vietnamese president, who never allowed anyone to interrupt his train of thought. The senator later spent time with the American newsmen and heard their side of the story, or at least their generally negative interpretation of the situation. The reporters went on at length about the repressive and disconnected Diem regime, the ineffectual Vietnamese Army (ARVN), the delusions of MACV and the U.S. embassy. The administration was very sensitive to anything printed or reported on television, especially since the election year 1964 was now only a few months away.

Mansfield's first impressions were immediately conveyed in person to JFK upon his return and included the recommendation that the

---

9. Jones, op. cit., pp. 256-257.
10. Ellen Hammer, *A Death in November. America in Vietnam 1963* (New York: E. P. Dutton, 1987). By far the most complete account of the fall of the Diem regime, with a revisionist view of the reasons for its failure. The author had access to major personalities in Vietnam and Washington and was close to the Diem regime.

United States step back from the commitment to Southeast Asia. Only a full-scale conflict, almost certainly far greater than the one the French had fought, would allow the U.S. to remain in that part of the world. Furthermore American military presence in Vietnam was not essential to national security: the current policy, if followed, according to Mansfield, would require "expenditure in American lives and resources on a scale which would bear little relationship to the interests of the United States."[11] Coming from a widely respected senator who had been one of Diem's key supporters from the start, such a negative assessment was the equivalent of a kiss of death. It was also surprising that Mansfield appeared to swiftly dismiss Diem as being so ineffectual after having championed him for so long. Perhaps the journalistic verve of the young reporters he spent so many hours with had impressed him enough to avoid going beyond their conclusions and digging deeper to reach a more balanced picture of the situation in South Vietnam.

In early January 1963 there was more bad news from the military front when the ARVN faced the Viet Cong army in battle at Ap Bac, just thirty-five miles west of Saigon.[12] That engagement came in the wake of yet another fact-finding mission, headed this time by Roger Hilsman and Michael Forrestal, who were sent to Vietnam to corroborate the Mansfield report. Hilsman reached the same negative conclusions as the Montana senator but recommended against withdrawal, under the assumption that victory could be achieved in an extended conflict.[13] That observation suited Kennedy's thinking, which remained unsettled but unwilling to disengage from Vietnam at that time. The Ap Bac clash turned into a combined ARVN-U.S. Adviser debacle according to press reports from Vietnam and the extensive account given later on by Neil Sheehan.[14] The ARVN commander failed to

11. Jacobs, op. cit., p. 139, quoting the Mansfield report of February 1962.

12. David M. Toczek, *The Battle of Ap Bac Vietnam* (Annapolis: Naval Institute, 2001-2007) is a detailed study of the engagement that stirred controversy, particularly because of the author's criticism of MACV advisors. The result of Ap Bac was that Americanization became the goal of the American military commanders who became very concerned about the poor performance of the ARVN and voiced these criticisms to the press. Lt. Col. John Paul Vann was also critical of the advisory effort and received extensive coverage by the main reporters in Vietnam at the time.

13. Jones, op. cit., pp. 222-223.

14. Neil Sheehan, *A Bright Shining Lie. John Paul Vann and America in Vietnam* (New York: Random House, 1988).

follow established plans, losing personnel and equipment, including five large H21 Shawnee helicopters known as the Flying Bananas, to a smaller group of Viet Cong guerrillas that for once didn't fade away but stood its ground to fight: 400 VCs held off three times more South Vietnamese manpower. Ironically just as the French had done many years before, the Americans were seeking to draw the Viet Cong into open battle on the assumption they could easily be defeated in a conventional fight due to basic Western superiority in firepower and tactics. But at Ap Bac it appeared obvious that the enemy, being far more motivated and ready for sacrifice than the South Vietnamese, had the edge.

Revisionist historians now conclude that Ap Bac was less of a momentous defeat than reported at the time and that the stories filed by *Washington Post* and *New York Times* correspondents were slanted and exaggerated.[15] Yet the negative propaganda effect was devastating for the Diem regime's image as well as for the ARVN, particularly in the United States. The consensus within the American military went through an evolution: if the policy was to defeat the VC, then it would be necessary to have a "full-scale Americanization of the war."[16] To avoid such an outcome it was best for the U.S. to withdraw after a face-saving victory on the ground that would also imply regime change in South Vietnam. Diem's army, operating under the multiple constraints of avoiding casualties and preventing the emergence of any strong military leadership that might become a political threat to the Vietnamese president, was not ready for the kind of commitment that was required. The existing government could not be counted upon to enact the improvements that the United States considered crucial. However, the possible negative consequences of a military coup against Diem were never seriously considered or analyzed in great detail and it was simply *assumed that anything* would be better than the existing regime. This impatience was exacerbated by the newspaper and media reporting from South Vietnam and the looming 1964

---

15. See Mark Moyar, *Triumph Forsaken* (New York: Cambridge, 2006). Moyar's book became the target of acrimonious debate in 2007-2008, mainly for his critical assessment of the MACV Advisors and the reporting in the press out of South Vietnam in 1963, as well as for his defense of the Diem regime.
16. Jones, ibid., p. 231.

election. Ap Bac was the opening salvo in a continuous barrage of anti-Diem articles throughout 1963.

The accepted view of Kennedy's intentions during that fateful year is that he was planning to pull out of Vietnam only *after* November 1964 to avoid being called "soft on communism" during the political campaign by his likely Republican opponents, who were then thought to be either Henry Cabot Lodge or Barry Goldwater. Therefore, and exclusively for domestic political reasons, there would be no withdrawal of the some 20,000-plus American military, paramilitary, AID, CIA, and diplomatic advisors any time soon.[17] The theory was to escalate the effort to a certain point, presumably until JFK's reelection victory, and then to gradually draw down the forces in place until 1965 when the bulk of American advisors would leave. The problem with this approach was that it also implied further increases in the number of Americans in Vietnam while paradoxically insisting that it was the best way to wind down the whole effort at a later date. There is little to corroborate this scenario, however, besides the statements by JFK's entourage and the ambiguous language of NSAM 263.[18] But later on, at the Honolulu Conference that took place in November 1963 at the same time as the Dallas assassination, covert action already in the works against North Vietnam was authorized and signed off on by the new president on November 26 and one may assume that Kennedy had he been alive would have done the same.[19]

In the spring of 1963 Ho Chi Minh was calling for negotiations to establish a neutral regime to replace Diem and include Viet Cong participation. But within the Lao Dong and North Vietnam, Ho was once again superseded by Le Duan, a hardliner from the south who was closer to China and had Mao's assurance of support should full-scale war with the Americans break out. In May, the devastating Buddhist crisis that would eventually topple the Diem regime was about to begin. The confrontation between the monks and the Diem forces

---

17. The actual number of strictly military advisors in late 1963 was 16,300; the other civilian personnel were attached to various agencies including the CIA, AID, and the State Department, among others.

18. Written by McGeorge Bundy on October 5, 1963, National Security Action Memorandum No. 263 recommended that "a program be established to train Vietnamese so that essential functions now performed by U.S. military personnel can be carried out by Vietnamese by the end of 1965. It should be possible to withdraw the bulk of U.S. personnel by that time." This is the basis for claims that JFK was committed to withdrawal from Vietnam by 1965.

19. Shultz, op. cit., p. 34.

quickly turned into the most destructive event in the history of South Vietnam since 1954.

A local dispute about displaying Buddhist flags in Hué led to a police and military crackdown of excessive brutality, prompting vigorous protests from Tri Quang, the leader of the monks. By insisting on the repression of the monks whom he considered Viet Cong agents, and incapable as he was of any flexibility—let alone negotiation—Diem unnecessarily escalated a crisis that could have been contained. The widespread violence and crackdown proved very embarrassing to the United States, particularly when the international press was suddenly linking the brutal Diem regime to its American benefactors.

On June 11, 1963, came a horrific incident when a monk set himself on fire in the middle of an avenue in downtown Saigon and journalist Malcolm Browne snapped a picture that made every front page and television news broadcast in the world. The images were shown relentlessly just about everywhere and were commented as the result of American policies in Southeast Asia. That specific event probably signaled the end of the Diem regime five months later. Madame Nhu's comment on the suicide—"All they have done is barbecue a bonze"—became unacceptable even to Diem's staunchest supporters in the United States. She was disowned by her parents: her father, the diplomat Tran Van Chuong and her mother, who was predicting the assassination of the entire family if the Nhus didn't leave the government of Vietnam. Ambassador Chuong became extremely critical of the government he was representing and didn't hesitate to call for the fall of Diem in private conversations in Washington.

American policy makers were suddenly coming under intense pressure and felt the need to react to the events in Vietnam. Kennedy decided that a change of ambassadors had become necessary and Ambassador Frederick Nolting found out from a radio broadcast in Europe that he was being replaced. The new top U.S. diplomat was to be Henry Cabot Lodge, defeated by JFK for the senate in Massachusetts in 1952, the former UN ambassador and Republican vice presidential candidate on Richard Nixon's ticket in 1960. Lodge came from a long line of wealthy and influential Massachusetts Republicans. There were electoral considerations involved in the selection: Lodge would almost certainly be a candidate for the Republican nomination for president in 1964 should his mission to Saigon be successful and he had expressed keen interest in the ambassadorship. If his tenure proved less than stellar it would also most certainly hurt his chances. In an added twist to the appointment, he was to report directly to the president and not, as was customary, to Secretary of State Dean Rusk.

Just as the new appointee was preparing to leave for Saigon the Diem regime began a massive crackdown on all dissidents and critics, including leading Buddhists in what became known as the "pagoda raids." It was no secret that the Kennedy administration was fed up with its association with Diem in the face of the Buddhist protests of May and June 1963 and that JFK was actively seeking an alternative— or at least for ways to ease Ngo Dinh Nhu and his wife out of Diem's entourage. The new U.S. ambassador, with Washington's full support, wasted no time in seeking out high-ranking officers in the Vietnamese military who could successfully overthrow and replace the Diem regime. The haste and apparent lack of debate with which this took place suggests that the regime change policy had been set by the White House long before Lodge was appointed. In fact it may have originated as early as February 1962 according to a recently declassified memorandum by Roger Hilsman.[20]

Lodge apparently had no specific written or verbal orders from the Kennedy administration or from the president himself to remove Diem. There was, however, no doubt that he was prepared to do what was expected in the short term to end the religious and political crisis, even if that meant encouraging and indeed actively seeking a coup by ARVN generals to overthrow the regime. From the moment he arrived in Saigon Lodge became deeply involved in plotting Diem's overhrow, but hadn't had time to familiarize himself with the situation and the likely candidates. CIA intelligence officer Lucien Conein provided a report and a list of generals to carry out a coup.

The atmosphere was further poisoned by an article in the U.S. press, asserting that Nhu was increasing his hold on power in South Vietnam. That information was enough to prompt a fateful top secret

---

20. Roger Hilsman, *A Strategic Concept for South Vietnam* Memorandum. Attorney General's Classified File Box 205, National Archives." He [Diem] is concerned that the United States will someday decide to engineer a coup [against him]."

State Department cable to Lodge on August 24 coming from Hilsman, Harriman, Michael Forrestal, and McNamara, but apparently without consulting Rusk and with JFK's verbal approval over the phone from Hyannis Port. The operative sentence was: "U.S. government cannot tolerate a situation in which power lies in Nhu's hands...we must face the possibility that Diem himself cannot be preserved. [...] make detailed plans as to how we might bring about Diem's replacement if this should become necessary."[21] Those instructions, even though they were qualified in the conditional, were for Lodge and Conein the equivalent of marching orders to bring down the regime.

The main dissenter was General Paul Harkins, who thought Diem could function without Nhu and should be given a chance to do so. But Lodge was adamant about moving ahead lest the U.S. lose the support of the ARVN generals, with whom he had been negotiating through Conein. JFK approved the scenario Lodge had provided, placing the momentum for the coup with the generals, basically assuring them of American support. But even under those circumstances the generals, including General Duong Van Minh ("Big Minh"), who in the end would be the moving force behind the overthrow of Diem, held back on August 31. The heavy-handed plotting by Lodge and Conein had finally attracted the attention of Nhu's intelligence service. The main weapon in Diem's hands at that point was to outmaneuver Lodge by attempting the unthinkable: seek a deal with North Vietnam.

The first news of this possibility appears to have reached the CIA in Saigon on August 25: that Nhu was looking for a way to end the war through an understanding with Ho Chi Minh, thereby forcing an American withdrawal from South Vietnam. General Nguyen Khanh told CIA Station Chief John Richardson that the generals were convinced this was true. There were other reports confirming the secret contacts: Nhu was communicating with Hanoi through Polish diplomat Mieczyslaw Maneli, whom Nhu met through French ambassador Roger Lalouette. Maneli saw Nhu twice, on August 25 and September 2, and the reaction from Hanoi was that they were ready to negotiate at any time. Actually, it appears that North Vietnam was interested in

---

reaching an agreement with the south behind the backs of the Americans as early as July 1963. Maneli was convinced that as long as Diem and Nhu were pitted against the Americans, the Viet Cong would remain on the sidelines.[22]

Nhu invited Maneli to a reception, where Lodge was also present, in a demonstration of South Vietnamese independence, since it was the first time a communist diplomat had been officially invited to a Saigon diplomatic function. This kind of information added to the deep distrust that some in Washington harbored toward Nhu, which was increasing with pressing demands that he and his wife be removed from Vietnam. The pressure to do something about Ngo Dinh Nhu was rekindled when Joseph Alsop wrote a column in the *Washington Post* on September 18 asserting that Nhu was in contact with Hanoi and that he had delusions of grandeur as the irreplaceable political figure who could save Vietnam. It was also rumored that Nhu had become a heavy opium user, that he was increasing his addiction by adding heroin, and was possibly seriously unbalanced. Even though the information was not corroborated, Lodge was reporting those tidbits to JFK, presumably to further darken Nhu's image and ease his exit from the scene. By mid-September Nhu had far more enemies than friends at all levels of government and society.[23]

There was still deep disagreement within the Kennedy administration: the Pentagon was basically opposed to the overthrow of Diem, while the State Department was pressuring for his removal in one way or another. The early days of September brought a lull in the coup fever because the South Vietnamese army generals were still reluctant to act. In Washington there were misgivings and hesitations: Vice President Johnson and Bobby Kennedy both had serious reservations about a coup and saw no alternative to Diem. On August 29 General de Gaulle began a major diplomatic initiative calling for negotiations and the neutralization of Vietnam—France expected to play a major role as peace maker in Southeast Asia once the Americans had packed

---

22. Mieczyslaw Maneli would later leave the Polish diplomatic service and became a political refugee and later a professor of political science at Queens College in New York.

23. There is doubt voiced by some scholars about any serious contacts taking place between Nhu and the Viet Cong or the North. Lien-Hang T. Nguyen, *Hanoi's War* (Chapel Hill: UNC Press, 2012), pp. 62–63.

up and left.[24] The French declaration came precisely when the movement toward a coup was again gaining momentum among the South Vietnamese generals and getting the backing of JFK and the entire American administration.[25]

Kennedy then gave his most extensive interview on Vietnam to date to Walter Cronkite on CBS News on September 2 when he said: "I don't agree with those who say we should withdraw. That would be a great mistake." He also called for personnel changes, implying the departure of Nhu from the government. The signals sent out in that broadcast were very clear: U.S. patience with Diem's procrastination was coming to an end. Those historians who support the theory that JFK's true goal remained gradual withdrawal are unable to explain the public and politically charged remarks by the president to the most trusted journalist of the major television network in the United States. If the 1964 election was on his mind, it would be rather difficult for President Kennedy to backtrack later on and avoid the "Who lost Vietnam?" accusation even after his reelection.

Later, on another news program, Kennedy said he believed in the domino theory. The ARVN had to fight the enemy on its own by 1965, thereby allowing a full U.S. withdrawal. But those often repeated milestones were more wishful thinking than reality. By mid-September 1963, the generals and Duong Van Minh had delayed or indefinitely postponed the operation. The whole matter could have probably ended there had the Nhus not continued their public utterances, and in particular Madame Nhu, who was touring the United States giving talks and press conferences. The opprobrium her statements were provoking encouraged Ambassador Lodge to propose that General Edward Lansdale be sent over to mastermind a coup in Saigon.

An unconfirmed episode then apparently took place in Washington one evening where Lansdale was driven to the White House by Robert McNamara and asked by JFK whether he would organize a military

---

24. Pierre Journoud, *De Gaulle et le Vietnam 1945-1969* (Paris: Tallandier, 2011). French Ambassador Lalouette confirmed the contacts between Nhu and the Viet Cong with the implication that a neutral Vietnam could eventually be possible.

25. Fredrik Logevall, *Choosing War. The Lost Chance for Peace and the Escalation of War in Vietnam* (Berkeley: California, 1999). The statement by De Gaulle on August 29, 1963, calling for negotiations and neutralization of Vietnam was viewed with hostility by the Kennedy administration that had made Vietnam a matter of American prestige and world power from which "there was no turning back" in the words of Henry Cabot Lodge.

coup against Diem, even if that meant Diem's complete demise and possible assassination. That at least according to Lansdale appeared to be the drift of the conversation. Lansdale claimed to have replied, "I couldn't do that. Diem is my friend." McNamara denied the meeting ever took place or said that he couldn't recall any such encounter. Lansdale told the story to Daniel Ellsberg later on and several historians appear to accept it as being true.[26]

Shortly after, on September 23, one more military mission went to Vietnam, headed jointly by General Maxwell Taylor and Robert McNamara ostensibly to produce a new situation report mainly focused on the military situation but also political in the search for a replacement to Diem or alternatively a solution that would exclude Nhu. McNamara was recommending accelerating the phased withdrawal of U.S. advisors, since the coup scenario now appeared unlikely. The consensus was to reduce the Viet Cong guerilla war so that the Vietnamese could fight unassisted by Americans. General Taylor's goal was for this to happen by the end of 1965. During the trip meetings took place with General Duong Van Minh, where the coup possibility was again alluded to. The conversations with President Diem were inconclusive, although McNamara kept on insisting that Madame Nhu be silenced as a condition for normal relations with the U.S.

In October the backchannels to the generals in Saigon were operating again, mainly through CIA operative Lucien Conein. The key request from the conspirators was to have assurances that the U.S. would continue to assist South Vietnam after the coup succeeded. The White House was now convinced that any government would be better than the Diem regime in its current form. During the days preceding November 1 many meetings were held in Washington regarding the coup in Saigon. At one point CIA Director John McCone said that according to his analysis "a successful coup would have a harmful effect on the war effort." But Averell Harriman brushed any hesitation aside: "Diem cannot carry the country to victory over the Viet Cong."[27]

26. Jones, op. cit., pp. 364-367.
27. Ibid., pp. 403-404.

On the evening of November 1, 1963, the Diem regime was over-thrown by a coalition of South Vietnamese generals led by General "Big Minh." Ambassador Lodge made little effort to save Diem and his brother although it was clearly possible for him to do so. Diem and Nhu managed to escape from the palace hours before the troops attacked and ended up taking refuge in a Catholic church where they surrendered. They were both shot, with their hands tied behind their backs inside an armored personnel carrier. Nhu's body had multiple stab wounds as well. The following day when news reached the White House that the president of South Vietnam and his brother had been executed, JFK looked surprised and distressed, as Theodore Sorensen wrote: "Kennedy was shaken that Diem should come to such an end..."[28] It was too late for anyone to have second thoughts and the die was cast for America's spiraling involvement in South Vietnam. As John Prados aptly remarked: "Those who argue that Jack Kennedy would have withdrawn from Vietnam have never been able to get past the consequences of the Diem coup, which President Kennedy, after all, supported. The maneuver eliminated all possible flexibility in U.S. policy."[29] Reflecting on the situation created by the Diem overthrow Henry Kissinger commented: "By encouraging Diem's overthrow, America cast its involvement in Vietnam in concrete. ... Diem's removal did not unify the people behind the generals, as Washington had hoped."[30] The chaotic situation that engulfed South Vietnam after the coup, which lasted for several years, would have undoubtedly influenced U.S. policy had JFK remained in charge as it actually did for Lyndon Johnson. While no one can predict how the Kennedy admin-istration would have actually reacted to the crisis, and the instability created but there are good reasons to believe that the end results could very well have been identical. In the final analysis twelve governments would follow the Diem regime from 1963 to 1975 and none managed to secure any kind of meaningful consensus within the population.

The final word on the coup against Diem may well belong to Vo Nguyen Giap, who commented in November 1995:

---

28. Sorensen, op. cit., p. 660.
29. Prados, op. cit., p. 342.
30. Kissinger, *Diplomacy*, p. 655.

Diem would never have permitted the accumulation of American dead on his soil. He would likely have dismissed them from Vietnam early in 1964 if Kennedy had not preempted this option by the November coup.[31]

In fact some clues about JFK's thoughts on the Diem overthrow have surfaced in his Oval Office tapes: he appears to have readily admitted that his administration had badly bungled the situation in South Vietnam. He understood that Diem's demise had instantly created a highly unpredictable context that was likely to turn against the United States in Southeast Asia. Ho Chi Minh always viewed Ngo Dinh Diem as his most formidable opponent and wondered in conversation with Wilfred Burchett why the Americans had opted for his downfall: "I can scarcely believe the Americans would be so stupid."[32] And further on, "The Americans have done something we haven't been able to do for nine years and that was to get rid of Diem."[33]

But JFK would never live to see the consequences of the coup that brought down the Diem government. On November 22, exactly twenty days later, Kennedy's life ended in tragedy in Dallas, Texas.

31. Francis X. Winters, *The Year of the Hare* (Athens: Georgia UP, 1997), p. 188.
32. Marguerite Higgins, *Our Vietnam Nightmare*, p. 320.
33. Moyar, op. cit., p. 286.

Part III

The American War

1.

Americanizing the War

Background

On November 22, 1963, the assassination of President John F. Kennedy brought to the presidency fifty-five year old Vice President Lyndon B. Johnson of Texas. Born in 1908, he grew up in the hill country near Austin. Thus, he was a product of the cowboy west.

In 1930, after graduating from Southwest Texas State teachers College, Johnson taught high school in Houston. Later, he said that teaching was harder than being president. After working as an assistant to a congressman and a relief administrator during President Franklin D. Roosevelt's New Deal, Johnson won a seat in the U.S. Congress in 1937. He moved to the Senate in 1948 and became Senate Majority leader in 1954. In 1960, Kennedy picked him as his vice president. With Kennedy's assassination, Johnson became the thirty-sixth president of the United States. He would hold the office for five years and two months.

An expert at one-on-one politicking, Johnson entered the White House as an able legislator. Declaring a war on poverty, he persuaded

Congress to adopt legislation to combat illiteracy and unemployment and pushed through it the Civil Rights Act of 1964. It outlawed segregation in public places, forbade discrimination in employment on the basis of sex as well as race, and ordered federal funds withheld from school districts that made inadequate progress toward segregation.

Called the Great Society, Johnson's administration was one of the great eras of American humanitarian reform. But his political genius was mainly in domestic politics. In foreign affairs he tended towards overblown rhetoric, emphasis on military preparations, and references to the Alamo and Munich. Johnson, like Kennedy, subscribed to the monolithic theory of Communism, seeing the Soviets fanatically dedicated to world conquest. To LBJ and his supporters it was vital to stop Communist aggression wherever it struck to prevent another world war.[1]

Once in office, Johnson retained Kennedy's foreign policy cabinet: Secretary of State Dean Rusk, Secretary of Defense Robert McNamara, and National Security Adviser McGeorge Bundy. Later, in 1966, Johnson would replace Bundy with the more hawkish Walt W. Rostow.

Johnson's greatest foreign policy problem was the Vietnam War, and he never seemed to understand the complicated nature of the conflict. At times, he referred to the so-called domino theory. If the Communists won in South Vietnam, it went, all the countries in Southeast Asia would collapse "like a row of falling dominoes."[2] At other times, he said, "I am not going to be the president that saw Southeast Asia go the way China went."[3]

To Johnson, North Vietnam's aggression against South Vietnam was the problem. Yet, the Vietcong guerilla fighters did not appear to be invaders from North Vietnam. According to military doctrine, guerillas cannot operate successfully unless they have popular support from the people. Otherwise, they would soon be isolated, alone, and destroyed.

Throughout the 1950s and 1960s, South Vietnam's political-military situation was unstable. The political ties linking Saigon to the

---

1. Wesley M. Bagby, *America's International Relations Since World War II* (New York: Oxford University Press, 1999), p. 239.
2. Jack Valenti, *A Very Human President* (New York: W. W. Norton, 1975), p. 185.
3. Bagby, op. cit., p. 249.

provinces was never secure, and American military and economic aid during this time did not seem to help. What's more, while desertion in the South Vietnamese army was rampant, Vietcong recruitment was high.

The Vietnam War presented Johnson with a dilemma. Escalating American involvement would diminish funds for his Great Society programs. Yet, losing South Vietnam to Communism would raise objections that he was "soft on Communism." Still, without additional U.S. troops, the Saigon government might not survive, but sending them might make its leaders appear to be puppets of white imperialists. To Bill Moyers, Johnson's press secretary, no one in the administration "knew exactly what to do."[4] But for the moment at least, it seemed to Johnson that his best choice was to continue Kennedy's policy of gradual escalation in the hope that it would avoid catastrophe.

But Kennedy's military and economic efforts had failed to construct a viable independent South Vietnamese nation. Despite his efforts, for example, to get the South Vietnamese leaders to implement land reform and redistribute the wealth, the land was still held by a few and corruption was deep and widespread among Saigon's leaders. In contrast, Johnson placed less emphasis on reforms designed to win popular support and more on military measures.

To lead the troops, he gave the Vietnam Command to General William Westmoreland. As deputy to then-Commander Paul Harkins, Westmoreland had been in Vietnam since January 1964. A tall, erect, handsome West Point graduate, he had earned a chest-full of ribbons during World War II and Korea. General Douglas MacArthur said that Vietnam would be a fine command, but one also "fraught with peril" for Westmoreland.[5]

Also, Johnson replaced Henry Cabot Lodge as ambassador to South Vietnam with General Maxwell Taylor. He then transferred control of South Vietnam's pacification programs, designed to win the hearts and minds of the South Vietnamese villages, from Saigon to the U.S. military. "If you get them by the balls," he said, "their hearts and minds will follow."[6] Nonetheless, Johnson's military buildup was slow.

---

4. Timothy P. Maga, *The Vietnam War* (New York: Alpha Books, 2010), p. 141
5. Ibid., p. 149.
6. Bagby, op. cit., p. 249.

By the end of the first year he had increased U.S. troops from Kennedy's 16,700 to only 23,000.

In December 1963, McNamara visited Saigon. In meetings with the South Vietnamese generals he observed that they were more intent on maneuvering for political power than in defeating the enemy, and that they lied about their military successes in the field. In press conferences however, he was more upbeat. To reporters he said, "We reviewed the plans of the South Vietnamese, and we have every reason to believe they will be successful."[7]

In talking with Johnson, however, McNamara was more forthright. "The situation is very disturbing," he said. He predicted Saigon's collapse in the next two or three months. The South Vietnamese generals, he added, were inadequate for the task of both government administration and combat efficiency against the Vietcong. Furthermore, the U.S. mission lacked leadership. Ambassador Lodge and General Harkins did not share information, and Lodge, most particularly, did not "take advice."[8]

Along with others, McNamara advocated escalation of American military force. Later, he wrote, "We never carefully debated what U.S. force would ultimately be required, what our chances of success would be, or what political, military, or financial and human costs be if we provided it." He added, "We were at the beginning of a slide down a tragic and slippery slope."[9]

On January 29, 1964, the political situation in South Vietnam stabilized somewhat after a group of officers, headed by Ngyuyen Khanh, overthrew a divided and ineffectual government. To McNamara, Khanh, a small man with darting eyes, a goatee, and often wearing a red beret, struck him as a man with extensive military experience but with little knowledge of politics and economics. The most worrisome factors to McNamara, however, were Khanh's lack of popular support, and that his control of the army appeared uncertain.[10]

On March 2, 1964, the Joint Chiefs of Staff wrote McNamara that preventing the loss of South Vietnam was in America's national self-

7. Robert S. McNamara, *In Retrospect: The Tragedy and Lessons of Vietnam* (New York: Random House, 1995), p. 108.
8. Ibid., pp. 105-106.
9. Ibid., p. 106.
10. Ibid., p. 112.

interest. To achieve this objective, they advocated destroying military and industrial targets in North Vietnam, mining its harbors, and implementing a naval blockade. If China intervened, they added, using nuclear weapons might be an option. Yet, even using them, they admitted, might not prevent the loss of South Vietnam.[11]

The Tonkin Gulf Resolution

In May 1964 Johnson asked the Defense Department to prepare an integrated political-military plan for gradual escalation against North Vietnam. In conjunction with it, the State Department drafted a resolution to submit to Congress seeking its consent for expanding U.S. military action in Indochina. This was the precursor of what became known as the Tonkin Gulf Resolution.

At the time, American actions in the Tonkin Gulf included plan 34A and De Soto patrols. Code-named 34A, the National Security Council (NSC) had approved Central Intelligence Agency (CIA) support for South Vietnamese covert operations against North Vietnam. Since 1963, U.S. Navy Patrol Torpedo (PT) boats had transported South Vietnamese commandos from Da Nang, South Vietnam, to locations above the seventeenth parallel. Their missions included intelligence gathering, sabotage, and kidnapping. During this same period, the U.S. Navy adopted De Sota patrols. They consisted of sending destroyers up the Gulf of Tonkin with the so-called mission of collecting intelligence on such matters as radar and coastal defenses.[12]

North Vietnam's Tonkin Gulf had been a primary invasion route by the enemies of Vietnam for years. The North Vietnamese saw the U.S. doing the same.

The incidents that occurred in the Gulf of Tonkin on August 2 and 4 were clouded in controversy.

The first attack took place in the early morning hours of Sunday, August 2. Shortly thereafter Johnson received a message from the White House duty officer that North Vietnamese torpedo boats had fired at the destroyer USS *Maddox* in the Gulf of Tonkin. Television

---

11. Ibid., p. 111.
12. George W. Ball, *The Past Has Another Pattern* (New York: W. W. Norton, 1975), p. 379.

and radio accounts said carrier-based fighter planes had driven off three North Vietnamese PT boats that had attacked the *Maddox*. Washington called the show of aggression "unprovoked" and reported that the *Maddox* was on routine patrol in international waters. But Hanoi, denying responsibility for any attack, claimed that South Vietnamese fishing boats had, under the cover of the *Maddox*, bombarded North Vietnamese islands.

Shortly after receiving the news of those events, Johnson assembled his key advisers. They included Secretary of State Dean Rusk, Under Secretary of State George Ball, Deputy Secretary of State Cyrus Vance, and General Earl Wheeler of the Joint Chiefs of Staff. After studying the latest reports, which were unclear, they decided against retaliation. They agreed to give Hanoi the benefit of the doubt this time and assume that the "unprovoked" attack had been a mistake.[13]

Nevertheless, although Johnson and his advisers had decided to treat the *Maddox* incident as a possible error, they drafted a stiff note to Hanoi. It said that U.S. ships operated freely on the high seas and would continue to do so. The North Vietnamese, it added, should be "under no misapprehension as to the grave consequences which would inevitably result from any further unprovoked offensive military action against United States forces."[14]

Johnson approved of sending the *Maddox* back in to the Gulf of Tonkin. Accompanying it was another destroyer, the USS *C. Turner Joy*. There, according to Ball, ships were to "show the flag" and to demonstrate that the U.S. did not intend to back down.[15]

On August 4 the commanders of the *Maddox* and *C. Turner Joy* reported that North Vietnamese boats had attacked them, but neither ship suffered harm. The commanders, however, may have misread the situation. The *Maddox*'s sonar gear, for instance, was not working properly. Moreover, a huge thunderstorm that night had churned up the high seas, and no one on board the was really sure that the North

13. Lyndon B. Johnson, *The Vantage Point: Perspectives of the Presidency 1963-1969* (New York: Holt, Reinhart and Winston, 1971), pp. 112-113.
14. Johnson, *Vantage*, p. 113.
15. Ball, *Past*, p. 379.

Vietnamese had attacked it that night.[16] After two or three days, according to Ball, even Johnson had doubts about the second attack. At one point he told Ball, "Hell, those, stupid sailors were just shooting at flying fish!"[17]

Johnson was aware that the U.S. military response might precipitate a North Vietnamese invasion of South Vietnam and encourage the Soviets and Chinese to aid North Vietnam. He phoned Soviet premier Aleksei Kosygin to assure him that the air strikes meant no aggressive intent against the Soviet Union. At the same time, Johnson warned Ho Chi Minh that North Vietnam might face even more serious consequences if its torpedo boats continued to attack American destroyers in international waters off the Gulf of Tonkin.[18]

Among United Nations members, however, there was disagreement over the definition of international waters. Was it 3 miles, 7 miles, or even 12 miles from the North Vietnamese coastline? It was unclear, moreover, how close to the coastline the *Maddox* and the *C. Turner Joy* had strayed. But despite the ambiguity of it all, Johnson always portrayed the U.S. Navy in the Gulf of Tonkin as an innocent bystander attacked in international waters.

Shortly after authorizing the airstrikes on August 4, Johnson and his advisers assembled with nine senators and seven congressmen from both political parties. Hanoi, said Rusk, had made a serious decision to attack U.S. ships on the high seas and that demonstrating U.S resolve in Southeast Asia by a limited retaliatory strike against North Vietnam was necessary. Johnson then informed them that he would submit a resolution to Congress requesting its support for U.S. combat operations in Southeast Asia if that should prove necessary. "Each expressed his wholehearted endorsement," said Johnson later, "of our course of action and of our proposed resolution."[19] But, as McNamara remembered it, there was not unanimous support.[20]

On August 6, Johnson submitted the Tonkin Gulf resolution to Congress for debate. As written, it authorized the president to take "all necessary measures to repel armed attacks against the forces of the

16. Maga, *Vietnam*, p. 159.
17. Ball, *Past*, p. 379.
18. Johnson, *Vantage*, p. 114.
19. Ibid., 117.
20. McNamara, *Retrospect*, p. 135.

United States and prevent further aggression." When Senator John Sherman Cooper of Kentucky asked "if Johnson considered it necessary to use force that could lead us into war, would the resolution authorize him to do it," Senator William Fulbright of the Senate Foreign Relations Committee answered, "That is the way I would interpret it."[21]

Still, according to McNamara, there was no doubt in his mind that both houses of Congress understood that Johnson would not use the Tonkin Gulf Resolution without first consulting them.[22] But to Ball, Congress had abdicated its responsibility to insert "qualifying language" and given Johnson a "terrifyingly open-ended grant of power."[23] The Resolution was like "grandma's nightshirt," said Johnson. "It covered everything."[24]

On August 7, 1964, the House passed the Tonkin Gulf Resolution 416 to 0 and the Senate 88 to 2. Expressing the sentiment of Congress, Senator Frank Church, who later took an antiwar stance, said that this was not the place challenge the "route of the flag" but "a time for all of us to unify."[25]

The two dissenting votes were Senators Wayne Morse of Oregon and Ernest Gruening of Alaska. They challenged the administration's description of events in the Tonkin Gulf, the military's response to them, and the resolution's potential for escalation. "We knew those boats were going up there," said Morse, "and that naval action was a clear act of aggression against the territory of North Vietnam."[26] Vietnam was not in America's vital interest, added Gruening, and therefore "not worth the life of the American trooper."[27]

Because Johnson got wide support for the Tonkin Gulf Resolution, some faulted him for not asking Congress for a declaration of war. "Our goals in Vietnam were limited," he said, "and so were our actions and I wanted to keep them that way."[28] Yet 1964 was an

21. Johnson, *Vantage*, p. 119.
22. McNamara, *Retrospect*, pp. 138-139.
23. Ball, *Past*, p. 380.
24. Maga, *Vietnam*, p. 160.
25. Richard M. Nixon, *No More Vietnams* (New York: Arbor House, 1985), p. 75.
26. McNamara, *Retrospect*, p. 137.
27. Maga, *Vietnam*, p. 162.
28. Johnson, *Vantage*, p. 119.

election year, and he knew that going to war at such a time was not good politics.

Interlude

As their 1964 presidential candidate, the republicans chose Senator Barry Goldwater of Arizona. An extreme right wing conservative, he said, "Extremism in the defense of liberty is no vice." Holding a major general's commission in the Air Force Reserve, he argued that Johnson was not fighting to win in Vietnam. Regardless of any international complications, he called for removing restraints on the military and allowing them to take whatever actions they considered necessary, such as bombing North Vietnam, to win the war.[29]

By contrast, Johnson's campaign statements on Vietnam seemed relatively moderate. He criticized those "eager to enlarge the conflict," stating that he was not going to get America bogged in an Asian land war. He would not, he said, "ask American boys to do the job that Asian boys should do." The U.S. aim in Vietnam, he added, was "to help restore the peace and to reestablish a decent order."[30]

Calling his domestic program the Great Society, Johnson promised a war on poverty and an end to racism. Goldwater, on the other hand, called for an end to government interference in the economy and an end to most existing government-funded social programs.

Goldwater's program, however, was too far to the right for the American people. On November 3, by a margin of sixteen million votes, Johnson crushed him. The Democrats, moreover, obtained huge majorities in both chambers of Congress.

Later, some argued that Johnson, during the election, had deceived the American people, hiding the fact that he was really bent on escalating American involvement in Vietnam. But if he had a plan to do so, said McNamara, he never told him. What's more, he added, there was still no consensus among the president's advisers on how to handle the Vietnam problem.[31]

---

29. Bagby, *International Relations*, p. 249.
30. Johnson, *Vantage*, p. 275.
31. McNamara, *Retrospect*, p. 145.

In the fall of 1964, Saigon's political situation was bad. Within sixteen months of Diem's assassination in 1963, nine different governments followed. Unable to find competent civilian leadership, the Johnson administration turned over the Saigon government to two military leaders: General Nguyen Van Thieu and Air Marshal Nguyen Cao Ky. Both were former supporters of the French against the Viet Minh, the Vietnamese Independence movement. With Thieu and Ky at the helm, said McGeorge Bundy, Washington was "scraping the bottom of the barrel."[32]

Saigon's military situation was also bad. The Vietcong steadily rose in number from 12,000 in 1961, 88,000 in 1963, 116,000 in 1965, and eventually to 221,000 in 1966. As a result, they took control of much of the countryside. Saigon controlled scarcely half of the population. In short, the administration's present course of establishing a government strong enough to defeat the insurgency was a failure.

But in October 1964 Undersecretary of State George Ball warned that Americanizing the war would only lead to heavy loss of life and unclear results. Instead, he advocated searching for a political solution as a way out.[33] To Rusk, Bundy, and McNamara, however, a political solution was tantamount to unconditional surrender. They supported a policy of gradual escalation. Siding with Ball, Vice President Hubert Humphrey said that the war was just as much a political and social struggle as a military one, and that "no lasting solution can be imposed by foreign armies."[34]

Escalation

In July 1964 Maxwell Taylor replaced Henry Cabot Lodge as U.S. ambassador to Vietnam. Reporting back from Vietnam on September 9, Taylor met with Johnson, his advisers, and the Joint Chiefs of Staff. While air force and Marine Corps chiefs argued for extensive air strikes against North Vietnam, General Wheeler said that his army and navy colleagues feared that such action might precipitate renewed fighting

---

32. Bagby, *International Relations*, p. 251.
33. McNamara, *Retrospect*, pp. 156-157.
34. Hubert H. Humphrey, *The Education of a Public Man: My Life and Politics*, Ed. Norman Sherman (Garden City: Doubleday, 1976), p. 317.

by the North and its allies the Vietcong. All agreed that Saigon's combat readiness was not good. At this point, Johnson asked "whether anyone at the table doubted that Vietnam was worth all this effort." Everyone present said that it was. If the U.S. lost South Vietnam, added the Joint Chiefs of Staff, all of Southeast Asia would fall to the Communists.[35] Still, Johnson was hesitant to draw the gun during an election year.

Shortly thereafter, on November 1, 1964, the Vietcong staged a major attack against the Americans. Earlier, in August, for the purpose of training South Vietnamese pilots, the Joint Chiefs had ordered a squadron of vintage American B-57 jet bombers from Clark Field in the Philippines to Bien Hoa Air Base, twelve miles north of Saigon. Its personnel had foolishly lined up the B-57s on the airfield like sitting ducks.

During the night Vietcong guerillas set up mortar positions near the bank of one of the many streams which intersected the area. Previously, Vietcong, posing as farmers had mapped out the airfield. Without ever being seen, the Vietcong gunners had fired their mortars with maximum speed, reloaded their equipment on their boats, and speeded off in a matter of minutes. Loss of life on the field was light, but the Vietcong had wiped out the B-57 squadron.

The attack on Bien Hoa marked a major turning point in Vietcong tactics. While they had fired on American troops advising South Vietnamese forces, this was the first time they had singled out a major U.S. base for attack. To Taylor, who saw it as instigated and approved by Hanoi, it warranted immediate retaliation against North Vietnamese targets.[36]

But, on the eve of a presidential election, Johnson rejected air strikes against North Vietnam. Yet he asked Taylor if the military needed more combat troops to guard American bases at Bien Hoa, Da Nang, and Nha Trang. He rejected them unless air strikes accompanied them. "I was greatly surprised that the offer of ground troops was made so casually," he recalled, "as it seemed to me a much more diffi-

---

35. Johnson, *Vantage*, p. 120.
36. Maxwell D. Taylor, *Swords and Plowshares* (New York: W. W. Norton, 1972), p. 324.

cult decision than the use of our air forces against military targets north of the seventeenth parallel."[37]

On Christmas Eve the Vietcong struck again. This time they bombed the Brink officer billet in Saigon. The blast killed nine soldiers and wounded one hundred and forty. At the time Taylor was meeting with Bob Hope and a troupe of entertainers who had just arrived from the Ton San Nhut airport. Hope's hotel was across the street from the Brink. Watching the square lit-up by towering flames, he said to Taylor, "I never had such a warm reception in my life."[38]

But, like the previous attack on Bien Hoa, Johnson decided against a retaliatory strike. Apparently, widening the war at this time was too soon after the November election, of which he ran as a dovish candidate.

On February 6, 1965, while Soviet premier Aleksei Kosygin, accompanied by his air force chief, were visiting Hanoi, the Vietcong attacked the American installations at Pleiku and Camp Holloway, killing eight Americans and destroying five aircraft. That night Johnson assembled his advisers in the Cabinet Room. Among others, McNamara, his deputy Cyrus Vance, and General Wheeler were there. Also, present at the meeting was Senator Mike Mansfield, who urged caution. But he was outnumbered. "The call for prompt retaliation was overwhelming," recalled Ball.[39] "We have kept our gun over the mantel and our shells in the cupboard for a long time now," said Johnson. "I can't ask our American soldiers out there to continue to fight with one hand tied behind their backs."[40]

Afterwards, in a memo to the president, Humphrey tried to persuade him not to bomb North Vietnam. It was not an industrial country, he wrote. Admittedly, there were some electric power plants in Hanoi that supplied energy for small factories making ammunition and some steel. But even if American bombers knocked out the electrical grids, he wrote, "the war effort would go on virtually unimpaired,

37. Ibid., pp. 324-325.
38. Ibid., pp. 332-333.
39. Ball, *Past*, p. 389.
40. Johnson, *Vantage*, p. 125.

and inevitably they would have been back at full production in a short time."[41]

By then, however, both Ambassador Taylor and General Westmoreland wanted air strikes. Unless the U.S. began sustained air reprisals against North Vietnam, they argued, Saigon's defeat appeared inevitable.[42] Their view coincided with the then prevailing one that the U.S. needed reprisals not only to punish Hanoi but to "pump adrenalin" into the South Vietnamese.[43]

Fearful that he would be the first president "to lose a war," Johnson implemented a policy, code-named Rolling Thunder, of sustained, continuous bombing against selected targets in North Vietnam.[44] Although Ambassador Taylor was elated over a policy which the American mission had been urging for months, Westmoreland recalled, "I still saw no hope, in view of the restrictions imposed, that it would have any dramatic effect on the course of the war."[45] To Ball, Washington could not easily control measured and limited air action. "Once on the tiger's back," he said, "we cannot be sure of picking the place to dismount."[46]

On March 2, the first Rolling Thunder bombing raid with a joint attack by American and South Vietnamese planes hit a North Vietnamese ammunition depot and naval base. In the beginning, the administration handpicked targets carefully for their political and psychological benefits. It constructed a situation room in the basement of the White House to monitor the war. Johnson would often appear there in the early morning hours, wearing bedclothes and toting a flashlight, so he could read the latest battle reports coming in from Vietnam.

The Joint Chiefs, however, sought a more sustained air campaign against long-range military targets. "Interference from Washington seriously hampered the campaign," said General Westmoreland. "This or that target was not to be hit for this or that nebulous nonmilitary reason." Similarly, Ambassador Taylor called "for a more dynamic

41. Humphrey, *Education*, p. 318.
42. McNamara, *Retrospect*, p. 170.
43. Ball, *Past*, p. 390.
44. Townsend Hoopes, *The Limits of Intervention* (New York: David McKay, 1970), p. 6.
45. William C. Westmoreland, *A Soldier Reports* (Garden City, N.Y.: Doubleday, 1976).
46. Ball, *Past*, p. 382.

schedule of strikes, a several week program, relentlessly marching north, to break the will of the North Vietnamese."[47]

By mid-March Johnson feared that the North Vietnamese would overrun the south if he did not change the direction of Rolling Thunder from a sporadic, halting effort into a regular and continuous program of air strikes. "If the bombing could destroy supplies and impede the flow of men and weapons coming south," he said, "our action would help save American and South Vietnamese lives."[48] "Three months of heavy bombing," said Bundy, "would cause Hanoi to seek peace."[49]

In a memo to Johnson, Ball argued that his advisers were misjudging both the political and military consequences of bombing. Sustained bombing would only increase North Vietnamese efforts to send troops south. They would fight a guerilla war which was best adapted to their resources. He warned, moreover, that increased infiltration of North Vietnamese regulars would require substantial American ground troops to defend U.S. bases that would, he concluded, put the U.S. in the position of France in the 1950s, "with all the disastrous political consequences of such a posture."[50]

In the first 20 months of Rolling Thunder, the North Vietnamese shot down over 300 U.S. planes, pressed over 200,000 persons into anti-aircraft defense work, and another 500,000 into repairing what the U.S. had bombed. To keep war materiel away from being bombed, the North Vietnamese moved it into South Vietnam. This made it more available to the Vietcong, which was not what the U.S. had in mind.[51]

Despite the bombing, Hanoi would not surrender. As a result, the administration increased the bombing, which became less discriminate, until North Vietnam despite its lack of industrial targets, became history's most heavily bombed country. In addition, Johnson stepped up the bombing in South Vietnam. From mid-1965 to the end of 1967, the U.S. dropped more bombs on Vietnam than the Allies dropped on Europe during all of World War II.[52]

---

47. *U.S.-Vietnam Relations IV* (3), p. v.
48. Johnson, *Vantage*, p. 132.
49. Bagby, *International Relations*, p. 250.
50. Ball, *Past*, pp. 381-382.
51. Maga, *Vietnam*, p. 181.
52. Bagby, *International Relations*, p. 250.

The intensified bombing campaign inadvertently killed large numbers of civilians. In South Vietnam this alienated much of the population, whose support was vital to U.S. success. "Every time Americans bombed a village," said Roger Hilsman, assistant secretary of state, "they created ten new Communists for every one they killed."[53]

In February 1965, as preparation for U.S. air strikes, General Westmoreland requested ground forces to protect the bases from which the air strikes would be launched. Ambassador Taylor, however, urged caution. "Once you put that first soldier ashore," he said, "you never know how many others are going to follow him."[54] But Johnson considered Westmoreland's request—protecting the lives of U.S. airmen—reasonable and acceded to it.

Throughout March, Westmoreland clamored for additional troop deployments. Although Ambassador Taylor reluctantly agreed with him, he cabled Johnson his apprehension that the U.S. not rush in and take over the conduct of the war. It might make the South Vietnamese too dependent on the U.S. and reduce their responsibility for making the maximum war effort. Taylor also feared that escalation in Vietnam might dissipate America's available military strength in other parts of the world.[55]

Nevertheless, on March 29, after Vietcong guerillas blew up the American embassy in Saigon, Johnson decided to increase support forces in South Vietnam by an additional twenty thousand men.

By this time, the Americanization of the war increased fears among seventeen nonaligned nations that the Southeast Asian conflict could spark a wider war, bringing in China or the Soviet Union. After meeting in Belgrade, Yugoslavia, in mid-March, the government leaders of the seventeen nonaligned nations sent an appeal to the United States, North and South Vietnam, and the United Nations to get peace talks started.

Shortly thereafter, on April 7, Johnson replied in an address to students at Johns Hopkins University. Calling for an independent South Vietnam, he remained ready to open up unconditional discussions with North Vietnam. Moreover, he would ask the United

53. Ibid., p. 252.
54. McNamara, *Retrospect*, pp. 174-175.
55. Taylor, *Swords*, p. 338.

Nations to launch a plan for cooperation in economic development. "I will ask the Congress to join in a billion dollar American investment in this effort." He hoped that all other industrial countries, including the Soviet Union, would join in it "to replace despair with hope and terror with progress."[56]

Although well-meaning, Johnson's speech viewed the world through the American experience. He hoped to bargain with the North Vietnamese the way he did with American business and labor leaders. Afterwards, he kept repeating "Old Ho can't turn me down," but he did. Ho's terms were that the U.S. must disengage from all of Vietnam, and the Vietcong must participate in any coalition government in South Vietnam.

In April, despite the infusion of American combat troops, and the larger size of the South Vietnamese Army, the Vietcong continued to grow in strength, and the Saigon government had little support. To bolster South Vietnamese forces McNamara and his colleagues recommended further troop deployments. By the end of May, U.S. troops in Vietnam passed the 50,000 mark. At the same time, Johnson got Congress to approve 700 million to meet the increasing costs.

By June 1965, however, despite the air strikes and additional troop deployments, the North Vietnamese and the Vietcong were winning the war. "The entire bastion was crumbling," said General Wheeler, chairman of the Joint Chiefs. "It wasn't a matter of whether the North Vietnamese were going to win the war. It was a question of when they were going to win it."[57] As a result, Westmoreland requested an additional 175,000 troops, but he added that they were only enough to "hold the fort" and more would be needed later.[58]

Westmoreland's request generated considerable dissent. Ambassador Taylor's deputy, Alexis Johnson, urged Assistant Secretary of Defense John T. McNaughton not to bring in more troops. "The situation," said Johnson "was in many ways no more serious than the previous year." [59] "Only the Vietnamese could save their own country," said Ambassador Taylor, "and too aggressive use of foreign troops

56. Johnson, *Vantage*, pp. 133-134.
57. Earle G. Wheeler interview with Dorothy Pierce McSweeny, August 21, 1969, University of Texas Oral History Project, Johnson Library, Austin.
58. Westmoreland, *Soldier*, p. 140.
59. *U.S.-Vietnam Relations* IVC (5), p. 117.

might even work against them."[60] To Ball, however, Vietnam was a country with an army but no government. "Even if we were to commit five hundred thousand men to South Vietnam," he said, "we would still lose."[61]

After a five-day fact-finding trip to Vietnam, McNamara arrived back in Washington on July 20. In his report he advised Johnson to accept Westmoreland's request for 175,000 more troops. "The Communists," he wrote, "considered South Vietnam ready for a complete takeover."[62]

After reading McNamara's report, Johnson assembled with his advisers to discuss it. All agreed with its conclusions except Ball. "I have grave doubts," he said, "that any Western army can successfully fight Orientals in an Asian jungle."[63] Turning to General Wheeler, Johnson asked him to ponder that question. He then asked, "Wouldn't we lose all credibility by breaking the word of three presidents?" Ball replied that the U.S. would suffer loss of credibility "when it is shown that the mightiest power on earth can't defeat a handful of miserable guerillas." Yet, said Rusk, "if the Communist world finds out we will not pursue our commitment to the land, I don't know where they will stay their hand." This concerned Johnson too. Later, he wrote, "I was convinced that our retreat from this challenge would open the path to World War III."[64]

On July 28, 1965, at a televised news conference in the East Room of the White House, Johnson informed the nation that he was now raising America's fighting forces from 75,000 to 125,000 troops and would send additional troops later. Also, he was raising the monthly draft calls from 17,000 to 35,000 a month. He sought an end to aggression and a peaceful settlement. "We do not want an expanding struggle with consequences that no one can foresee," he said. "Nor will we bluster or bully or flaunt our power, but we will not surrender, and we will not retreat."[65]

---

60. Ibid., p. 106.
61. Ball, *Past*, p. 397.
62. Johnson, *Vantage*, p. 324.
63. Ball, *Past*, pp. 400-401.
64. Johnson, *Vantage*, p. 148.
65. Valenti, *Human*, pp. 356-358.

With further troop deployments to follow, Westmoreland perceived a long war. "I could make no estimate," he said, "more precise than several years."[66] By the end of 1965, American troop levels had risen to 180,000; by the end of 1966 to 380,000; and by the end of 1967 to 500,000. By then, the war was costing $30 billion a year, and the casualty toll had risen to more than 25,000 American battle deaths and 100,000 wounded.

---

66. Westmoreland, *Soldier*, p. 160.

2.

Rising Opposition to the War

In all spheres of American life, the Vietnam War generated debate. It took place in press editorials, church sermons, political podiums, and universities and colleges. It was felt at family gatherings, at the workplace, and at play. It divided families, broke friendships, and affected the way people judged each other.

The debate centered around the hawks and the doves. While the hawks favored war, the doves opposed it. The hawks emphasized the country's moral responsibility to resist aggression and its obligations under the Southeast Asia Treaty Organization (SEATO) pact. It was not a binding defense pact, said the doves, but only bound its members to consult in case of Communist aggression. Invoking the domino theory, the hawks said that if the U.S. allowed the Communists to take over Vietnam, they would soon take its neighbors, continuing until they had conquered the whole world.

The doves, rejecting the domino theory, noted the growing split between the Chinese and the Soviets and the traditional hostility of the Vietnamese to the Chinese. While the hawks argued that the North Vietnamese provoked the conflict, the doves said it was a popular revolt against a corrupt and repressive South Vietnamese regime, and that the North Vietnamese had only increased their military activities in the south in proportion to the United States' intervention on the side of the Saigon regime.

Proposals to end the war varied. Extreme hawks favored the abolition of all bombing restrictions, sending ground troops into North Vietnam, and, if necessary, using atomic weapons. Some doves favored the immediate withdrawal of all United States troops, but most urged Johnson to negotiate for the best terms to get out of the war. All of them agreed, however, that he should end the bombing as a means of drawing Hanoi into negotiations.

Because of America's great power status, Johnson argued that it had the responsibility to fight communism in Vietnam. "If we are driven from the field in Vietnam," he said, "then no nation can ever again have the same confidence in American promises."[1] Confident of victory, he had the support of former presidents Truman and Eisenhower and of former Republican presidential candidates Thomas E. Dewey, Richard Nixon, and Barry Goldwater.

In 1938, Johnson and his advisers were young men. At that time, in Munich, Germany, the Western powers agreed to Hitler's demands to annex the Sudetenland from Czechoslovakia. Later, violating the agreement, he took all of it and then invaded Poland, which led to World War II. To Johnson and his advisers, the lesson of Munich was that success "only feeds the appetite of aggression," and that "aggression unchecked was aggression unleashed."[2]

Humphrey argued, however, that that the Munich lesson, whether true or not, did not apply to Vietnam. "We were hooked on a valid lesson of history," he said, "but one that had little relevance to what was going on in Vietnam." The conflict," he said, "was a struggle that had started between the Vietnamese themselves, North and South, and the French."[3] The Vietnamese, added the doves, began the war against French imperialism and were now continuing it against U.S. intervention. That made the fight, they said, one by nationalists, seeking national independence, against foreign domination.

Wars for national liberation, to be sure, began long before the rise of Communism. The American Revolution was such a war. The Viet-

---

1. Johnson, op. cit., p. 148.
2. Bagby, op. cit., p. 254.
3. Humphrey, op. cit., pp. 340-341.

cong, moreover, desired land reform and other measures helpful to the poor, who constituted the majority of the Vietnamese. The Saigon government, on the other hand, favored the minority of wealthy land-owners. The Vietcong could not long survive without aid from civilians, and their higher morale indicated that they had both popular support and more faith in their cause than did Saigon's troops.[4]

Between 1965 and 1968 a growing number of Americans began to adopt the dove position. They maintained that Vietnam was not two nations, but one. The war had started, they maintained, not with an invasion from North Vietnam, but as a popular uprising in South Vietnam, with most of the Vietcong being native South Vietnamese.

The hawks insisted, however, that the fighting resulted from aggression by Communist North Vietnam, which in turn, they charged, was the agent of Communist Russia and China. But America's own statistics did not support this. The vast majority of arms taken by dead or captured Vietcong were not ones they had acquired from North Vietnam but had captured from the South Vietnamese army, plus a lot of captured French weapons that had been originally supplied by the U.S. Not until 1964 did substantial numbers of North Vietnamese troops enter South Vietnam.[5]

To a growing number of Americans, the Vietnam effort, compounded with anti-Communism and ignorance of Asia, appeared irrational. "A feeling is widely and strongly held," wrote Assistant Secretary of Defense John McNaughton, "that the establishment is out of its mind...that we are trying to impose some U.S. image on distant peoples we cannot understand, and that we are carrying the thing to absurd lengths."[6]

With increasing troop deployments, the international outcry against America's war in Vietnam rose. Church leaders, including the pope and the World Council of Churches, denounced it, as did the governments of Sweden, Canada, and the nonaligned nations. U.N. Secretary General U Thant and Prime Minister Indira Gandhi of India called for a bombing halt. President Charles de Gaulle of France labeled it a "detestable war." (De Gaulle said this with a straight face as he tried to

---

4. Bagby, op. cit., p. 255.
5. Ibid., p. 250.
6. Ibid., p. 255.

reinvent himself as an anti-colonialist.) The Americanization of the war was undermining America's international stature and prestige.

The Antiwar Movement

Johnson's Americanization of the war aroused intense opposition. Peace marches, White House picketing, campus protests, and draft-card burning became common. Thousands of young men left for Canada, went underground, or were sent to prison. In one rally, in October 1967, 50,000 Americans marched in Washington against the war. Among the war's opponents were retired Generals James Gavin and Lauris Norstad, as well as many of the nation's leading Far Eastern experts. In late 1967, 30 members of the house appealed to Johnson to halt the air attacks on North Vietnam. Privately, Senator Fulbright said, "We go ahead treating this little peasant country as though we were up against Russia and China put together."[7]

Although the antiwar movement was a broad-based coalition of various peace, church, and socialist groups, it was the colleges and universities, led by students for a Democratic Society (SDS), that were in the forefront of it. Rejecting, the hawkish view, they argued that the North Vietnamese and the Vietcong were nationalists first, communists second, and that they were fighting not for worldwide Communism but against Western imperialism and sought self-determination against foreign control.

Beginning in the summer of 1965, approval for Johnson's handling of the war diminished. A survey published in October 1967 showed that 46 percent of the public regarded the commitment to Vietnam as a "mistake," while 44 percent continued to back it.[8] On the other hand, the majority of Americans opposed withdrawal and favored tougher attacks against North Vietnam. Nonetheless, the country's mood on the war was uncertain and confused. "I want to get out," said a housewife, summing up the mood, "but I don't want to give up."[9]

Although smaller antiwar demonstrations had occurred throughout the country, the first major demonstration took place on April 17,

---

7. Hoopes, *Limits*, p. 83.
8. Bagby, op. cit., pp. 252-253.
9. Stanley Karnow, *Vietnam: A History* (New York: Viking Penguin, 1997), p. 502.

1965. On that day, thousands of protesters gathered for SDS's march on Washington. This was the first of many large-scale national antiwar gatherings of the 1960s. A sense of urgency marked the event. Johnson had sent combat troops to Vietnam in February and began Rolling Thunder in March. The demonstration had been "an electrifying moment," recalled David Dellinger, a leading antiwar organizer, and after that "the teach-ins, campus rallies, pickets, and large-scale mass protests invigorated the war's opponents."[10]

One of the most poignant acts of antiwar dissent came on the afternoon of November 2, 1965. A young Quaker, Norman Morrisson, father of three and an officer of the Stoney Run Friends Meeting in Baltimore, poured gasoline on himself and then lit a match. He did it within forty feet of McNamara's Pentagon window. He did it, said his wife, "to express his concern over the great loss of life and human suffering caused by the war in Vietnam."[11]

Johnson took the criticisms and condemnations of his Vietnam policies hard. The antiwar demonstrations referred to him as an insensitive militarist, using massive military power to defeat a small nation. Yet he considered himself caught in the middle. He would neither withdraw from Vietnam nor would he abide by the extreme hawks, most of whom wanted him to use even more massive force. As the man in the middle, he could not call up the National Guard or ask Congress for a declaration of war, for economic controls, or for a tax increase.

On the domestic front, Johnson was doing well. The 1960s was a period of economic prosperity, more jobs, higher income, greater national growth, and a better distribution of income. Nevertheless, the country was becoming polarized over the war and race riots in major cities, beginning in 1965 with Watts, a suburb of Los Angeles. "We remained a nation with a split personality," recalled Humphrey, "a nation with two characters, two lives."[12]

One of the biggest demonstrations before 1968 took place on October 21, 1967. About 20,000 antiwar demonstrators marched on the Pentagon. Their goal was to shut it down. The authorities were

10. David Dellinger, *More Power Than We Know* (New York: Anchor Press, 1975), p. 149.
11. McNamara, *Retrospect,* p. 216.
12. Humphrey, *Education,* p. 344.

ready for them. Guarding the Pentagon were eighteen hundred National Guard troops, four battalions of military police (totaling three thousand men), two thousand District of Columbia police officers, and contingents from the Eighty-Second Airborne Division.

The demonstration included two separate parts. About 50,000 attended the first part, which was a rally at the Lincoln Memorial. From it, about 20,000 would march to the Pentagon. A well-known figure among Americans, Dr. Benjamin Spock, noted baby doctor, spoke at the rally. "The real enemy," he said, "is Lyndon Johnson, whom we elected as a peace candidate in 1964, and who betrayed us within three months, who has stubbornly led us deeper and deeper into a bloody quagmire."[13]

After the rally, the crowd split off, and about 20,000 of them walked across the Memorial Bridge to the Pentagon. Army helicopters hovered overhead. Along with U.S. marshals, troops surrounded the building, rifles at ready, standing shoulder-to-shoulder. Inside the Pentagon were more soldiers at the ready. If the crowd forced a breach in the troop line, the soldiers inside the building would pour out to close it.

Several confrontations took place as the marchers tried to break the line. At one point, the troops fell back against the Pentagon's doors, and those inside flowed out to hold back the crowd. Using rifle butts and nightsticks, soldiers and U.S. marshals beat back the demonstrators. They arrested 128 of them, including David Dellinger, the rally's organizer.

To McNamara, if the protesters had been more disciplined, they might have achieved their objective of shutting the Pentagon down. "All they had to do was lie on the pavement around the building," he said. "We would have found it impossible to remove enough of them fast enough to keep the Pentagon open."[14]

Led by General Lewis Hershey, the Selective Service System, referred to as the draft, was unfair. It deferred those who went to college and fell heavily on those young men who went into the labor market after high school. To escape from it, some men fled to Canada

---

13. Dellinger, *More Power*, p. 175.
14. McNamara, *Retrospect*, p. 304.

while others sought conscientious objector status on religious grounds or faked medical problems. Some resisted openly by burning their draft cards and accepting jail as an alternative to Vietnam.

LBJ's Peace Offensive

At times, Johnson would make a peace offer. In April 1965 he offered Hanoi one billion in economic aid to develop the Mekong River valley. In December 1966, he ordered a bombing pause that lasted thirty-seven days. At the same time, he sent Vice President Humphrey and diplomatic envoys Averell Harriman and Arthur Goldberg to visit forty capitals. In September 1967, he offered a bombing halt in return for productive negotiations. But his offers only applied to governments. He excluded negotiations with the principal enemy, the Vietcong. To do so would be a tacit admission that America was intervening in a Vietnamese civil war, not to stop international Communism.

The doves charged that Johnson's peace offers were motivated by domestic considerations. His purpose, they said, was to blunt opposition to the war and to provide justification for escalating it. If Johnson was serious about negotiations, said the doves, he would have to not only negotiate with the Vietcong but also allow Vietnam to become a nonaligned nation. But he opposed neutralization, which he called surrender on the installment plan, allowing South Vietnam to be taken over through Communist subversion. Thus, said one official, "the very word 'negotiation' was anathema to the administration."[15]

On November 30, 1965, McNamara submitted a memo advocating a short bombing pause. Even if it failed to get Hanoi to the negotiating table, he wrote, it would "demonstrate our genuine desire for peaceful settlement" and temper domestic criticism. Also, by making a serious move now, he added, "it would make it easier for us to carry out necessary additional military measures in the future."[16]

Johnson's other cabinet members, however, were skeptical of a bombing pause. They noted that Hanoi's leaders had given no signal

---

15. Bagby, *International Relations*, p. 256.
16. Johnson, *Vantage*, p. 234.

they would respond to one, and if they did, they would only talk, not enter into serious negotiations. But Johnson was inclined to try a pause if stopping the bombing might open a road to peace. "I wanted to explore every possible avenue of settlement," he said, "before we took additional measures."[17]

At the same time, Johnson wanted a "diplomatic extravaganza." He would send Ball, Averell Harriman, McGeorge Bundy, Ambassador Foy Kohler, Arthur Goldberg, and Vice President Humphrey to visit forty capitals to persuade their leaders to bring Hanoi to the negotiating table. To Ball, the spectacle of flying people all over the world to solicit their help was "futile and unbecoming."[18] Yet, the pause, he said, at least broke the "momentum of escalation." He feared, however, that after it, the administration would be under pressure to "increase the pace of the war."[19]

Lasting thirty-seven days, from December 24, 1965 to January 31, 1966, the bombing pause failed to persuade Hanoi to come to the negotiating table. On January 28, three days before Johnson resumed the bombing, Radio Hanoi broadcast Ho Chi Minh's reply to Washington's peace move. Denouncing the "so-called search for peace," he accused the U.S. of being "deceitful " and "hypocritical." He insisted that the U.S. pull all of its troops out of Vietnam and accept the National Liberation Front (Vietcong) as "the genuine representative of the people of South Vietnam."[20]

On February 8 Johnson ordered a short bombing pause on all of Vietnam as part of a general truce surrounding Tet, the Vietnamese New Year. In a letter to Ho Chi Minh, he wrote that he was prepared to order a cessation of bombing against North Vietnam if Ho would halt military troops and aid into South Vietnam.

In reply, Ho Chi Minh demanded that the U.S. "unconditionally" stop all bombing, that it withdraw all its troops from Vietnam, and that it recognize the National Liberation Front. "The Vietnamese people,"

17. Ibid., p. 237.
18. Ball, *Past*, p. 405.
19. Ibid., p. 404.
20. Johnson, *Vantage*, pp. 239-240.

he wrote, "will never yield to force nor agree to talks under the menace of bombs."[21]

At the Manila summit in October 1966, Johnson assembled with the leaders of all the nations with troops in Vietnam, which included South Korea, Thailand, Australia, New Zealand, and Saigon's Thieu and Ky. Out of the summit came the so-called Manila formula. It stated that "allied forces shall be withdrawn, after close consultations, as the other side withdraws its forces to the north, ceases infiltration, and the level of violence thus subsides."[22] Nothing was said about the Vietcong, and Hanoi never responded to it. While the summit was a good public relations exercise, said Clark Clifford, Johnson's political confidant, it was not "an honest review of the political and military difficulties confronting the allies."[23]

From Manila, Johnson made a secret trip to Vietnam. His visit to the troops at Can Ranh Bay was the first trip by a president to troops in a war zone since Franklin D. Roosevelt had visited them during the World War II Casablanca Conference in January 1943.

Johnson's visit lasted two and a half hours. While a military band played the national anthem, he moved among the soldiers at attention and those lying in hospital beds. Finally, to a group of officers in a packed officers club, he gave an emotional patriotic speech. He said that the military will get everything it needs. Reaching back to his Texas roots, he told the officers to "go out there and nail that coonskin to the wall."[24] For the rest of the war, people joked, "nailing the coonskin on the wall." Nevertheless, it signaled Johnson's determination to win the war and not be, as he feared, the first president to lose a war.

On April 6, 1967, Johnson, in a letter to Ho Chi Minh, wrote that he was prepared either to talk first about a settlement and then stop fighting or to undertake steps of mutual de-escalation that might make negotiation of a settlement easier. Ho Chi Minh did not respond.

During a June 1967 summit conference at Glassboro, New Jersey, Aleksei Kosygin informed Johnson that if he stopped bombing, Hanoi

---

21. Ibid., pp. 594-595.
22. Henry Kissinger, *White House Years* (Boston: Little Brown, 1979), p. 256.
23. Clark Clifford, *Counsel to the President: A Memoir* (New York: Random House, 1991), p. 441.
24. Ibid., p. 443.

was willing to talk. He agreed to it as long as Hanoi's forces near the seventeenth parallel did not move southward. In return, he would not order U.S. forces to move northward. But again, Washington did not receive a response from Hanoi.

The War at the End of 1967

By the fall of 1967, criticism of the war was mounting. As it did, the administration became more defensive. Some of its response was shrill. Johnson and his advisers called critics of the war "nervous nellies" and "special pleaders." Westmoreland insisted that within two years the United States could phase down its military effort and withdraw some troops.[25] "We could now see light at the end of the tunnel," added ambassador to Vietnam Ellsworth Bunker.[26] But the Joint Chiefs of Staff remained silent.

For many Americans, it seemed inconceivable that a small under-developed country could long withstand America's overwhelming military power. Although the Vietcong suffered high casualties, won no sizable battles, and numbered fewer than 300,000 lightly armed men, they continued not only to exist but to expand, a fact many found astonishing.

By the end of 1967, the Americanization of the war was a fact. American troop levels rose to 500,000, peaking at 540,000 in February 1969, and the total number of Americans killed to 9,400 in 1967 and rising to 15,600 in 1968. At the same time, the U.S.-trained and -armed Saigon military force rose to nearly 800,000 men.

But the South Vietnamese Army proved of limited value. Despite American training and equipment, they did poorly in combat. The battles became American led and fought. The administration sent more troops to protect the few that were already there until the few became the many. As U.S. troop levels increased, the North Vietnamese sent more units to the south.

While the Americans were mainly trained to fight conventional war, the Vietcong used guerilla warfare, infiltration, and mortar attacks

25. Westmoreland, *Soldier*, p. 28.
26. *New York Times*, November 20, 1967.

on American bases. Hitting Americans at their weak points and then hiding among the people was standard Vietcong practice. For the most part, the Vietcong were South Vietnamese. It soon became apparent to some that America's presence in Vietnam only reinforced the Communist argument that Vietnam was fighting a war of independence from foreign control.

Fighting a guerilla war in the jungles of Vietnam was a difficult task for American soldiers. Guerilla war was elusive, quiet, and deadly. On search and destroy missions, American troops faced mines, snipers, and booby traps, which accounted for enormous casualties and psychological disorientation.

To fight the guerilla war, the army adopted free-fire zones and defoliation of South Vietnam's jungle forests. Using helicopters in the free-fire zones was standard procedure. Anybody found in them was a fair target. Also, U.S. planes had defoliated over one-eighth of Vietnam's land. By this time, moreover, Congress had budgeted 20 million for the war.

By 1967, the war was deadlocked. "Before I came out here a year ago, I thought we were at zero," said General Fred Weyrand to a visiting official, but "I was wrong, we were at minus fifty, and now we're at zero."[27]

In mid-July 1967 Johnson agreed with the Joint Chiefs on the need for additional troops. But he faced mounting criticism that U.S. allies were not contributing enough troops. Their contribution at that time was slightly more than 50,000 troops. Consequently, he asked Maxwell Taylor and Clark Clifford to make the rounds of U.S. allies in South Korea, Thailand, the Philippines, Australia, and New Zealand to get them to send additional troops.

The allied countries resisted Taylor's and Clifford's attempts to get more troops. Each country's leaders had good reasons why they could not send additional troops. Thailand's leaders, for example, said that they could not send additional troops because they were fighting their own communist insurgency in the northeast. Visiting Thailand's Pote Sarasin, the minister of national development, in his home in Bangkok, Clifford listened to him criticize Secretary Rusk for talking about the

---

27. Karnow, *Vietnam*, pp. 525-526.

"yellow peril" from China. Sarasin did not think the Chinese would send troops to North Vietnam like they did during the Korean War. "Don't you Americans know," he said, "that the Chinese and Vietnamese have hated each other for centuries?"[28]

Similarly, the Australians and the New Zealanders could not send more troops because of new defense problems arising out of the planned British withdrawal of troops from Malaysia and Singapore, and the South Koreans faced terrorist threats from North Korea.

While Clifford was negative about the visit, Taylor was upbeat. "Eventually," he recalled, the allied forces increased from 50,000 to 70,000 troops in the next two years. Yet, he admitted that "the allied troop strength was always less than we Americans wished."[29]

In a speech before the National Legislative Conference in San Antonio, Texas, on September 29, 1967, Johnson made another peace proposal. Referred to as the San Antonio formula, he offered to stop the bombing in return for constructive discussions. But his offer, like the previous ones, referred to governments, excluding negotiations with the Vietcong, the principal enemy. Without including them into negotiations, however, he could not hope for a peace settlement. Thus, his critics charged that he was not sincere about peace, and that the main purpose of his peace offers was to diminish opposition to the war and provide justification for escalating it.

Despite the administration's official optimism, Secretary of Defense McNamara was beginning to doubt the wisdom of escalation in Vietnam. Beginning in 1967 he expressed his doubts to journalists, friends, and former attorney general Robert Kennedy. "As McNamara's pessimism grew," recalled White House aide Doris Kearns, "his access to the President diminished since Johnson did not want to hear other people's doubts."[30] By the summer of 1967, recalled presidential assistant John P. Roche, McNamara was "a very disturbed guy."[31] "He lacked the innate toughness required in a 'War Minister,'" reported Joseph Alsop, and fellow columnist William S. White added

---

28. Clifford, *Counsel,* pp. 449-450.
29. Maxwell D. Taylor, *Swords and Plowshares* (New York: W. W. Norton), p. 376.
30. Doris Kearns, *Lyndon Johnson and the American Dream* (New York: Harper and Row, 1976), p. 320.
31. John P. Roche: interview with Paige Mulhollan, August 16, 1970, Oral history Project, Lyndon B. Johnson Library, Austin, Texas.

that McNamara was "more bookish than martial in spirit and attitude."[32]

McNamara's evolution from hawk to dove on the war was a long, evolving process. Periodically, while in public, he ran across people who would shout "murderer" or "baby burner," or tell him that he had "blood on his hands." His wife and son developed ulcers. On one occasion, Jackie Kennedy, the former first lady, erupted in fury and tears at him over his role in escalating the war. Dining with her in her Manhattan apartment, recalled McNamara, she suddenly exploded, turned and "began literally to beat on my chest, demanding that I do something to stop the war."[33]

Beginning in August 1967, under questioning before the Senate Armed Services Committee, McNamara was unable to make a strong argument for the continued bombing. His disagreements with the Joint Chiefs on this issue became a matter of public record. Rather than examining the reasons for his doubts on the war, Johnson began to express his doubts to Clifford about McNamara's loyalty and stability. "The President still liked and respected McNamara enormously," said Clifford, but he was losing confidence in the judgment of his tormented aide, and was increasingly suspicious of his relationship with Robert Kennedy."[34]

During a lunch meeting with Johnson and his advisers on October 31, 1967, McNamara proposed a new course of action on Vietnam. He said that the current policy was "dangerous, costly, and unsatisfactory." Johnson asked him to put his thoughts on paper.

The next day McNamara submitted a memo outlining his thoughts on the war. He expressed fears that the military would call for additional troops and increased bombing which would only increase our casualties and at best result in only "slow progress." As an alternative, he advocated stabilizing U.S. war efforts, including not expanding air attacks against the North or increasing the number of American ground troops. Moreover, he proposed a bombing halt and favored

---

32. *Washington Post*, November 30, 1967.
33. McNamara, *Retrospect*, pp. 257-258.
34. Clifford, *Counsel*, pp. 456-457.

giving the South Vietnamese greater responsibility for their own security.[35]

Johnson passed McNamara's memo around to Rusk, Clifford, Westmoreland, and Taylor. Although they agreed that the U.S. needed to give the South Vietnamese greater responsibility for their own security, they rejected both the idea of a bombing halt and stabilizing American forces in the south. They argued that Hanoi would interpret both actions as "a resigned and discouraged effort to find a way out of a conflict for which the U.S. had lost both its will and dedication."[36]

Alone among Johnson's closest advisers, McNamara had come to the conclusion that the administration's present course of action was untenable and dangerous, costly in lives, and not in America's national self-interest.

On November 28, 1967, amidst mounting press speculation of an open break, Johnson approved McNamara's resignation, taking effect in March 1968, and appointed him president of the World Bank. "There never was any open break between them," insisted Press Secretary George Christian.[37] "The job," recalled presidential assistant John P. Roche "was just too much for McNamara."[38]

Earlier, on November 2, 1967, Johnson had assembled together a group of elder statesmen, called the Wise Men, in the White House Cabinet Room. They included Dean Acheson (secretary of state under President Truman). General Omar Bradley (World War II commander), Arthur Dean (chief Korean War negotiator), Douglas Dillon (secretary of the treasury under President Kennedy), Abe Fortas (a sitting associate justice of Supreme Court), Robert Murphy (a senior career ambassador of the Truman-Eisenhower administrations). Others present were Ambassador Averell Harriman, Henry Cabot Lodge, and Maxwell Taylor as well as presidential assistant McGeorge Bundy and Undersecretary of State George Ball.

At this time, Johnson, reeling from McNamara's change of policy memo, needed to get the Wise Men's views on Vietnam. After all, they were experienced members of America's foreign policy establishment.

---

35. Johnson, *Vantage*, pp. 372-373.
36. Clifford, *Counsel*, p. 458.
37. George Christian interview with Joe B. Frantz, July 1, 1971, Oral History Project, Lyndon B. Johnson Library, Austin, Texas.
38. Roche interview with Mulhollan, July 16, 1970.

They had spent the past two decades dealing with the challenges and perils of the Cold War.

Concealing McNamara's memo from the Wise Men, Johnson sought their independent opinion. Maintaining public support for the war was the major theme of the meeting. Except for Ball, who advocated a bombing halt, the Wise Men expressed satisfaction with the war's progress. They agreed that the administration should emphasize "light at the end of the tunnel," instead of "battles, deaths, and danger."[39]

Afterwards, as the Wise Men came out of the Cabinet Room, Ball said, "You're like a flock of old buzzards sitting on a fence, sending the young men off to be killed," and "you ought to be ashamed of yourselves."[40]

The meeting reaffirmed Johnson's policy, and that was what he hoped would be the result. He always seemed to need reaffirmation. He himself would often go back and forth, but he seemed to always lean to the Joint Chief's views.

By the fall of 1967, the U.S. seemed to be winning the war. The Vietcong seemed to replenish their forces when Americans were killing four Vietcong for every South Vietnamese soldier. The number of South Vietnamese under Vietcong control dropped by a million to 2.4 million. In November General Westmoreland announced, "we are winning." He said that the enemy had not won "a major battle" in more than a year.[41] Yet, at the same time, General Wheeler, chairman of the Joint Chiefs of Staff, said that "a desperate Battle of the Bulge effect by the communists was expected."[42]

When Humphrey returned from a visit to Vietnam in November 1967, he urged Johnson to stop the "search and destroy" missions and switch to a "clear and hold" strategy. He called for a phase down of America's combat mission in order to precipitate a policy of gradual disengagement. He hoped for a negotiated settlement that would lead to broad-based South Vietnamese support for the Saigon government. He did not, however, mention if this government would include the

---

39. Clark M. Clifford, interview with the author, August 18, 1982.
40. Ball, *Past*, p. 407.
41. Westmoreland, *Soldier*, p. 234.
42. Walt W. Rostow, *The Diffusion of Power: An Essay in Recent History* (New York: The Macmillan Company, 1972), p. 481.

Vietcong. Most important, he saw clearly that a large number of Americans were beginning to waver in their support for the war, and that some of them were convinced that it could not be won.[43]

But Humphrey's doubts were his private thoughts. He was the vice president: in public, he pushed the administration's policy. This would bode ill for him later as more liberals in the Democratic Party turned against the war. Soon, the war's turning point would commence. It would fall on Tet, the South Vietnamese New Year.

---

43. Humphrey, *Education*, pp. 349-350.

3.

The Breaking Point

The Tet Offensive

On January 19, 1968, President Johnson appointed Clark Clifford secretary of defense. Unlike McNamara, who became president of the World Bank, Clifford seemed to fit Johnson's innate biases on the war. Although he initially opposed the buildup of American troops in Vietnam, he had consistently supported Johnson's Vietnam policy. When the press corps asked him if he was a hawk or a dove, he said that he did not fall under either definition.

Most Washington insiders, however, described Clifford as a hawk, and almost every article at the time described him as one. To the *New York Times*, "President Johnson has replaced a brilliant doubter with a confident confidant."[1] But speculation was premature, said the *Boston Globe*. "It will depend entirely on what he senses as he takes the nation's pulse."[2]

In November 1967 U.S. intelligence observers reported heavy traffic on the Ho Chi Minh trail. They spotted several North Vietnamese divisions being positioned near the Laotian border. A region of rolling hills, it straddled Route 9, an old French road which connected the Vietnamese coast to the Laotian market towns along the Mekong River. American troops had set up a camp there to recruit and train local mountain tribesmen. As reports came in of enemy troop buildups

---

1. *New York Times*, January 20, 1968.
2. *Boston Globe*, January 19, 1968.

nearby, General Westmoreland began to stockpile the base with ammunition, howitzers, and mortars, and refurbished its airstrip. Three thousand marines defended the base. Another three thousand were dug in on the four nearby hills.

With the increased traffic on the Ho Chi Minh trail, Westmoreland and General Wheeler determined that the North Vietnamese had decided on a major offensive. They were certain it would come at Khe Sanh. To Westmoreland, the Communists considered taking it as part of their broader strategy of conquering South Vietnam's northernmost provinces. Once taken, like they did after defeating the French in 1954 at the battle of Dien Bien Phu, the Communists would then enter into negotiations.[3]

On January 21, 1968, North Vietnamese troops and the Vietcong launched an attack on Khe Sanh. Johnson held several meetings with his advisers and the Joint Chiefs, who assured him that the marines could handle the enemy assault. According to Clifford, nobody at these meetings ever suggested that Khe Sanh might be part of an enemy strategy to divert American attention and resources from an offensive elsewhere.[4]

But North Vietnamese general Vo Nguyen Giap had devised a masterful plan of deception. Khe Sanh was only a diversionary effort designed to pull Saigon's troops away from the cities in the south. He would launch his major offensive on Tet, January 30, the most important holiday in Vietnam.

To Westmoreland, however, Khe Sanh was the main theatre of the offensive and the surrounding northernmost provinces. Along with others, he assumed that the Communists would not alienate the people of South Vietnam by violating a truce that they themselves agreed to on Tet, Vietnam's sacred festival. And a good number of South Vietnamese and American soldiers were given leave that day.

But American leaders had failed to study Vietnam's history. They were unaware that the most famous exploits in its history occurred during Tet of 1789. At that time, Emperor Quang Trung deceptively routed a Chinese occupation army while they were celebrating the

---

3. Stanley Karnow, *Vietnam: A History* (New York: Viking Penguin, 1997), pp. 552-553.
4. Clifford, *Counsel*, p. 469.

holiday in Hanoi. The Americans did not understand that after centuries of both internal conflict and outside invasions from China that the Vietnamese were "inured to duplicity."[5]

On January 30, 1968, Tet, the North Vietnamese and Vietcong launched a major offensive. Unreported by both peasants and urban dwellers, the Vietcong, secretly moved large forces into the cities and achieved complete surprise with massive simultaneous attacks that struck five of South Vietnam's six major cities, thirty-three of its forty-four provincial capitals, and sixty-four district capitals. Some of the worst fighting occurred in Hue, the old imperial capital. About 7,500 Vietcong seized it. They held out to American forces for twenty-six days, leaving the city almost destroyed and with more than 70 percent of its inhabitants homeless.

The damage to Saigon was considerable. At the American embassy in Saigon a squad of Vietcong blasted a hole in the wall surrounding the compound and entered the grounds, but United States military police and marine guards prevented them from penetrating the building itself and killed all the attackers.

Despite reports of enemy buildup, the administration was caught off guard by the ferocity of the offensive. "There was some warning that something was coming," said Press Secretary George Christian. "But the intensity and strength of the attack surprised everybody."[6] "The major surprise," recalled National Security Adviser Walt Rostow, "was the number of provincial capitals attacked."[7] "Everybody was amazed together," said Clifford.[8] "No one really expected the enemy to launch the attack during Tet," recalled General Wheeler.[9] "It was a shock to all of us," agreed Johnson.[10]

Despite its early successes, the Tet offensive was a military disaster for the Vietcong. It exposed their secret organizations and membership. They failed to capture radio stations, and the South Vietnamese civilians did not rise to their support.

---

5. Karnow, *Vietnam*, p. 556.
6. George Christian, interview with the author, August 5, 1982.
7. Walt W. Rostow, interview with the author, December 22, 1982.
8. Clark Clifford, interview with the author, August 18, 1982.
9. Earle G. Wheeler, interview with Dorothy Pierce McSweeny, August 21, 1969, Oral History Project, Lyndon B. Johnson Library, Austin, Texas.
10. Johnson, *Vantage*, p. 284.

But American losses were the heaviest since the war began. In eight weeks of fighting, Casualties totaled 3,895 killed. The South Vietnamese forces sustained 4,954 recorded deaths, and 58,000 North Vietnamese regulars and Vietcong, who suffered the most casualties, died.[11] Ironically, the loss of so many South Vietnamese fighters, the Vietcong, gave North Vietnam more influence over the war in South Vietnam.

The administration claimed a decisive victory against the enemy. "They lost as many people at Tet as we have lost in the entire war," said Johnson.[12] "The best units of the Vietcong were decimated," said Press Secretary George Christian, "and the ground loss was quickly recovered."[13] The Tet Offensive, said Maxwell Taylor, was "the greatest victory we ever scored in Vietnam."[14] But "another victory or two like that," recalled Secretary of Defense Clifford, "and we would be out of business." He added, "It was a disastrous defeat for us."[15]

Growing Pressures for Policy Change

After Tet, popular sentiment for the war fell sharply and much of the public media turned against it. The press, television, and magazines carried pictures of ruined cities, and they published the statement of an American commander who said that "it was necessary to destroy Hue in order to save it." One particularly telling picture showed South Vietnam's National Police Chief Nguyen Loan shooting a handcuffed Vietcong prisoner in the head.[16] This act, if committed by an enemy, would be considered an atrocity. The guerrilla who was summarily executed had just massacred entire families inside the national police compound but the media later made no mention of that fact.

Major publications like the *Wall Street Journal*, the *New York Post*, *Life*, *Look*, *Time*, and *Newsweek* and major television networks like CBS and NBC concluded that the U.S. had "made a mistake" in committing

---

11. Clifford, *Counsel,* p. 473.
12. *New York Times,* February 7, 1970.
13. Christian, interview with the author, August 16, 1982.
14. Maxwell D. Taylor interview with Dorothy Pierce McSweeny, February 10, 1969, Oral History Project, Lyndon B. Johnson Library, Austin, Texas.
15. Clark Clifford interview with the author, August 18, 1982.
16. Bagby, *International,* p. 257.

combat troops to Vietnam."[17] "The whole Vietnam effort," editorial-
ized the *Wall Street Journal*, "may be falling apart beneath our feet."[18]
The popular television news anchorman Walter Cronkite added that
America was "mired in stalemate," and "the only rational way out is to
negotiate."[19]

Opposition to the war also came from Congress. A total of 139
House members, Republicans and Democrats, joined in supporting a
resolution calling for an immediate Congressional review of the administration's Southeast Asian Policy.[20] To LBJ, however, their resolution
symbolized "a chorus of defeatism." He blamed the news media for "a
great deal of emotional and exaggerated" reporting on the Tet
Offensive.[21]

To some, Tet was a psychological victory for the enemy. Nobody
in Saigon, said Westmoreland, "even remotely anticipated the psychological impact that the Tet Offensive had on the American public."[22]
While the enemy was losing on the battlefield, said Taylor, the
American public was "shocked by the unexpected vitality shown by an
enemy whom many had supposed to be on his last legs."[23] The
administration, said Humphrey, had given the public an optimistic
picture of the war and then Tet "destroyed its credibility."[24] The size
and scope of the massive assault, agreed Clifford, had "devastated the
administration's credibility."[25]

On February 12, 1968, General Westmoreland, fearing another
round of attacks, asked for an additional 10,000 American troops."
"With additional reinforcements," he said, "I could strengthen the
North without risking further weakening of forces in the South,
around Saigon."[26] Johnson agreed to send him more troops.

But to General Wheeler, 10,000 additional troops was not enough.
On February 28, he asked the president to consider sending 205,000

17. *Wall Street Journal*, February 18, 1968.
18. Ibid.
19. *Washington Post*, March 8, 1968.
20. *New York Times*, February 17, 1968.
21. Johnson, *Vantage*, p. 384.
22. Westmoreland, *Soldier*, p. 321.
23. Taylor, *Swords*, p. 383.
24. Humphrey, *Education*, p. 357.
25. Clifford, *Counsel*, p. 473.
26. Westmoreland, *Soldier*, p. 352.

additional troops to Vietnam. In Wheeler's judgment, without an increase in troops, Westmoreland might have to give up South Vietnam's two northern provinces.

McNamara was not convinced. To him, adding more troops would only compel the North Vietnamese to match our increase with more of their own troops.[27] Walt Rostow, however, not only supported the military's recommendation for more troops but also advocated invading Laos, Cambodia, and North Vietnam.[28] Clifford, on the other hand, recommended opening up new peace efforts. But Johnson needed more information. He asked Clifford to head a task force to consider the military's request for more troops since this was now an issue of national mobilization.

Reassessment

Between February 28 and March 4 Clifford's task force met daily to prepare their report for Johnson. It included Rusk, McNamara, Wheeler, Taylor, William Bundy, CIA director Richard Helms, Deputy Secretary of Defense Paul H. Nitze, Assistant Secretary of the Treasury Henry H. Fowler, and Assistant Secretary of Defense for Public Affairs Phil G. Goulding.

The Task Force examined every aspect of the Vietnam War. According to Taylor, the participants expressed "little or no enthusiasm" for sending 205,000 more troops and their discussions revolved around whether the U.S. should re-adjust its strategy and, if so, what direction it should take.[29]

Until then, Clifford, a hawk with ties to America's top financial leaders, had never analyzed the war in detail. He was shocked to discover that the Joint Chiefs could not give him any assurances. "If 205,000 might not be sufficient," he asked, "how many more troops would the military need?" But they had no way of knowing. "Will stepping up the bombing stop the war," he asked, or "decrease American casualties?" They replied that bombing by itself would not stop the war, and it would decrease American casualties "very little, if at all."

---

27. Johnson, *Vantage*, p. 391.
28. Walt W. Rostow, interview with the author, December 22, 1982.
29. Taylor, *Swords*, p. 388.

This exchange disturbed Clifford greatly. "Although I kept my feelings private," he recalled, "I was appalled, nothing had prepared me for the weakness of the military case."[30]

Rejecting the military's request for 205,000 additional troops, Clifford's Task Force recommended that Johnson give Westmoreland only 22,000 troops but hold periodic reviews to decide whether additional troops were necessary.[31] By this time Clifford had become convinced that there was "no light at the end of the tunnel," and that a change in policy was necessary to avoid disaster.[32]

His change of heart hit Johnson hard. "The impact on the President," said Westmoreland, was "considerably stronger than if some admitted dove had come up with a similar conclusion."[33] Johnson was "deeply concerned and angered," recalled Clifford. He had supported his position before hand, but after talking with the Joint Chiefs he had discovered things that he had not known. "Their strategy," he said, "was to stay at it, and ultimately attrition would be so devastating that the enemy would give up, but they were just dead wrong."[34] Still, said Christian, Clifford lost little of his influence with Johnson and "continued to present his views forcefully to the end."[35]

In a memo to Johnson on March 5 Rusk proposed a temporary bombing halt. For the next month, he wrote, monsoon rains would cover northern Vietnam, hindering North Vietnamese movement. Thus, a short bombing halt would not entail too much risk. If Hanoi failed to respond, the U.S. would resume air strikes, "It was important," he said, "not to embroider the statement with all sorts of conditions or assumptions."[36]

Johnson said that he would give Rusk's proposal "careful thought." But on the question of whether to send additional troops, he remained noncommittal. "I had almost been ready to call up a large number of reserves," he said later. "My opinion had changed as a result of what I had heard from my advisers and what I saw happening on the ground

30. Clifford, *Counsel*, pp. 493-494.
31. U.S. Vietnam Relations, IUC (6), p. 59.
32. Clark Clifford interview with Paige Mulhollan, July 14, 1982, Oral History Project, Lyndon B. Johnson Library, Austin, Texas.
33. Westmoreland, *Soldier*, p. 358.
34. Clark Clifford, interview with the author, August 18, 1982.
35. George Christian, *The President Steps Down* (New York: Macmillan, 1970), p. 115.
36. Johnson, *Vantage*, p. 400.

in Vietnam."[37] He complained to Christian: "The military talk too big about success, body count, and all that."[38]

The bombing halt issue resurfaced at cabinet meetings on March 20 and 22. If Hanoi agreed to withdraw its forces far north of the seventeenth parallel, Clifford proposed a bombing halt north of the twentieth parallel.[39] Rusk, however, continued to argue for a bombing halt without conditions. It would not cost much, he added, and if the enemy continued to attack, it would justify committing more U.S. troops.[40] But Johnson continued to remain noncommittal. "I was judging the possible impact of a peace move linked with an announcement of my decision to withdraw from politics at the end of my turn."[41]

Dropping out of the presidential race and announcing a partial bombing halt appealed to Johnson's sense of the dramatic. He would be sacrificing a second term to spend the rest of his administration seeking peace in Vietnam. At that time he felt very much like a man in the corner, besieged on all fronts. By early 1968, in fact, he could not travel anywhere in the U.S. without confronting large crowds of anti-war protesters. Moreover, on March 12 Senator Eugene McCarthy, a dark horse antiwar Democrat, lost to LBJ by only a few thousand votes in the New Hampshire primary. On March 16, Senator Robert Kennedy, Johnson's nemesis, decided to enter the race as well.

The Wise Men

Johnson had still not made up his mind about a bombing halt. Discouraged by the results of his own advisers, he asked Clifford and Rostow to again assemble the special group of presidential advisers, called the Wise Men. It was the same group that had met in November, except for two newcomers: Cyrus Vance (deputy secretary of defense under McNamara) and General Matthew Ridgeway (Korean War commander).

---

37. Ibid., p. 406.
38. Christian, interview with the author August 16, 1982.
39. Johnson, *Vantage,* p. 412.
40. Herbert Y. Schandler, *The Unmaking of a President* (Princeton: Princeton UP, 1988), p. 243.
41. Johnson, *Vantage,* p. 413.

On March 25 the Wise Men assembled in Rusk's office to listen to three government officials describe the Vietnam situation. They included Deputy Assistant Secretary of State Philip De Puy, and CIA analyst George Carver. They painted a gloomy picture of Vietnam. It would take five to ten more years, they said, to pacify the country and expel the North Vietnamese from the south.[42] To Taylor, they "seemed slightly more pessimistic about the political situation than I had expected."[43] Later, Johnson said that "their assessment did not square with the situation as I understood it."[44]

The following day, March 26, the Wise Men assembled with Johnson and Generals Wheeler and Creighton Abrams, who was shorter, heavier, and less telegenic that either Wheeler or Westmoreland. Abrams, recalled Clifford, was "blunt and reassuring where Westmoreland was dramatic and Wheeler cautious."[45] Asking the generals to give the Wise Men a firsthand description of the military situation, Johnson said, "We don't want an inspirational talk or a gloom talk, but just give them the factual, cold honest picture as you see it."[46]

Wheeler and Abrams gave a more upbeat picture of the war than the government officials did the previous evening. To the two generals, the press was to blame for "all the doom and gloom." One of the enemy's objectives, they said, was to demoralize our home front.[47] But when Abrams said that he was training the South Vietnamese Army to take on a large part of the war, one of the Wise Men wondered if that was realistic. "Yes," said Abrams "I would have to quit if I didn't believe that." Once Saigon completed its military buildup, he insisted, the South Vietnamese Army would take on a larger share of the buildup.[48]

After lunch, the Wise Men retired to the Cabinet Room with Johnson. Explaining that their position had changed since November 1967, Bundy said that the dominant sentiment among them was that the burden of proof rests on those who are urging a troop increase.[49]

---

42. Ball, *Past*, p. 408.
43. Taylor, *Swords*, p. 390.
44. Johnson, *Vantage,* p. 416.
45. Clifford, *Counsel*, p. 516.
46. Johnson, *Vantage,* p. 416
47. Ibid. p. 417.
48. Ibid.
49. Clifford, *Counsel*, p. 516.

"All of us had the impression," added Dean Acheson, "that there was no military conclusion in sight."[50] By a vote of six to four, the best advice the Wise Men could offer was to disengage from a war that was "not only endless but hopeless."[51] Their opposition was based on the belief that the war weakened America both at home and abroad.

The Wise Men's changed opinions clearly affected Johnson. "This dramatic and unexpected reversal of position on the part of so many respected friends," recalled Taylor, "made a deep impression on the President."[52] Their turn around, added Ball, "profoundly shook him."[53] "I had always regarded the majority of them as very steady and balanced," but now "disgustedly," said Johnson, "the establishment bastards have bailed out."[54]

The Speech and Reaction

Not running for reelection had been on Johnson's mind for quite some time. In 1964, he told Humphrey that he would not run again. But the vice president did not believe him and acted on that assumption.[55] "Johnson had often threatened not to run," recalled Edgar Berman, Humphrey's political confidant and physician, "but no one ever took these protestations seriously, least of all Humphrey."[56]

As Johnson escalated the war, he found himself isolated and alienated in his ability to physically communicate with the American people. By 1968, the antiwar movement had gained strength and momentum. Greeting Johnson at his speaking spots, antiwar hecklers chanted "Hey, hey LBJ! How many kids did you kill today?" These hecklers became so numerous that Johnson could only make his speeches on military bases. The "frustrations and genuine anguish" of his last year in office, he recalled, sometimes made him feel that he was

---

50. Mc George Bundy, "Summary of Notes," March 26, 1968, Lyndon B. Johnson Papers, Lyndon B. Johnson Library, Austin, Texas.

51. Bagby, *International*, p. 258.

52. Taylor, *Swords*, p. 391.

53. Ball, *Past*, p. 408.

54. Bagby, *International*, p. 258.

55. Humphrey, *Education*, p. 361.

56. Edgar Berman, *The Triumph and Tragedy of the Humphrey I Knew* (New York: Putnam, 1979), p. 152.

"living in a continuous nightmare."[57] To some observers, the Vietnam war had ruined Johnson's otherwise promising administration.

The exact moment when Johnson decided to offer a bombing halt north of the twentieth parallel and couple it with his withdrawal from the race remained unclear. On the morning of his March 31 speech he showed Humphrey two endings: one with and one without his withdrawal statement.[58] His decision about which one to use shifted back and forth throughout the day. At one point, he said, "I'm not going to know probably until I get in there whether I'm going to use that speech."[59]

Deploying an additional 13,500 troops to Vietnam, Johnson ordered Westmoreland home to become army chief of staff. Then, on Sunday, March 31, he addressed the nation from the oval office. In the interest of getting peace negotiations started, he announced a partial bombing halt of North Vietnam to a few miles north of the seventeenth parallel. He neither placed any conditions on the bombing halt nor mentioned any conditions under which he would resume bombing. If negotiations failed, he did not indicate what would happen, stressing only that the U.S. would equip the South Vietnamese army to defend its territory.

Then, in a dramatic statement, to take his peace efforts out of politics, Johnson said that he would not seek, and would not accept, the Democratic Party's nomination for another term as president.[60]

The North Vietnamese response to Johnson's peace move was positive. On May 3, 1968, the two sides agreed on Paris as the meeting place. The North Vietnamese wanted the Vietcong and the U.S. wanted the Saigon Government represented at the conference. But the U.S. considered the Vietcong puppets of the North while it considered the Saigon government puppets of the America. In a compromise mood, each side accepted the presence of the puppet of the other but only as members of the other side's delegation.

Heading the U.S. delegation was W. Averell Harriman. He would have his first contacts with the North Vietnamese on May 10. Talks

---

57. Bagby, *International*, p. 260.
58. Humphrey, *Education*, pp. 358-359.
59. Horace Busby, interview with the author, August 18, 1982.
60. Public Papers of Lyndon Johnson, pp. 469-476.

soon bogged down, however, and a stalemate ensued that would last into the next administration.

On April 4, 1968, Johnson placed a ceiling of 550,000 on United States forces in South Vietnam. This meant that none of the requested 205,000 reinforcements would be sent to Vietnam. Nevertheless, he intensified the war. In 1968, B-52 bombing missions tripled and search-and-destroy missions were the largest yet. At the same time, President Thieu, raising the South Vietnamese army to 850,000, took back the territories lost in the Tet Offensive. To Johnson, America was not going to be defeated "by a raggedy-ass little fourth-rate country."[61]

Although Johnson's withdrawal took the Democrats by surprise, the Republicans were equally amazed. While this was a year of surprises, said Richard Nixon, "I must say I didn't expect Johnson to withdraw from the race."[62] Other candidates for the Republican nomination, Nelson Rockefeller and Ronald Reagan, were stunned. "I almost fell off the couch," said Richard Kleindienst, a Nixon aide.[63] Another Nixon man, John Sears, recalled, "In the years I've spent in politics I have to say this was the single most surprising thing that has ever happened."[64]

The press seemed to support Johnson's withdrawal. To the *Washington Post*, "He made a personal sacrifice in the in the name of national unity that entitles him to a very special place in the annals of American history."[65] According to newsman William S. White, "His decision may return domestic tranquility and unity to a nation torn by war."[66]

Johnson's challengers, Eugene McCarthy and Robert Kennedy, were now without a target. "At once," said political activist Jack Newfield, "Kennedy had lost his chief issue."[67] Deprived of the Johnson target, said the Nation, Kennedy's candidacy "has dimmed."[68] "John-

61. Bagby, *International*, pp. 258-259.
62. *New York Times*, April 1, 1968.
63. Richard G. Kleindienst, interview with the author, August 25, 1982.
64. John W. Sears, interview with the author, September 14, 1982.
65. *Washington Post*, April 1, 1968.
66. Ibid., April 3, 1968.
67. Jack Newfield, "Kennedy's Search for a New Target," *Life*, April 12, 1968, p. 35.
68. Carey McWilliams, "The Bitter Legacy of LBJ," *The Nation*, September 9, 1968, p. 199.

son's decision," said the *Wall Street Journal,* "instantly cooled the controversy."[69]

Johnson claimed that many factors entered into his withdrawal from the presidential race. He feared another heart attack, like the one he had in the late 1950s, and that more race riots might occur during the fall campaign and hinder his response to them. Also, since 1964, his influence with Congress had lessened, and he would be unable to get much more legislation through it. But most important, he insisted that his withdrawal was "a serious and sincere effort to find a road to peace."[70] "Plainly," said the *Nation,* "the President's move was a monumental gamble for nine month's time to redeem his policies in Vietnam."[71]

Nevertheless, Johnson did not have to withdraw from the presidential race as a peace gesture, and nobody expected him to do that, including the enemy. The presidency, in fact, gave him the means to influence events and polls and to undercut his opponents with further peace efforts. But Johnson feared domestic collapse for his Vietnam policy, and withdrawal from the race helped him regain political momentum to better deal with it.

By linking his withdrawal with a bombing cutback and rejection of further massive troop increases, Johnson changed the war's direction from military escalation to negotiation. His actions signaled to the North Vietnamese a sincere desire to begin peace negotiations.

The 1968 Presidential Campaign and Election

Law and order and the Vietnam War were the two biggest issues of the 1968 presidential campaign and election.

Running on the American Independent Party's third-party ticket, Governor George C. Wallace of Alabama was the leading proponent of the law and order issue. A segregationist, he advocated strong measures to deal with northern black ghetto riots and antiwar demonstrations. Because of his rising national support, the two mainstream parties took up the issue as well. But the general public held the

---

69. *Wall Street Journal,* July 9, 1968.
70. Johnson, *Vantage,* p. 427.
71. *The Nation,* July 8, 1968, p. 19.

Democrats most responsible for its breakdown, which benefited the Republicans.

The Vietnam War issue split the Democratic Party. Senators Eugene McCarthy of Minnesota and Robert Kennedy of New York were both antiwar. While McCarthy had strong appeal to liberal intellectuals, Kennedy had more connections to party leaders and had a better chance of nomination. Kennedy won most of the spring primaries. But on June 5 an Arab nationalist assassinated him in a Los Angeles hotel. Many of his followers shifted to McCarthy. Controlling his party's nomination process, however, Johnson backed Vice President Hubert Humphrey for the presidency.

Held in Chicago, the 1968 Democratic convention was one of the most contentious conventions in U.S. history. Seeking to disrupt it, thousands of antiwar activists converged on the city. They occupied parks and held rallies; the police claimed that they did not have permits for these activities and charged and clubbed them. The protestors fought back. National television carried scenes of these violent clashes. The police behaved with little restraint, and brutality prevailed. A later investigation found the Chicago force guilty of a "police riot."

The convention's antiwar delegates clashed with the party's pro-Johnson leadership. Humphrey depended on them to win the nomination. When the antiwar delegates proposed a complete bombing halt plank to put in the platform, he, while privately agreeing to it, feared Johnson's wrath and thus took a public stand against it. Consequently, by a wide margin, Humphrey won the nomination over McCarthy. Beating back challenges from Rockefeller and Reagan, former Vice President Richard M. Nixon won the Republican nomination.

The vice president started the fall campaign with little funds, low poll ratings, and a split party. Moreover, Johnson seemed to give Humphrey less than total support; he may have thought Nixon more committed than Humphrey to carry on the war. In a September 30 speech, Humphrey called for a complete bombing halt. The liberal antiwar faction of the party started to support him. But not until October 31, only a few days before the election, did Johnson announce a bombing halt. Meanwhile, figuring it could get a better deal from

Nixon, the Saigon government refused to agree to arrangements for getting the stalled peace negotiations started.

With a united party and Johnson's full support, Humphrey began to make late gains. Nixon, however, claiming to have a secret plan to end the war and win the peace, won by seven-tenths of a percent. At the same time, 12.5 percent of the vote went to the hawkish third-party ticket of George Wallace and his vice presidential candidate General Curtis Le May. Now it was Nixon's turn to deal with the Vietnam War.

America's man in South Vietnam: Ngo Dinh Diem with President Eisenhower and John Foster Dulles in 1957.

President Diem *(right)* with U.S. Ambassador Frederick Reinhardt and Colonel Edward Lansdale *(standing and removing his cap)*. General John O'Daniel, the first head of MAAG, is standing at the far left.

Ngo Dinh Nhu, Diem's brother and main advisor.

Madame Nhu played the role of first lady of South Vietnam from 1954 to 1963.

John F. Kennedy and Defense Secretary Robert S. McNamara.

JFK with National Security Advisor McGeorge Bundy.

John F. Kennedy had the highest regard for General Maxwell Taylor.

JFK's top problem in 1961 appeared to be Laos, but Vietnam was close behind.

Foreign policy advisor Averell Harriman with JFK.

General Maxwell Taylor was sent to meet with Diem and report back to JFK.

(Left to right) Henry Cabot Lodge, General Paul Harkins, and CIA Director John McCone.

The H-21 Shawnee helicopter, also known as the "flying banana," was symbolic of the Ap Bac military defeat of the ARVN in January 1963.

Protesting the war, a Buddhist monk, doused with gasoline, set himself on fire in downtown Saigon in the summer of 1963.

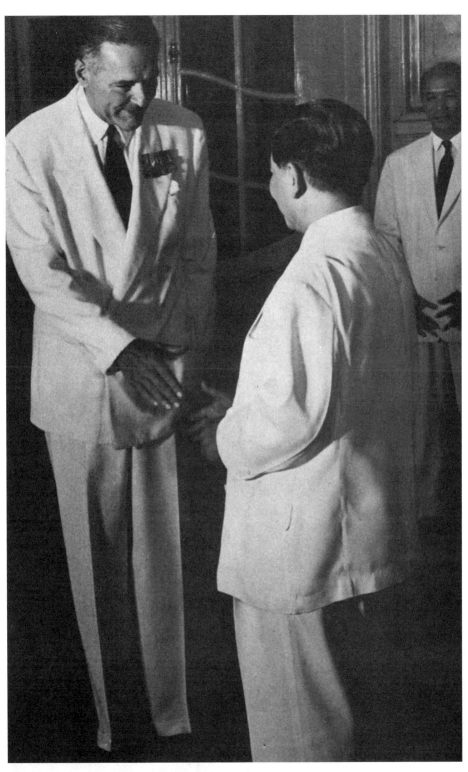

Ambassador Henry Cabot Lodge met Diem very few times before the military coup.

Lodge and Diem.

Diem and Nhu
were murdered on
November 1, 1963.

Lyndon Johnson kept most of the Kennedy team on board from 1963 to 1968. Here with Secretary of State Dean Rusk.

LBJ and General William Westmoreland.

Clark Clifford became a key advisor
at the end of the Johnson presidency.

The Tet offensive in early 1968 was seen as a defeat by the American public, although the
Vietcong and North Vietnamese didn't achieve their objectives, despite massive casualties.

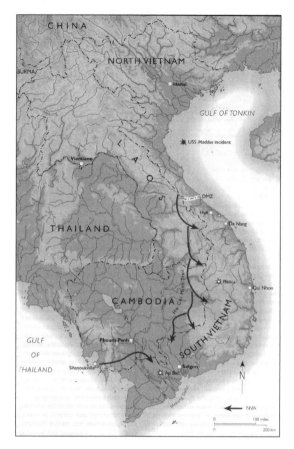

The Ho Chi Minh Trail.

Generals Ky *(left)* and Thieu managed to bring some stability to South Vietnam.

Growing antiwar protests in the United States in 1968-1971.

Robert F. Kennedy minutes before being assassinated in Los Angeles after winning the California primary.

President Richard Nixon and Henry Kissinger negotiated with North Vietnam and achieved a peace agreement leading to the withdrawal of U.S. troops.

4.

Vietnamization

Nixon Takes Over

On January 20, 1969, Richard M. Nixon became the fifth American president in twenty-three years to deal with the Vietnam issue. It had little impact in the Truman, Eisenhower, and Kennedy administrations. However, it seriously undermined the Johnson administration. Now it was in the forefront of Nixon's administration.

By this time, America had 541,500 troops in Vietnam, and 31,000 Americans had died there, nearly 5,000 of them in 1968. By the end of 1969, the total number of American deaths in Vietnam rose above 40,000, and the annual cost of the war was $30 billion.

From its beginning, Nixon had been a hawk, supporting every subsequent escalation of U.S. involvement. This gave him a deep emotional commitment to the war.

After earning a law degree from Duke University, Nixon served in World War II. Starting in 1946, he won elections to Congress and the Senate as an ardent anti-communist and served as vice president for two terms under President Eisenhower. In 1948, he won national prominence by pressing charges that Alger Hiss, a State Department official, had spied for the Communists.

Calling world communism a united force (monolithic), Nixon echoed the current anti-communist clichés of the time. These included the four age-old standard war propaganda points: (1) that the enemy is evil and commits atrocities, (2) that the enemy is an enemy of God, (3) that the enemy is out to conquer the world, and (4) that the enemy is an enemy of civilization.

In 1949, Nixon blamed Truman for the loss of China to the Communists, backed MacArthur's attempts to enlarge the Korean War to include China in 1950, and urged Eisenhower to send U.S. troops to Vietnam after the fall of the French at Dien Bien Phu in 1954.

Unlike many politicians, he did not have an outgoing personality. His associates described him as a loner, insecure, secretive, suspicious, and devious. Adept at misrepresentation, many referred to him as "tricky Dick." Reluctant to interact with people, he told his press secretary, "It would be damned easy to run the White House if you didn't have to deal with people."[1]

For his national security adviser, Nixon selected Henry Kissinger. Raised in Nazi Germany as a Jew, he immigrated to the United States with his family in 1938. "I always remembered the thrill when I first walked the streets of New York City," Kissinger recalled. "Seeing a group of boys, I began to cross to the other side to avoid being beaten up, and then I remembered where I was."[2]

After serving in the armed forces Kissinger attended Harvard and later taught there as a professor. During the Kennedy-Johnson years, he had been on call as a foreign policy adviser. A historian, he was known at Harvard as a traditionalist but somewhat ambivalent on the Cold War. He challenged, for instance, the idea that world communism was monolithic, a united world force. Instead, he argued that nationalism was a more powerful force than Communism. Also, he was a proponent of traditional balance of power politics. He saw Communist China and the Soviet Union as natural enemies because of their own national interests. He advocated playing each side against the other.

During the 1968 presidential campaign, Kissinger was more attracted to Nelson Rockefeller, who touted himself as the education

---

1. Robert Dallek, *Nixon and Kissinger: Patterns in Power* (New York: Harper Collins, 2007), p. 92.
2. Kissinger, *White House,* pp. 228-229.

candidate, than the ardent anti-Communist Richard Nixon. Still, when he offered him the job as national security adviser, Kissinger immediately accepted it.

Like Nixon, Kissinger was insecure, conspiratorial, and egotistical. But unlike him, he gravitated towards the press and enjoyed a measure of popularity among the public. He spoke with a European accent, dated famous movie stars, and exhibited wit and brilliance. Also, he was less ideological than Nixon, who was himself undergoing a change. At this time, Kissinger's balance of power theory made more sense to him than the monolithic theory of communism. When Nixon took office, he wrote that he had two long-term foreign policy goals: "detente with the Soviet Union and an opening to Communist China" as the key to ending the Vietnam War. He told his son-in-law to be, Edward F. Cox, that his famous "secret plan" to end the war was to go to Moscow and to Peking and make a deal.[3]

As secretary of state, Nixon picked William P. Rogers, who had been attorney general in the Eisenhower administration. A quiet bureaucrat, Rogers had little interest in leading U.S. foreign policy. This was perfect for Nixon, who would give him lesser matters while he and Kissinger would handle foreign policy.

Nixon and Kissinger showed a higher degree of sophistication in foreign affairs than their immediate predecessors. They recognized the changing distribution of world power, including the relative decline of America's post-World War II power and the need to keep foreign commitments within the nation's economic capacity. Although they leaned towards balance of power politics and sought to preserve stability and order, they agreed that no nation can have "absolute security" because that would produce "absolute insecurity for all the others."[4]

Although as unrelenting as his predecessors in opposing the expansion of communism, Nixon did introduce more civility into U.S. relations with the Soviet Union and Communist China. Calling for a policy of détente, he meant not an end to the Cold War, for it was a policy of

---

3. Richard Nixon, *No More Vietnams* (New York: Arbor House, 1985), p. 98.
4. Bagby, *International Relations*, p. 262.

conducting relations with an adversary, but a moderation of its intensity.

Like Nixon, Kissinger perceived the war as an attempt by North Vietnam to conquer South Vietnam. He had supported Johnson's sending U.S. combat troops. But he subsequently became convinced that the war was weakening America's strength, and he doubted whether America's initial planners understood the nature of guerrilla war. The guerrilla wins if it does not lose while the regular army loses unless it wins. "We were fighting a military war against an elusive enemy," recalled Kissinger, "but our adversary fought a political one against a stationary population," and "I doubted our planners grasped this."[5]

Nixon and Kissinger agreed that they could not resolve America's Vietnam dilemma by military means alone. It required negotiations to allow the U.S. to withdraw militarily without undermining the credibility of its commitments to other allies. But negotiations were not progressing. The only change since peace negotiations had started after Johnson's withdrawal speech was an agreement on the shape of the negotiating table.

Also, the nation was bitterly divided. On inauguration day, Nixon and his wife could not ride in an open car in the parade because scores of demonstrators lined the route, chanting "Ho, Ho, Ho Chi Minh. The NFL is going to win." "I'm not going to end up like LBJ," said Nixon, "holed up in the White House afraid to show my face in the street."[6]

Nixon knew that a good number of Americans favored a military victory. But they favored a quick one. Otherwise, he would lose their support. The only two options for a decisive victory, he recalled, was either to bomb the elaborate system of North Vietnam's irrigation dikes, resulting in floods and many deaths, or use tactical nuclear weapons. "If we had chosen to go for a knockout blow by bombing the dikes or using tactical nuclear weapons," he said later, "the resulting domestic and international uproar would have damaged our foreign policy on all fronts."[7]

---

5. Kissinger, *White House*, p. 232.
6. Nixon, *No More*, p. 101.
7. Ibid.

In July 1969, on Guam, the president set forth the Nixon Doctrine. The United States, he said, would no longer "undertake all the defense of the free nations of the world." While continuing to send economic and military aid to those states resisting Communist aggression, America would no longer send U.S. troops. Nations under attack must provide their own troops. While Johnson had halted escalation, Nixon would now begin de-escalation. In the future, he said, "we must avoid that kind of policy that will make countries in Asia so dependent on us that we are dragged into conflicts such as the one we have in Vietnam."[8]

At the same time, he drafted a personal letter to Ho Chi Minh. Dated July 15, his letter signaled a carrot-and-stick approach. If Ho did not end stalemated Paris negotiations, Nixon threatened a renewed military response. He decided on November 1, 1969, the first anniversary of Johnson's bombing halt, as the deadline for what in effect was an ultimatum to North Vietnam.

Replying to Nixon on August 30, Ho was unyielding. "Our Vietnamese people," he wrote, "are determined to fight to the end." He demanded that the United States withdraw its forces without any reciprocal steps from Hanoi, abandon Thieu and Ky, and allow the Vietnamese to decide their own fate "without foreign influence."[9]

Shortly thereafter, on September 3, the seventy-nine-year-old Ho died of a heart attack. His successors, led by Premier Pham Van Dong, continued to reiterate his demands.

Vietnamization

At a news conference on September 26, 1969, Randall J. Dicks, a Georgetown University student, asked Nixon to comment on the October 15 student moratorium and other campus demonstrations being planned for that fall against the Vietnam War. "Now I understand that there has been and continues to be opposition to the war in Vietnam," replied Nixon. "As far as this kind of activity is concerned,

---

8. Richard Nixon, *The Memoirs of Richard Nixon* (New York: Grosset and Dunlap, 1978), pp. 394-395.
9. Dallek, *Nixon and Kissinger*, p. 152.

we expect it, but under no circumstances will I be affected whatever by it."[10]

His insensitive response to Dicks' question further alienated Nixon from students opposed to the war. Yet, the president was fully aware of the furor that his statement would cause. "Faced with the prospect of demonstrations at home that I could not prevent," he said later, "my only alternative was to try to make it clear to the enemy that the protests would have no effect on my decisions."[11]

Nixon's dismissal of the antiwar protests, however, was disingenuous. He feared that opposition was approaching the point at which Congress might cut off funds for the war. By the fall of 1969, in fact, leading political figures, some of whom had formerly supported the war, including Senator Fulbright, Republican senator Jacob Javits, and former vice president Hubert Humphrey, grew more critical in denouncing it. Student protests spread from large universities to small conservative colleges. The October 15 moratorium demonstrations spread across the country and in every city, bringing out 4 million people.

The protests made Nixon nervous. On the top of the page of his preliminary notes for his November 3 speech, he wrote, "Don't get rattled, don't waver, don't react."[12] His speech, he hoped, would reduce opposition to the war long enough to allow him to arrange an honorable withdrawal. He sought to get out without the appearance of losing the war. "We simply cannot tell the mothers of our casualties in Vietnam," he told Rogers, "that it was all to no purpose."[13] Nevertheless, staying in the war longer meant more mothers would lose sons.

Calling his plan Vietnamization, Nixon sought to slowly reduce American troops and let the South Vietnamese army do the fighting. By reducing the number of Americans drafted and killed, he hoped he could undercut the antiwar movement. Troop withdrawals, he predicted, would "drop a bombshell on the gathering spring storm of anti-

---

10. *New York Times,* October 14, 1969.
11. Nixon, *Memoirs,* p. 399.
12. Ibid., p. 402.
13. Dallek, *Nixon and Kissinger,* p. 183.

war protest." To some generals, however, Vietnamization was "surrender on the installment plan."[14]

At 9:30 p.m. on November 3, 1969, Nixon addressed a national television audience from the White House. He traced the history of American involvement in Vietnam, discussed the negotiating efforts of his administration since taking office, outlined his Vietnamization policy, and placed the blame for the continuation of the war on the North Vietnamese. He appealed to America's "great silent majority" to show that they backed him and not the antiwar protesters. "North Vietnam," he concluded, "cannot defeat or humiliate the United States, only Americans can do that."[15]

The public's reaction to Nixon's speech was favorable. His overall approval rating climbed from 56 percent to 67 percent. From the minute he left the air the White House switchboard lighted up. Calls of support lasted throughout the night. All told, said Nixon, the White House mail room reported more than 50,000 telegrams and 30,000 letters had poured in, and the percentage of critical messages among them was low.[16] To Kissinger, "the American people might be tiring of the war, but they were not ready to be defeated."[17]

Although Nixon's speech garnered a measure of popular support, skepticism of his Vietnamization plan was still high. "Does his peace plan depend on his assumption that the South Vietnamese can successfully defend their country either with or without the logistical support of noncombatant U.S. troops," asked columnist James Reston, "and if they cannot, do we keep our troops there indefinitely?"[18] "Having failed to beat the Communists with a well-led, well trained and superbly equipped American army of half a million men," said *New York Times* reporter Richard Halloran, "we can hardly expect the South Vietnamese army on its own to do the job."[19]

In appealing to the "patriotic reflexes" of the great silent majority, his critics charged that "the majority of Americans will not subscribe,

---

14. Bagby, *International Relations*, p. 284.
15. *New York Times*, September 4, 1969.
16. Nixon, *Memoirs*, p. 410.
17. Kissinger, *White House*, p. 307.
18. James Reston, "Washington: The Unanswered Vietnam Questions," *New York Times*, December 10, 1969.
19. Richard Halloran, "Fulbright, Fearing a 'Disaster' Urges Nixon to End War This Year," *New York Times*, April 3, 1970.

to the underlying philosophy that the United States has a destiny to serve as the world's policeman."[20]

While Senator Edward M. Kennedy questioned whether the president "really did have a plan for peace," Senator Edmund S. Muskie "complained that the vital decision on withdrawal was left with Saigon and Hanoi rather than Washington." And Senator George McGovern protested that the speech "offered us an echo from the past, the tired rhetoric of former secretaries of state John Foster Dulles and Dean Rusk, and the hopeless policy of Thieu and Ky."[21]

In August 1969 Kissinger had opened secret conversations with North Vietnam's negotiator, Le Duc Tho. Kissinger's emotional commitment to the war was less intense than Nixon. As a realpolitik diplomat, he seemed to be willing to settle for a "decent interval" of perhaps two or three years between U.S. withdrawal and a Communist takeover.[22]

Meanwhile, Nixon hoped to persuade the Soviet Union and China to drop their support of North Vietnam. Following a policy of "linkage," if the Soviets helped, Nixon told them that America would grant them trade concessions. Both the Soviets and the Chinese, in fact, did pressure Hanoi to compromise; however, the Nixon administration exaggerated the control they could exert over the North Vietnamese, which was far from being as ironclad as Americans imagined.

At the same time, Nixon redoubled his efforts to implement Vietnamization. He enlarged the bombing of North Vietnam and increased Saigon's forces from 850,000 to 1.1 million, improving their pay, training, and armament. Counting militia, South Vietnam's armed forces reached nearly 2 million, more than half of its able-bodied men. In short, Saigon became the world's fourth-ranking military power.

What's more, learning the lessons after years of failure, to win over the South Vietnamese, Nixon arranged for more troops to be stationed near the villages for protection, and gave back to them the power to elect village chiefs. Also, assuming the cost of a land reform program, redistributed nearly 2.4 million acres of land to poor peasants. These

20. John W. Finney, "Nixon and the War," *New York Times*, November 9, 1969.
21. Ibid.
22. Kissinger, *White House*, p. 444.

measures helped to bring some progress in winning the "hearts and minds" of the peasants and restoring production.

Also, Nixon continued to press negotiations. He proposed a stand-still cease-fire. This would be followed by a phased withdrawal of all non-South Vietnamese forces and the democratic election of a new Saigon government. But in countries with little experience in democracy, elections are usually won by those who count the ballots. To conduct the election, the Vietcong insisted on first replacing Thieu and Ky with a coalition government.

At this time, Nixon considered himself in the middle of the argument between the doves and the hawks. Yet, he always leaned to the latter. They wanted him, for instance, to invade Cambodia to destroy enemy communications and sanctuaries; to invade Laos to cut the Ho Chi Minh trail, along which supplies moved from North to South Vietnam; and to bomb Hanoi and its principal harbor Haiphong. Nixon would eventually do all three.

War in Cambodia

After the Geneva Conference of 1954, France granted Cambodia independence. A small agricultural country of about 6.5 million, Cambodia had been given aid by the U.S., which also helped equip and train its army. Although anti-communist, Prince Norodom Sihanouk tried to keep his underdeveloped country out of the Vietnam War. Urging America to negotiate a settlement, he argued that Southeast Asians considered America's involvement as an imperialist endeavor, and that the result was only creating more favorable support for the Communists throughout the region.

In March 1969 Nixon began a sustained bombing of the area of Cambodia that North Vietnam used to transport arms and supplies to their Vietcong allies in the south. He kept the bombing secret. He did this, he said later, for two reasons: to avoid the domestic uproar that might result from publicized air strikes and to avoid putting Sihanouk in "a perilous political position."[23]

According to Kissinger, the U.S. only attacked military bases. These were in areas, he said, that were unpopulated by civilians and at

---

23. Nixon, *No More*, p. 108.

most only five miles from Vietnam's border.[24] Later, columnist Anthony Lewis wrote that the areas bombed were "virtually free-fire zones for the B-52s." Although their pilots were supposedly avoiding population centers, he added, they were "using outdated maps on a scale that did not show the crowded villages."[25]

Later, critics contended that the secret bombings were an illegal abuse of presidential power, and that bombing a neutral country violated international law. Nixon denied both charges. A reasonable interpretation of the Constitution, he said, could not conclude that the president, as commander-in-chief, was forbidden from attacking areas occupied by enemy forces and used by them as bases from which to strike at American and allied troops. Concerning Cambodia's neutrality, he argued that a neutral country has the obligation not to allow its territory to be used by a belligerent.[26] Yet Sihanouk's army was too weak to prevent this. To offset his military weakness, he was, in effect, playing the Americans and North Vietnamese against each other, hoping to keep both away from him. But that method effectively left him without any friends, since he was deemed unreliable by almost everyone who was in a position to help him.

Hoping to receive large amounts of U.S. aid, Cambodian army leaders, led by Marshal Lon Nol, overthrew Sihanouk in March 1970. They were impatient at Sihanouk's inability to keep the Vietcong from using Cambodian territory. From abroad, Sihanouk formed an anti-Nol alliance with the Cambodian Communists, called the Khmer Rouge. Lon Nol sought help from Washington but the Cambodians were in a difficult position with a North Vietnamese army corps occupying the northern third of the country and no protection in the event of a settlement between North and South Vietnam.

On April 29, after secluding himself at Camp David for two days, watching *Patton*, Nixon informed his secretaries of defense and state that he had decided to send 40,000 South Vietnamese and 20,000 U.S. troops in Cambodia. This invasion placed Lon Nol in an impossible situation that would end in his defeat.

---

24. Kissinger, *White House*, p. 254.
25. Anthony Lewis, "It Did happen Here," *New York Times*, May 3, 1979.
26. Nixon, *No More*, pp. 110-111.

Addressing the nation the next night, Nixon announced his decision to counter the Communist offensive by attacking North Vietnamese-occupied base areas in Cambodia. American troops would withdraw after completing their mission, which, he said, was "cleaning out sanctuaries" that held the "headquarters for the entire Communist military operations." This, he said, would facilitate U.S. withdrawal from Vietnam. "If when the chips are down," he added, "the United States acts like a pitiful helpless giant, the forces of totalitarianism and anarchy will threaten free nations and free institutions throughout the world." He concluded: "It is not our power, but our will that is being tested tonight."[27]

Although polls showed that a slight majority of Americans supported the invasion, the press criticized Nixon for violating his announced policy of de-escalation. When it comes to Vietnam, said the *New York Times*, "time and bitter experience have exhausted the credulity of the American people."[28] According to the *Washington Post*, "It was a self-renewing war supported by suspect evidence, specious argument, and excessive rhetoric."[29] "The script in Cambodia shockingly is the same as the story in Vietnam in the days of Kennedy and Johnson," said the *Miami Herald*. "We have heard it all before—endless times."[30] "Americans want an acceptable exit from Indochina," said the *Wall Street Journal*, "not a deeper entrapment."[31] And the *St. Louis Post-Dispatch* called it "a shocking escalation."[32]

Calling the Cambodian invasion "reckless" and "foolhardy," Clark Clifford termed the Vietnamization program "A formula for perpetual war."[33] "This speech confirms a judgment that I've been reluctant to reach," said Edmund Muskie. "The President has decided to seek a military method of ending the war rather than a negotiated method." It is, added Senator Walter Mondale of Minnesota, "an outright admission of the failure of Vietnamization."[34] Students were part-

---

27. *New York Times*, May 1, 1970.
28. Editorial, *New York Times*, May 1, 1970.
29. Editorial, *Washington Post*, May 1, 1970.
30. Editorial, *Miami Herald*, May 1, 1970.
31. Editorial, *Wall Street Journal*, May 1, 1970.
32. Editorial, *St. Louis Post-Dispatch*, May 1, 1970.
33. David E. Rosenbaum, "War Protest Leaders Denounce Nixon's Rigid Vietnam Stance," *New York Times*, September 8, 1969.
34. Nixon, *Memoirs*, p. 453.

icularly vocal against Nixon's speech. Demonstrations against it erupted on at least 448 campuses. During a visit the next day, May 1, at the Pentagon, he said, "you see these bums blowing up the campuses," and they are the "luckiest people in the world, going to the greatest universities, and here they are burning up the books and storming around on this issue."[35] That afternoon Nixon and his family sailed down the Potomac to Mount Vernon on the presidential yacht, the *Sequoia*. By the time he returned to Washington, the indignant reaction to his "bums" statement that morning at the Pentagon had almost overwhelmed the response to his decision to invade enemy sanctuaries in Cambodia. The *New York Times* headlined NIXON DENOUNCES BUMS ON CAMPUS, and the *Washington Post* echoed with NIXON DENOUNCES CAMPUS BUMS.[36]

Nixon's "Bums" statement fueled the call by student leaders for strikes and marches. The National Student Association called for Nixon's impeachment, and the editor of the eleven Eastern colleges ran editorials in their campus newspapers calling for a nationwide academic strike.

At Ohio's Kent State University students burned the ROTC building. The next day, May 4, National Guard troops fired into the protesters, killing four and wounding nine. Some of them were passersby. Several days later, at Mississippi's Jackson State College, city and state police fired 200 rounds into a crowd, killing two and wounding twelve others in front of the women's dormitory.

The events at Kent State University and Jackson State College sparked hundreds of colleges and universities to go on strike in protest both for the Cambodian invasion and the killings of six students and wounding of twenty-one others. Administrators at some schools closed them down for the remaining school year. Outbreaks of violence took place at even normally conservative and placid institutions like the University of Kentucky, where students burned down a building and national guardsmen broke them up using tear gas.[37]

---

35. *New York Times*, May 2, 1970.
36. *Washington Post*, May 2, 1970.
37. Joseph Lelyveld, "Protests on Cambodia and Kent State are Joined by Local Schools," *New York Times*, May 6, 1970.

Over 100,000 demonstrators converged on Washington, D.C. They were so loud and angry that the Secret Service parked buses and other vehicles in front of the White House as extra measures of protection. "For too many," said the *New York Times*, "it seemed that Cambodia and Kent State were the last straw."[38]

Although the polls showed that a slight majority of Americans blamed the students for the Kent State killings, Nixon was shaken by them. He had reached a point of "exhaustion" that caused his advisers deep concern. "Those few days after Kent State were among the darkest of my presidency," said Nixon later.[39] The "enormous uproar," said Kissinger, was "profoundly unnerving" and "the Executive Branch was shell-shocked."[40] As a result, three top members of Kissinger's staff, including Anthony Lake, and a hundred Foreign Service Officers resigned in protest.

Unable to sleep, Nixon had the Secret Service drive him to the Lincoln Memorial at 4:00 a.m. to talk to the student demonstrators. He was, according to Kissinger, "deeply wounded" by their hatred of him. But he was unable to connect with them. One of the students told a reporter, "He wasn't really concerned with why we were here," and another said that "Nixon had been tired and dull and rambled aimlessly from subject to subject."[41] "His awkward visit to the Lincoln Memorial to meet students," recalled Kissinger, "was only the tip of the psychological iceberg."[42]

But other Americans rallied to Nixon's support. On May 7, when students demonstrated in New York City's financial district, for example, construction workers building the World Trade Center descended on them with clubs and makeshift weapons. Afterwards, the construction workers held a huge rally in support of the president. In July, the reverend Billy Graham and comedian Bob Hope drew 250,000 people at a pro-war "Honor America Day" assembly in Washington.

In June 1970, U.S. troops returned from Cambodia. Later, Nixon called the Cambodian "incursion" the most successful military opera-

---

38. *New York Times*, May 10, 1970.
39. Nixon, *Memoirs*, p. 457.
40. Kissinger, *White House*, pp. 513-514.
41. Nixon, *Memoirs*, p. 460.
42. Kissinger, *White House*, p. 514.

tion of the entire war. He argued that it undercut North Vietnam's offensive striking power and bought time to press forward with Vietnamization.[43] Yet, the troops did not find Vietcong headquarters, and they pushed some Vietcong deeper into Cambodia, helping Cambodia's Communist guerrillas. Subsequently the United States intensified its bombing of Cambodia, and the Soviets increased their aid to the Communist Khmer Rouge that would eventually enact genocidal policies against its opponents.

In January 1971, in a significant reversal of previous support for escalation, Congress repealed the Tonkin Gulf Resolution, and it banned the use of U.S. troops in both Cambodia and Laos.

Nonetheless, Nixon arranged an invasion of Laos to stop the North Vietnamese from using the Ho Chi Minh trail to transport supplies and men into South Vietnam. Operation Lom Son 719 was launched on February 8, 1971, and lasted until March 25. Massive "secret" bombing had failed to interdict the movements of supplies and troops on the trail. To circumvent Congressional restrictions, he employed only South Vietnamese troops, supported by U.S. planes and helicopters. In February 1971 the U.S. Army airlifted two South Vietnamese divisions into Laos. In support, the U.S. Air Force dropped 48,000 tons of bombs. Still, the North Vietnamese stopped the South Vietnamese troops short of their targets, and the North Vietnamese mounted a counterattack that inflicted a 50 percent casualty rate on the South Vietnamese troops. The remainder of them retreated in panic, leaving the impression that the invasion had been a fiasco. The most negative effect was to have seriously harmed the best units of the ARVN, and it would take some time to bring them back to fighting trim.[44]

Surveillance and Exposure

In 1969-70, with the rise of the Weathermen (a terrorist offshoot of the Students for a Democratic Society) and the Black Panther Party (a militant black revolutionary group led by Huey Newton, Bobby

---

43. Nixon, *No More*, p. 122.
44. See John L. Plaster, *Secret Commandos: Behind Enemy Lines with the Elite Warriors of SOG* (New York: Simon & Schuster, 2004).

Seale, and Eldridge Cleaver), Nixon's suspicion of critics of the war and antiwar demonstrators reached a new height. His nerves were raw. Looking out the window one day, he saw a man, later identified as Monroe Cornish, a Maryland schoolteacher, with a 10-foot antiwar banner stretched out in front of Lafayette Park. Nixon told his associates that "the sign had to come down." Dwight Chapin, the president's appointments secretary, said that he was going to get some "thugs" to remove the man, but instead the Secret Service got the Park Police to convince him to move away from the president's sight.[45]

On June 5, 1970, Nixon held a White House meeting with J. Edgar Hoover, director of the FBI, Donald V. Bennett, director of the Defense Intelligence Agency, and Admiral Noel Gayler, director of the National Security Agency. Also in attendance was Tom Huston, a young lawyer and Nixon's aide on domestic violence by radicals.

Called the Huston Plan, the group drafted a strategy calling for a wide-ranging domestic surveillance of radical groups. It planned to intensify electronic surveillance, opening mail, placing informants on college campuses, lifting restrictions on burglary, and enhancing coordination of all government security agencies.

Everyone approved the plan except Hoover. He felt that it would undercut his power over the FBI, and if it got out, it would undermine his "carefully guarded image."[46] Consequently, the president withdrew his approval and said "while Hoover would undoubtedly carry it out, he would soon see to it that I had cause to reverse myself," and "there was even the remote possibility that he would resign in protest."[47]

Written at the direction of Robert McNamara, the Pentagon Papers, labeled "top secret," described the history of American involvement in Vietnam from 1945 to 1968. In 1971, Daniel Ellsberg, a former marine and employee at the Rand Corporation, released them to the *New York Times*, which subsequently published them. To Nixon, that kind of exposure threatened national security. Stating First Amendment rights, the newspaper denied that publishing the documents constituted a threat to the country, since the authors wrote them before Nixon's Vietnamization policy took effect.

---

45. *New York Times*, July 22, 1973.
46. Ibid.
47. Nixon, *Memoirs*, p. 475.

Nixon blamed the *New York Times'* antiwar policy rather than its "attachment to principle" as the real reason for the Pentagon Papers.[48] Arguing that their publication was an illegal act, his administration took the case to the Supreme Court, but the Court ruled in favor of the *New York Times* six to three.

The Ellsberg matter laid the foundation for the later Watergate scandal of 1972. As a result of the leaking of the Pentagon Papers, Nixon had created a special White House unit, dubbed the Plumbers, to plug such leaks and to conduct other secret operations. Led by ex-CIA and ex-FBI agents, the Plumbers broke into Ellsberg's psychiatrist's office, looking for smoking gun evidence that would expose Ellsberg's treason, names of his possible accomplices, and links to the antiwar movement.

Later, on June 17, 1972, the Plumbers were caught burglarizing the Democratic National Committee's headquarters at the Watergate office and apartment building. The incident led back to the White House and sensational revelations linking Nixon's advisers to the break-in. In an effort to divert attention from himself, the president fired his two top aides, John Ehrlichman and H. R. "Bob" Haldeman, but additional disclosures showed that Nixon himself had been aware of the unlawful activity and had participated in the cover-up.

A prolonged series of developments eroded his image and ability to govern. In the summer of 1974, with declining poll ratings and Congress on the verge of starting impeachment proceedings, Nixon resigned from office and turned the presidency over to Vice President Gerald R. Ford.

---

48. Ibid., p. 509.

5.

The War Drags On

The Spring Protests

In April 1971 the antiwar movement's Spring offensive against the Vietnam War began in Washington D.C. The Vietnam Veterans Against the War (VVAW) started it off on April 18 with a week of lobbying, guerilla theater, camping out on the Mall, and a medal-throwing ceremony at the Capitol. These activities served as a prelude to an April 24 march and rally at the Capitol and the May Day protests.

Recognizing the significance of the Vietnam Veterans War protests, the administration tried unsuccessfully to limit them. Receiving hourly updates, Nixon was able to persuade the Supreme Court to rule that the veterans could not sleep in the Mall. When the VVAW voted to defy the Court and sleep there anyway, the president, fearing a public backlash for arresting them, ordered the District of Columbia's police to leave them alone.[1]

The VVAW's most dramatic protest occurred on April 23. Hundreds of them, calling for an end to "this barbaric war," threw away their medals on the Capitol steps. Not even right wing hawks could call them "pinko hippies." They were, said Senator George McGovern, "Our boys, America's heroes." He called their action the most effective protest to date."[2]

The next day a crowd estimated at over 200,000 marched from the Ellipse, behind the White House, down Pennsylvania Avenue to the

---

1. David Dellinger, *More Power Than We Know* (New York: Arbor Press, 1975), p. 234.
2. James M. Naughton, "200,000 Rally in Capital to End War," *New York Times*, April 25, 1971.

rallying point at the Capitol. Sponsored by the National Peace Action Coalition, the rally attracted not only students and antiwar activists but also businessmen, union members, and teachers.[3] Among the speakers was VVAW's leader John Kerry. Receiving an enthusiastic ovation, he said, "The veterans proved that without picking up sticks, without picking up rocks, we can be heard."[4]

On May 1, the "Mayday Tribe," led by antiwar activists David Dellinger and Rennie Davis, descended on Washington. Its purpose, said Dellinger, was "to shut down the city."[5] Around fifteen thousand demonstrators surged into Washington from all directions. Many of them were wearing handkerchiefs and goggles or army gas masks over their faces to protect them from tear gas and mace. Their tactics included lying down in the streets and disrupting rush-hour traffic. Five thousand police and 41,000 federal troops arrested over 12,000 of them.

In the summer of 1971, public opinion polls revealed that only 31 percent of Americans supported the war. Of those polled, 71 percent said that sending U.S. troops to Vietnam had been a mistake and 58 percent called the war immoral. Many of them sought a complete withdrawal, even if that meant a Communist takeover. Military leaders, moreover, feared the effects of the war were undermining troop morale and discipline as well as the military's public image. In short, a growing number of Americans concluded that it was time for America to retreat.[6] To salvage anything from the war, Nixon understood that he must negotiate a settlement.

Negotiations Narrow the Gap

Since August 1969, the Nixon administration had been involved in secret conversations with North Vietnam in Paris. During this time, the North Vietnamese had captured American crewmen from downed U.S. planes. Because Nixon sought their release, this gave the North Vietnamese additional bargaining power.

---

3. Ibid.
4. Ibid.
5. Dellinger, *More Power*, p. 235.
6. Bagby, *International Relations*, p. 288.

In May 1971, if North Vietnam would release all prisoners, the Nixon administration would agree to withdraw all U.S. troops within six months. Representing a major concession an America's part, it omitted any demand for withdrawal of the North Vietnamese from South Vietnam. But the North Vietnamese rejected it unless the U.S. supported a coalition government—including the Vietcong—in Saigon to prepare new elections. Rejecting it, Nixon, in turn blamed the North Vietnamese for stalling on the negotiations.[7]

In October 1971, if North Vietnam agreed to release U.S. prisoners, Kissinger offered to force Thieu to resign one month in advance of an internationally supervised election. Although the Vietcong could participate in it, Saigon's officials would have controlled its machinery. Hanoi rejected it. "Our proposal stretched the limits of our generosity," said Nixon later.[8] In March 1972, there were just 95,000 U.S. troops were still in Vietnam, and only 6,000 of them were combat troops. That month the North Vietnamese launched a major invasion of South Vietnam. Their force included 120,000 troops supported with over 200 tanks and large numbers of 130mm recoilless artillery. Americans criticized the Soviets for furnishing the North Vietnamese with most of their weapons. The Soviets countered that Americans were furnishing Saigon with most of their weapons.

For Kissinger, Hanoi's biggest single reason for mounting its invasion of South Vietnam at that time had to do with the growing number of Americans opposed to the war. "The North Vietnamese," he said, "could only conclude that one more military push might propel us into essentially unconditional capitulation."[9]

But Hanoi's goal was much more limited. Its main purpose was to force the transfer of South Vietnamese troops from the villages to the Northern border. This would them allow the Vietcong to disrupt pacification programs.[10] Although the South Vietnamese Army put up determined resistance, the North Vietnamese overran Quang Tni, South Vietnam's northernmost province.

7. Nixon, *Memoirs*, p. 583.
8. Nixon, *No More*, p. 142.
9. Kissinger, *White House*, p. 1041.
10. Bagby, *International Relations*, p. 289.

In response, Nixon issued orders for Pentagon planners to assemble a massive attack force of aircraft carriers, cruisers, and destroyers for sea bombardment and B-52s for aerial raids on North Vietnam. "I felt that if we could mount a devastating attack on their home territory while pinning down their army in the south," said Nixon, "we would be in a very good position for the next round of negotiations."[11]

Widening the bombing of North Vietnam to include both Hanoi and Haiphong, Nixon said, "The bastards have never been bombed like they're going to be bombed this time."[12]

Endangering Soviet and Chinese shipping, Nixon laid mines in Haiphong's harbor. Four Soviet merchant ships hit them and sank. When the Soviets protested, Kissinger held them responsible for the invasion.[13] Despite their protests, the Soviets did not cancel a scheduled summit conference. What's more, both Russia and China put pressure on North Vietnam to accept a compromise. Yet, although North Vietnam suffered much damage, its movement of troops and supplies into South Vietnam did not slow.

On October 11, 1972, after years of negotiations, Kissinger and North Vietnam's negotiator Le Duc Tho struck a deal in Paris. This time the Vietcong would be given a share in the control of an election. A new tripartite electoral commission composed of representatives of Saigon, the Vietcong, and neutral nations would conduct it. In return, the North Vietnamese dropped their demand for prior removal of Thieu. A cease-fire would result, but it would leave the Vietcong in control of parts of South Vietnam and not require the withdrawal of North Vietnamese troops. Within sixty days, the North Vietnamese would return all U.S. prisoners, and at the same time the U.S. would withdraw all its troops.

But Thieu rejected the agreement. In a political contest, he feared that he did not have sufficient popular support to compete with the Vietcong and criticized the tripartite election commission as, in effect, a coalition government. He also protested leaving North Vietnamese troops in the south and conceding much of South Vietnam to the

---

11. Nixon, *Memoirs*, p. 587.
12. Bagby, *International Relations*, p. 289.
13. Kissinger, *White House*, p. 1116.

Vietcong. "Have you ever seen any peace accord in the history of the world," he said, "in which the invaders had been permitted to stay in the territories they had invaded?"[14]

Meanwhile, in the fall of 1972, a presidential campaign was under way in America. Running for a second term, Nixon's opponent was George McGovern, a liberal Democrat, who had long opposed the war. Like the 1968 campaign, the Democrats split over the Vietnam issue. Another decisive point was the new convention reform rules, which helped nominate McGovern by marginalizing the influence of establishment Democratic figures. Consequently, many of them refused to support him. Taking advantage of the Democrat's factionalism, the Nixon camp established "Democrats for Nixon."

Recognizing that Nixon would win again and that their bargaining power would drop after the election, the North Vietnamese went public with the peace agreement. On Radio Hanoi, they broadcast the agreed-upon terms and set an October 31 deadline for the United States to sign them. They insisted that the U.S. was dragging out the talks in order to cover up its "scheme of maintaining the Saigon puppet regime for the purpose of its continued 'war of aggression.'"[15] But Nixon announced that he would not yield to pressure.

On October 26, partly to undercut McGovern's antiwar appeal, Kissinger announced that "peace was at hand." He said, "It is obvious that a war that has been raging for ten years is drawing to a conclusion."[16] It's a "most welcome statement," said columnist Tom Wicker, that "the longest war in our history is about to end."[17]

Nixon, however, was not happy with Kissinger's statement. He feared that the public's hopes for an early settlement would be premature. "McGovern's supporters," he said, "would naturally claim that we were trying to manipulate the election."[18]

In an address to the nation on November 2, Nixon announced that he would not allow either a North Vietnamese deadline nor an election deadline to force the U.S. into an agreement. "We are going to sign the

14. Tom Wicker, "With Peace at Hand," *New York Times*, October 29, 1972.
15. Nixon, *Memoirs*, pp. 704-705.
16. Anthony Lewis, "No End of a Lesson: I," *New York Times*, April 24, 1975.
17. Wicker, "With Peace at Hand."
18. Nixon, *Memoirs,* pp. 706-707.

agreement when it is right, we are going to sign, without one day's delay."[19]

The failure to come to an agreement had little impact on the election's outcome. In November, Nixon got 61 percent of the vote. He carried 49 of the 50 states to win 520 electoral votes. McGovern carried only Massachusetts and the District of Columbia for a total of 17 electoral votes.

With the election over, Thieu's continued intransigence angered Nixon and Kissinger. "When you deal with the Vietnamese," said Kissinger, "it's like training rattlesnakes."[20] In a letter to Thieu, Nixon wrote that his continued opposition to the settlement would likely result in a disaster for his country."[21]

But Nixon would not give up on Thieu. If the South Vietnamese president accepted the agreement, Nixon promised him more than $1 billion in additional military supplies and offered absolute assurances that if North Vietnam violated its terms, America's reactions would be "swift and severe."[22] Thieu appeared to be in board. That same month, November, Kissinger got the North Vietnamese to agree to make token troop withdrawals and to accept some reduction in the political status of the Vietcong and the powers of the tripartite electoral commission. But when he insisted that the North Vietnamese accept the seventeenth parallel as a national boundary, Le Duc Tho refused. His refusal convinced Nixon and Kissinger to turn from negotiations to military force.

The Christmas Bombing and the Peace Accords

On December 18, 1973, Nixon ordered the massive bombing of North Vietnam in Operations Linebacker I and Linebacker II. He wanted an all-out attack. "It cannot be a weak response," he said, "but rather must be a massive and effective one."[23] Lasting twelve days, he ordered all available B-52 bombers to Vietnam for a round-the-clock bombing of Hanoi and Haiphong. In one day alone, December 26, 116

---

19. Ibid., pp. 706-707.
20. Robert Dallek, *Nixon and Kissinger: Patterns in Power* (New York: Harper Collins, 2007), p. 453.
21. Ibid.
22. Ball, *Past*, pp. 417-418.
23. Dallek, *Nixon and Kissinger*, p. 441.

B-52s bombed targets in the Hanoi-Haiphong area. "A hundred B-52s was like a 4,000-plane raid in World War II," said Kissinger. "It's going to break every window in Hanoi."[24]

All told, Nixon's Christmas raid included 729 B-52 sorties (combat flights) and about 1,000 fighter-attack sorties. In the heaviest bombing of the war, U.S. planes dropped 36,000 tons of bombs. The attacks devastated Hanoi's and Haiphong's industrial, railroad, and residential areas, including the largest hospital, and killing at least 2,200 civilians. The U.S. lost 26 planes, including 15 B-52s, a huge loss of American air power. The North Vietnamese, moreover, captured nearly a hundred more Americans to join those already taken prisoner.[25] A British observer of North Vietnam stated that Linebacker II was the one raid that made the enemy fearful and nervous.

There were a number of reasons behind the massive Christmas bombing. If Nixon did not get the North Vietnamese to accept his terms quickly, he feared that Congress would force him to accept defeat by agreeing to a withdrawal in exchange for return of POWs.[26] The bombings were "his last roll of the dice," said Kissinger.[27] Also, they were an attempt by Nixon to convince Thieu that the U.S. would back him if North Vietnam reneged on the agreement. At the same time, he wanted to persuade Hanoi that he was something of a "madman." Its leaders, in other words, better abide by the agreement or else suffer huge consequences.[28]

There was widespread reaction against the bombing. THE RAIN OF DEATH CONTINUES headlined the *Boston Globe*, and in the *New York Times*, TERROR BOMBING IN THE NAME OF PEACE. Senator Muskie called the bombing "disastrous." Senator Jacob Javits threatened "a cut of funds." Senate Majority leader Mike Mansfield referred to the bombing as "a stone age tactic."[29]

Foreign criticism was equally vocal. The Swedish government compared the bombing with the Nazis. The Danish, Finnish, Dutch, and Belgian governments criticized the attacks on cities. Peking called it

---

24. Ibid., pp. 445-446.
25. Ball, *Past*, pp. 420-421.
26. Nixon, *No More*, pp. 156-157.
27. Kissinger, *White House*, p. 1449.
28. C. L. Sulzberger, "Look Back in Puzzlement," *New York Times*, December 23, 1972.
29. *New York Times*, December 22, 1972.

"barbarous." Moscow emphasized the need to conclude the agreement. At the same time, however, both Peking and Moscow were pressuring Hanoi "subtly but unmistakably to settle."[30] Similarly the U.S. Congress was literally threatening to cut off funds for the continued war effort unless Nixon signed the agreement.[31]

On December 29 Nixon ended the pounding of Hanoi and Haiphong. As a result, the Paris talks resumed. Then, on January 15, 1974, he ended all bombing and mining of North Vietnam. "The bombing had done its job," he said. "It had been successful, and now it could be ended."[32]

The U.S. and North Vietnam signed a new agreement on January 27. Recognizing the "unity" of Vietnam, the U.S. agreed that the seventeenth parallel was not a territorial boundary. Thus, the Nixon administration had forfeited the point that had disrupted negotiations before Christmas and conceded that, after all, the war was an internal South Vietnamese conflict and not, as the hawks had always contended, a defense against international Communism. As a result, a cease-fire was put in place that left the Vietcong and North Vietnamese in control of much of South Vietnam. Within sixty days the U.S. agreed to withdraw all military forces, technicians, and advisers and to dismantle its military bases in return for simultaneous release of all U.S. prisoners. South Vietnam was given none of the benefits that were extended to South Korea, including American troops stationed on their soil for protection and to deter attacks from the north, they only received vague promises of future assistance.

While Nixon called the Paris Peace Accords "peace with honor," Thieu referred to it as a "surrender agreement," and he refused to sign it. Nixon was angry. "Brutality is nothing," he said. "You have never seen it if this son-of-a-bitch doesn't go along, believe me."[33]

In two unofficial letters to Thieu, Nixon used the carrot and stick approach. While threatening to cut off aid if Thieu did not sign, Nixon promised him that the U.S. would use "full force" if Hanoi failed to honor the agreement. Also, he dropped the proposed election in favor

30. Kissinger, *White House,* p. 1454.
31. Nixon, *No More,* pp. 169-170.
32. Nixon, *Memoirs,* p. 748.
33. Kissinger, *White House,* pp. 1469-1470.

of vague provisions for future political settlement and reunification. Thieu, in other words, did not have to submit to a democratic election.[34] At the same time, Nixon promised to give North Vietnam $2.5 billion in reconstruction aid.[35]

Although the Paris Peace Accords left Saigon in a politically weak position, it was, according to Nixon, "adequate to ensure the survival of South Vietnam—as long as the United States stood ready to enforce its terms."[36] Apparently, he did not trust Saigon's military to defend Saigon.

Nevertheless, in January 1974, the military balance of power was in South Vietnam's favor. It had 450,000 army troops. Its air force included 54,000 military personnel, and its navy numbered 42,000 sailors. In addition, there were 325,000 troops in its regional forces and another 200,000 in its popular forces. In comparison, North Vietnam's strength stood at between 500,000 to 600,000 troops. About 290,000 were in North Vietnam, 70,000 in Laos, and 25,000 in Cambodia. North Vietnam had about 148,000 combat troops in South Vietnam. In short, Saigon had at least a four-to-one advantage on the battlefield.

But how well would the ARVN fight for Saigon? Throughout the war, in fact, the South Vietnamese were decidedly inconsistent in their enthusiasm to fight. The Vietcong fighters, on the other hand, appeared more dedicated and persistent in their fighting abilities and willingness to die for their cause.

The Paris Peace Accords ended America's direct participation in the fighting. Including its support for France in Indochina, the U.S. had been involved in Vietnam for 23 years, and it had been seven years since the Johnson administration had Americanized the war. Reluctantly, Nixon came to understand that Vietnam was not two separate nations and to accept Communist control much of South Vietnam. Henry Kissinger and Le Duc Tho won the Nobel Peace Prize for ending the war. This led Under Secretary of State George Ball to remark that the Norwegians (who chose the recipients) "must have a

34. Ball, *Past*, pp. 418-419.
35. Bernard Gertzman, "The Cease-Fire Accords and Beyond," *New York Times*, January 26, 1973.
36. Bagby, *International Relations*, p. 291.

sense of humor."[37] To some, in fact, the agreement was "probably no more favorable than was available at the beginning of Nixon's term."[38]

Although withdrawing U.S troops and halting the bombing of North Vietnam, Nixon still left 9,000 U.S. advisers, allowed the South Vietnamese to keep huge quantities of American military supplies, and continued the not-so-secret bombing of Cambodia.

In the war's aftermath, Congress sought to diminish Nixon's power. His legislative supporters urged him to accept a fixed date for ending the bombing of Cambodia. At first, he refused, forcing a vote on June 30, 1974, to require an immediate halt to U.S. military operations in or over Cambodia. In response, Nixon, who initially vetoed it, accepted a compromise that delayed the cutoff date to mid-August.[39]

Earlier, in November 1973, Congress sought to reassert its control over going to war. It enacted the War Powers Act, which stipulated that the president would have to inform it within forty-eight hours if he sent U.S. forces into a combat area, and specified that he could keep them there no longer than ninety days without Congressional consent. Nixon vetoed the bill, but Congress overrode his veto.[40] This dubious piece of legislation actually may be unconstitutional since the president does have the right to commit American military personnel to fight a war. Congress, however, is under no obligation to fund it.

Down to the Wire

Almost immediately, Thieu violated the cease-fire agreement. In 1974, seeking to make the most of his military superiority, he launched large-scale offensives against Vietcong areas. At first, the North Vietnamese remained relatively quiescent, fearing that the U.S. would reverse its evacuation. But eventually Hanoi sent more troops south, and the Vietcong recovered much of their lost territory.

Not long after the signing of the Paris Peace Accords, the political and economic situation in South Vietnam worsened. As the previous flow of American money stopped, shortages occurred, corruption worsened, and unemployment and inflation soared. Since the war had

---

37. Ibid., pp. 291-292.
38. Nixon, *No More*, p. 180.
39. Ibid., pp. 180-181.
40. Ibid.

ravaged the countryside, one-fourth of South Vietnam's rural population became refugees, crowding into its cities. Saigon's population, for
example, went from 300,000 to 3 million. Black marketing, war
spending, prostitution, and real estate speculation characterized its
urban economy. Other cities in South Vietnam had had similar problems.

While Buddhists demanded peace, some South Vietnamese
churches begged Americans not to send more military aid since it
would only prolong the war. It dropped from $2.3 billion in 1973 to $1
billion in 1974. Without American assistance in weapons and troops,
South Vietnam's military morale, which was never really high,
collapsed. In 1974, 240,000 South Vietnamese soldiers deserted.[41]

As mentioned earlier, the Watergate affair had produced evidence
that Nixon had been involved in illegal acts. By June 1974, with a
public approval rating at 23 percent, Watergate had eroded both
Nixon's image and his ability to govern. Throughout the summer Congress was preparing impeachment proceedings against him, charging
him with abuse of power, obstruction of justice and contempt of Congress. Consequently, on August 9, Nixon resigned the presidency. Vice
President Gerald R. Ford became president.

In March 1975 the Vietcong and North Vietnamese made a preliminary probe into South Vietnam's central highlands. To their surprise, they quickly captured Pleiku and Kontum. When Thieu decided
to withdraw his forces from the highlands to more defensible areas, the
retreat of his troops turned into a panic-stricken rout. Defenders of the
important cities of Hue and Da Nang fled. "In just three weeks, under
Communist pressure, that appears to have been no heavier than offensives successfully resisted in the past," wrote columnist Tom Wicker.
"South Vietnam is about to come tumbling down."[42]

In fact, it took the Vietcong and North Vietnamese fifty-five days
to defeat the Saigon regime. When President Ford requested additional
military aid, Congress rejected it. By April 30, ships and helicopters got
all Americans and about 150,000 Vietnamese out. As the North Vietnamese poured into South Vietnam, they acquired a huge number of

41. Bagby, *International Relations*, p. 292.
42. Tom Wicker, "An Illusion Shattered," *New York Times*, April 1, 1975.

U.S.-built military installations and over $5 billion worth of U.S. military equipment.

A month before Saigon fell, on April 1, Lon Nol fled Cambodia and the Communists moved in. In October, the Laotian Communists completed their takeover of Laos. It had been twenty-six years since the U.S. first committed aid to the defense of Indochina, and twenty-one years since the 1954 Geneva Agreement to unite Vietnam.

The fall of Vietnam was the most humiliating defeat in America's history. But it did not erode America's national interests in the rest of the world and may have strengthened them. The loss of Vietnam, in short, did not bring about a major shift in the distribution of world power.

The monolithic theory of Communism proved illusionary. Although the Communists seized Cambodia and Laos, no other dominos fell. The North Vietnamese and Vietcong victory did not give the Chinese control of Vietnam. Instead, the Vietnamese Communists sought to expel their influence in Cambodia and a violent clash with them in northern Vietnam later resulted. Although the Russians took over the gigantic former U.S. naval base at Cam Ranh Bay, the U.S. did not, as President Johnson had predicted, lose control of the Pacific.

America had lost 58,000 men, with 300,000 wounded and 1,400 missing. Many veterans came home with psychic scars. Including aid to France's efforts to re-conquer Indochina after World War II, America had spent $300 billion dollars on the Vietnam War. It ended up with as many as 2 million dead and perhaps twice the number wounded. Moreover, it damaged America's image and alienated its allies.

Retreat from the Vietnam War strengthened America's national security. Leaving Indochina meant that the U.S. was a lesser threat to both the Chinese and the Soviets. Without a common enemy, their conflicts over territory and power variables only intensified. Thus, it placed the Nixon-Kissinger balance of power strategy on a stronger footing.

What went wrong in Vietnam? To Kissinger and Nixon, they should have encouraged the military to strike quickly with full force. "We should have bombed the hell out of them the minute we got into office," said Kissinger.[43] "We failed to understand the determination of our enemy," said Nixon, "and what it would take to defeat him," he added.[44]

For the doves, the war was not politically winnable; the military solution was unattainable. They said that no amount of military force could compel the Vietnamese to accept the division of their country indefinitely or to support a U.S.-armed and -equipped Saigon regime.

Even if, according to the doves, the U.S. had sent enough troops to occupy North Vietnam, it could not have achieved peace. After World War II, a period of rising expectations had arisen in third-world countries. Asians, for instance, would no longer accept Western imperialism or regimes tied too closely to the West. But along with Europeans, Americans had a problem viewing the world other than in their own image. They had little knowledge of Indochina, whose history, politics, and culture they did not understand.

The North Vietnamese and the NLF fought the U.S. for independence and self-rule even though America went to Vietnam to ensure the independence of that country, not to colonize it. In the perception of the Vietnamese, no matter how justified, the United States had replaced France and behaved like a colonial power. In the end, Americans could have easily defeated Communist aggression, as they had in Korea. They lost not to foreign Communists, the USSR, or the People's Republic of China, but to native Vietnamese people fighting to expel foreigners and reunite the country under Communist Party rule. They were unable to defeat Vietnamese Communists, who had such strong popular support.

---

43. William Safire, "What Went Wrong?" *New York Times*, April 24, 1975.
44. Nixon, *No More*, pp. 46-47.

Chronology 1939-1975

August 1939	General Georges Catroux appointed governor general of Indochina
June 19, 1940	First Japanese ultimatum accepted by Catroux
June 24	Catroux dismissed and replaced by Admiral Jean Decoux
July 25	FDR signs U.S. embargo on aircraft fuel and scrap metal to Japan
August 30	Franco-Japanese agreement
September 22	Japan to station troops and open airfields in Tonkin
May 1941	Viet Minh league is created by Vietnamese communists and non-communists
July	Darlan-Kato Agreements on French-Japanese defense
	Further U.S. restrictions on oil and other commodities, Japan's accounts frozen in America
December 7	Pearl Harbor
1944	De Gaulle appoints General Mordant head of French resistance in Indochina
	First OSS contacts with Ho Chi Minh in China
August 25, 1944	Paris is liberated
October	U.S. the USSR and Great Britain recognize the French Provisional Government
February 1945	Yalta Conference, France is excluded
March 9	Japanese forces overthrow French administration in Indochina
March 24	French provisional government statement on Indochina
May 8	Germany surrenders war ends in Europe
June	OSS provides help and assistance to the Viet Minh
July-August	Potsdam conference agrees to Chinese occupation north of the 17th parallel and British occupation in the south; France doesn't participate
August 6	Atomic Bomb on Hiroshima
August 9	Atomic Bomb on Nagasaki
August 13	Viet Minh insurrection
August 15	Japan surrenders; De Gaulle appoints Admiral Thierry d'Argenlieu high commissioner in Indochina and General Leclerc military commander in chief
August 25	Emperor Bao Dai abdicates and accepts the Viet Minh
September 2	Ho Chi Minh proclaims the independence of Indochina in Hanoi
	French sign formal Japanese surrender on board the USS *Missouri*
September	Fighting between French civilians and military against Viet Minh in Saigon

	Massacre at the Cité Hérault in Saigon: 100 French civilians killed
	President Truman disbands OSS
October 5	General Leclerc arrives in Saigon, battles against Viet Minh in the south
December 26	Former emperor Vinh San dies in a plane crash on his way to Saigon
March 1946	French troops arrive at Haiphong
	Ho Chi Minh–Sainteny agreement: France recognizes the DRV as a free state within the French Union and Indo-chinese Federation
April	Conference at Dalat is inconclusive
July	Ho Chi Minh and Viet Minh delegation in Paris
August	Adm. d'Argenlieu holds a second Dalat conference without the Viet Minh
	In Paris the Viet Minh suspends the conference and returns home
September	Ho Chi Minh and Marius Moutet sign the *modus vivendi* as a stopgap
November	Incidents at Haiphong
December 19	Bombardment of Haiphong and insurrection in Hanoi
	From his hiding place Ho Chi Minh calls for all out war
March 1947	Emile Bollaert a civilian replaces Admiral d'Argenlieu as high commissioner
September	Bao Dai denounces the Viet Minh dictatorship
October	Operation Lea misses to trap the Viet Minh leadership by minutes
July 1949	Bao Dai heads a State of Vietnam within the French Union
September	Scandal of the Generals begins in Paris
	The USSR detonates the first Soviet atomic bomb
December	Chinese communist troops reach the border with Tonkin
	Ambassador Philip C. Jessup visits Bao Dai and promises U.S. assistance
January 1950	Communist China and the USSR both recognize Ho Chi Minh's regime
June 25	North Korea invades South Korea
June 30	First war supplies delivered by plane to Saigon directly from the United States
October	Disaster at Cao Bang, evacuation of Lang Son and posts on the Tonkin side of the Chinese border
December	General de Lattre appointed high commissioner and military commander in Indochina
January 1951	De Lattre gives new impetus and has a string of military successes

March	New structure replaces the Viet Minh with the Lao Dong
September	Triumphant visit by de Lattre to the U.S. seeking military aid
December 20	De Lattre leaves Indochina
January 11, 1952	De Lattre dies in Paris; General Salan is the new military commander
March	Increased U.S. assistance
April	Jean Letourneau is high commissioner and minister of the associated states
July	U.S. legation becomes an embassy in Saigon
October	U.S. Admiral Arthur Radford visits Indochina backs more assistance
November	Air base set up at Na San similar to Dien Bien Phu Eisenhower elected president
December	Viet Minh attacks repulsed at Na San
January 1953	René Mayer new French prime minister
February	Bao Dai agrees to reinforce the Vietnamese army
March	Stalin dies; Mayer and Eisenhower meet in Washington U.S. demands more aggressive war plans
May	General Henri Navarre appointed new military commander in Indochina
June	Joseph Laniel new French prime minister
July	Korean War armistice signed at Pan Mun Jom
August	Na San base evacuated
September	American assistance is increased
November	Dien Bien Phu base is set up according to the Navarre Plan
December	Viet Minh attacks in upper Laos
January 1954	Dien Bien Phu base being set up; Berlin Conference of 'Big Four' agrees to meet at Geneva in April to resolve the Korean armistice and discuss peace in Indochina
March 13	Viet Minh assault begins on Dien Bien Phu; French parliamentary debate on Indochina; French government declares it wants a negotiated end to the war
April	Dien Bien Phu under siege; U.S. refuses to provide relief bombing raids without congressional support; Eisenhower statement on Indochina
May 7	Dien Bien Phu falls to the Viet Minh; debates in French parliament on the talks
June 16	Bao Dai appoints Ngo Dinh Diem as prime minister of the State of Vietnam
June 17	Pierre Mendès France is the new French prime minister
July 21	Agreements reached at Geneva on a cease fire in Indochina
August	Exodus of Catholics from North Vietnam
September	SEATO Pact signed in Manila

October	French evacuation of Hanoi; Gen. J. Lawton Collins mission to South Vietnam
November	Rebellion in Algeria, prelude to 8 years of war
February 1955	American advisors take over instruction of Vietnamese Army from the French; Gen. Collins recommends dropping Diem
March	Diem defeats the religious sects
May	Gen. Collins leaves Vietnam
August	Diem refuses negotiations with North Vietnam
October	Diem victory in elections and rejection of Bao Dai; Republic of Vietnam is proclaimed with Diem as president
February 1956	Sianouk moves closer to Communist China
March	Souvanna Phouma prime minister of Laos
April	Diem refuses Geneva Accords elections; last French troops leave Saigon; MAAG military mission takes over
September	Disastrous agrarian reform in North Vietnam
December	Political struggle in South is decided in Hanoi by the Lao Dong
March 1957	Socialist reforms in the North
July 1958	Lao Dong debates on increased terrorism in the South
January 1959	Lao Dong central committee led by Le Duan decides on armed struggle against South Vietnam
May	Diem creates special courts to repress terrorism
	Ho Chi Minh Trail is prepared
July	First two Americans are killed in attack on Bien Hoa base by Viet Cong
January 1960	New North Vietnamese constitution
May	MAAG is increased
September	Le Duan elected general secretary of Lao Dong and resume struggle in the South
November	John F. Kennedy elected president; failure of coup attempt against Diem
December	NLF (National Liberation Front—Viet Cong) is created in South Vietnam
January 1961	Pathet Lao pushes back Laotian Royalist army; pro-Western government by Boun Oum
May	Vice President Lyndon Johnson visit to Saigon; JFK approves special forces and sabotage operations against North Vietnam
October	Maxwell Taylor and Walt Rostow mission to Saigon
November	JFK increases aide to South
February 1962	Diem and Nhu launch strategic hamlet program; MACV is created to replace MAAG and new commander is Gen. Paul Harkins

December	U.S. Advisors grow to 11,300
January 1963	South Vietnamese army defeated at Ap Bac
May	First Buddhist protests
June	Monk sets himself on fire in Saigon
August	Nhu's special forces raid the pagodas against Buddhists; fateful August 24 cable instructs Ambassador Lodge to encourage coup against Diem
November	Coup and murder of Diem and Nhu; assassination of JFK
January 1964	Military coup by Gen. Nguyen Khanh in Saigon
April	Gen. Westmoreland replaces Gen. Harkins at MACV
July	Maxwell Taylor ambassador to South Vietnam
August	Tonkin Gulf incident and resolution by congress; war intensifies
December	Ho Chi Minh Trail is bombed
February 1965	LBJ launches "Rolling Thunder" after attack at Pleiku and Quin Hon
March	First marines land at Da Nang; Westmoreland plan; bombing continues
April	Reinforcements sent to Vietnam; LBJ offers negotiations; Pham Van Dong answers
June	Westmoreland asks for more troops and freedom to deploy as needed
	Gen. Nguyen Cao Ky prime minister and Gen. Van Thieu head of the military committee
July	More reinforcements are approved
August	Search and destroy tactics
February 1966	Conference at Honolulu: Ky and Thieu and LBJ decision to win hearts and minds
June	Secret contacts with North Vietnam
August	De Gaulle speech in Cambodia asking for negotiated settlement
December	U.S. troops 362,000 plus 50,000 allies (South Korea, Philippines, Australia, New Zealand, Thailand)
January 1967	Operation Cedar falls
February	Operation Junction City
March	Westmoreland asks for 200,000 more troops; McNamara is opposed
April	Antiwar demonstrations in the U.S.
July	LBJ limits reinforcements to 55,000
September	LBJ offers peace talks
October	More anti war protests
November	Westmoreland states war will end soon; preparations by North Vietnam for major attack into southern cities

January 1968	Siege of Khe San (January to April); Tet Offensive starts on January 30
March	Clark Clifford replaces Robert McNamara; General Abrams replaces Westmoreland; LBJ will not seek reelection
May	Agreement with Hanoi to hold talks; first preliminary meeting in Paris
July	LBJ meets Thieu in Hawaii
October	Bombing halt just before the election
November	Nixon elected president
December	U.S. troops 536,000
January 1969	Paris negotiations open
March	Bombing of Cambodia
May	NLF peace program in ten points published; Nixon announces staged withdrawal of U.S. troops and requests that all non southern troops do the same
June	Bombing of North Vietnam resumes; Nixon-Thieu meeting at Midway; Vietnamization agreed upon
August	Kissinger-Xuan Thuy meeting in Paris
September	Death of Ho Chi Minh
October	Antiwar protests in the U.S.
December	U.S. troops 475,000
February 1970	First meeting Kissinger – Le Duc Tho
March	Sihanouk is overthrown; Lon Nol takes over in Cambodia
April	U.S. and Vietnamese operations in Cambodia
May	Massive antiwar protests in the U.S.
June	U.S. troops withdraw from Cambodia; U.S. Senate votes Cooper-Church amendment forbidding U.S. participation in ground operations in Cambodia
October	Nixon offers a cease fire in Indochina
December	More U.S. troops withdrawn from South Vietnam; Tonkin Gulf Resolution is cancelled
February-March 1971	Operation Lom Son 719 ARVN-U.S. attack on Ho Chi Minh Trail in Laos
April 1971	Peace protests in the U.S.
June	Pentagon Papers published by *New York Times*
December	U.S. troops reduced to 156,000
February 1972	Nixon at Beijing
March	Communist offensive in South Vietnam
April	Renewed bombing of North Vietnam
May	Quang Tri captured by the North; Kissinger states the U.S. will not demand that North Vietnamese forces withdraw from the South; Nixon orders mining of harbors in the north and destruction of communications

June	ARVN retakes Quang Tri; 47,000 U.S. troops left in South Vietnam
October	Agreement in principle for ceasefire
November	Thieu opposed to agreement
December	Talks are suspended; bombing of the north; Hanoi returns to the negotiations; 24,000 U.S. troops in South Vietnam
January 1973	Nixon pressures Thieu; Paris peace Accords signed
February	Cease fire in Laos
March	Last U.S. troops leave South Vietnam
June	Congress prohibits bombing into Cambodia
October	Lao Dong decides to use violence to achieve unification
November	Congress passes war Powers Act
January 1974	Phnom Penh bombed by communists
August	Congress places limits on military aide to South Vietnam
	Nixon resigns; Gerald Ford becomes president, promises aide to Thieu
December	Lao Dong decides on final offensive against South Vietnam
January 1975	Khmers Rouges attack Phnom Penh
March	Attacks in Central Vietnam; Hue and Da Nang are lost
April	Lon Nol leaves Phnom Penh; fighting in Laos; Ford requests funds for South Vietnam; U.S. evacuates Phnom Penh; Lao Dong decides to take Saigon; final evacuation of U.S. presence; Saigon occupied April 30; General Duong Van Minh asks for end to fighting. Vietnam war ends.

Selected Facts and Figures

Indochina Population

Years (millions)	1900	1945	1954	2000
Vietnam	17.5	23.6	30.4	78.7
Laos	1.0	1.5	2.1	5.5
Cambodia	1.1	3.0	4.7	12.2
Total Indochina	19.6	28.1	37.0	96.4

In 1940 French Indochina had a population of 24 million in including 40,000 Europeans.

In 1962 North Vietnam had a population of 16.5 million and South Vietnam 14 million.

In 2012 the total population of the three countries of the old French Indochina reached 112 million.

****

Geographic Note

Vietnam is the contemporary name of the long coastal region of the Indochinese peninsula in Southeast Asia that stretches from the Chinese border to the Gulf of Siam for a total of 1,650 kilometers and a surface of 331,000 sq. kilometers. From the earliest times the country was made up of three parts: Cochinchina in the far south with the fertile Mekong Delta that included the rich rubber plantations and the city of Saigon.

A narrow central strip of mountainous territory is known as Annam with the imperial capital at Hué: a spectacular coastline and steep highlands that border with Laos. The north known as Tonkin borders China and Laos, has always been a poor, populous region especially in the Red River delta (also known as the Tonkin delta) with its regularly flooded lowlands, rice paddies and depressed economy. Famine was a regular feature of life for the peasants of Tonkin who emigrated to work as coolies on southern farms and plantations.

Cambodia, west of Cochinchina, is a land steeped in history with its great temples and thick jungles originally colonized by Indian and Siamese rulers. To the west of Annam and Tonkin are the mountainous areas of Laos, the third component of French Indochina.

Indochina War 1945-1954

Total French troops having served in Indochina	489,560
French nationals	233,467
Legionnaires	72,833
North Africans	122,920
Africans	60,340
Total French Killed and MIA	110,000
Total Viet Minh estimated killed	500,000

Vietnam War 1958-1975

Killed in Action:

North Vietnam and Viet Cong	1,100,000
South Vietnam	220,357
United States	58,272
Korea	4,407
Australia	487
New Zealand	37
Thailand	351
Laos (Meo-Hmong)	30,000
Vietnamese civilians killed (estimated)	2 to 5 million

1968 Troop Strength in Vietnam

South Vietnam	850,000
United States	536,100
South Korea	50,000
Australia	7,672
New Zealand	552
Thailand, Philippines	10,450
North Vietnam	287,465
China PRC	170,000
USSR and North Korea	3,600

French Governments 1944 to 1958

Provisional Government of the French Republic

August 1944–January 1946	Charles de Gaulle
January 1946–June 1946	Félix Gouin
June 1946–November 1946	Georges Bidault
November 1946–January 1947	Léon Blum

Fourth Republic

President
Vincent Auriol	1947–1953
René Coty	1953–1958

French Prime Ministers 1947-1959*

January–October 1947	Paul Ramadier
October–November 1947	Paul Ramadier
November 1947–July 1948	Robert Schuman
July–August 1948	André Marie
September 1948	Robert Schuman
September 1948–October 1949	Henri Queuille
October 1949–February 1950	Georges Bidault
February–June 1950	Georges Bidault
July 1950	Henri Queuille
July 1950–February 1951	René Pleven
March–July 1951	Henri Queuille
August 1951–January 1952	René Pleven
January–February 1952	Edgar Faure
March–December 1952	Antoine Pinay
January 1953–May 1953	René Mayer
June 1953–January 1954	Joseph Laniel
January 1954–June 1954	Joseph Laniel
June 1954–February 1955	Pierre Mendès-France
March 1955–January 1956	Edgar Faure
January 1956–May 1957	Guy Mollet
June–September 1957	Maurice Bourgès Maunoury
November 1957–April 1958	Felix Gaillard
May 1958	Pierre Pflimlin
June 1958–January 1959	Charles de Gaulle

---

* Same names next to each other indicate the formation of a new government.

Governor General of French Indochina

General Georges Catroux	1939-1940
Admiral Jean Decoux	1940-1945

High Commissioner in Indochina

Jean Cédile	1945
General Philippe de Hautecloque Leclerc	1945
Admiral Thierry d'Argenlieu	1945-1947
Emile Bollaert	1947-1948
Léon Pignon	1948-1950
General Jean de Lattre de Tassigny	1950-1952
Jean Letourneau	1952-1953

General Commissioner in Indochina

Jean Letourneau	1953
Maurice Dejean	1953–1954
General Paul Ely	1955
Henri Hoppenot	1955–1956

French Expeditionary Corps in the Far East

Corps Expéditionnaire français en Extrême-Orient (CEFEO)

General Philippe Leclerc de Hauteclocque	(1945-1946)
General Jean-Etienne Valluy	(1946-1948)
General Raoul Salan (interim)	1948
General Roger Blaizot	(1948-1949)
General Marcel Carpentier	(1949-1950)
General Jean de Lattre de Tassigny	(1950-1952)
General Raoul Salan	(1952-1953)
General Henri Navarre	(1953-1954)
General Paul Ely	(1954-1955)

American Ambassadors to Vietnam

Donald Heath	1950-1952 & 1952-1954
G. Frederick Reinhardt	1955-1957
Elbridge Durbrow	1957-1961
Frederick Nolting	1961-1963
Henry Cabot Lodge	1963-1964
Maxwell Taylor	1964-1965
Henry Cabot Lodge	1965-1967
Ellsworth Bunker	1967-1973
Graham A. Martin	1973-1975

American Military Representatives

MAAG—Military Assistance Advisory Group 1950-1962

Brig. General Francis Brink
Major General Thomas Trapnell
General John W. O'Daniel
Lt. General Samuel T. Williams
Lt. General Lionel McGarr
Major General Charles Timmes

Special U.S. Representative to Vietnam 1954-1955

General J. Lawton Collins

MACV—Military Assistance Command Vietnam 1962-1973

General Paul Harkins
General William Westmoreland
General Creighton Abrams
General Frederick Weyand

Co-Author's Note

Two personal experiences prompted me to work on this book. In mid-November 1963 I had a brief exchange with Ngo Dinh Trac, the son of Ngo Dinh Nhu and of Madame Nhu. who had just been spirited out of Vietnam by the CIA and brought first to Rome to be reunited with his mother better known as the "dragon lady" Madame Nhu then to a catholic school where I was also a student. In the course of that conversation between youngsters Trac revealed some troubling aspects of the Vietnam tragedy and the overthrow of Ngo Dinh Diem. Like his mother he assigned all the blame for what was happening at the doorstep of the Americans. "You Americans want to Americanize everything. You can't accept foreign cultures, refuse to learn about them and all you can think about is to want to shape other countries in your own image. That's a mistake and it will work against you in Vietnam. In the end you will have to leave. Better you go now than after a war you shall lose." The boy had just lost his father and uncle in a bloody coup by the South Vietnamese army. He'd been told that his father had his head 'squashed' when he was killed. With his sister he had been placed in a safe house in Dalat then flown out of Saigon on an American plane. The trauma he felt at age sixteen must have been immense and yet he remained calm and rational about what had happened. I admired his self confidence and strength of character.

On November 7 and 8, 1968, in Paris I was able to obtain an interview with Georges Bidault. A former head of the French Resistance, president of the provisional government, prime minister and foreign minister many times from 1944 to 1954 and one of the main architects of the Indochina policy during that entire period, Georges Bidault embodied the policy of colonial presence and continuity. He was foreign minister before and during the battle of Dien Bien Phu and headed the French delegation at the start of the Geneva Conference on Indochina. Some of the notes from those two three hour sessions were used in parts of this book. In fact, Georges Bidault in impromptu conversation provides a unique window into the events that led to decolonization.

[Co-Author's Note by Robert L. Miller]

Bibliography

Manuscripts

Christian, George, Interview with Joe B. Frantz, June 30, 1970, Oral History Project Lyndon B. Johnson Library, Austin, Texas.

Clifford, Clark M., Papers, Lyndon B. Johnson Library, Austin, Texas.

Clifford, Clark M., Interview with Paige Mulhollan, July 14, 1982, Oral History Project Lyndon B. Johnson Library, Austin, Texas.

Humphrey, Hubert H. Papers, Minnesota Historical Society, Saint Paul, Minnesota.

Johnson, Lyndon B., Papers, Lyndon B. Johnson Library, Austin, Texas.

McCarthy, Eugene J. Papers, Library of Georgetown University, Washington D.C.

McPhearson, Harry, Papers, Lyndon B. Johnson Library, Austin, Texas.

Roche, John P. Interview with Paige Mulhollan, August 16, 1970, Oral History Project Lyndon B. Johnson Library, Austin, Texas.

Roche, John P. Papers, Lyndon B. Johnson Library, Austin, Texas.

Taylor, Maxwell D. Interview with Dorothy Pierce Mc Sweeney, February 10, 1969, Oral History Project Lyndon B. Johnson Library, Austin, Texas.

Westmoreland, William C. Interview with Dorothy Pierce Mc Sweeney, Oral History Project Lyndon B. Johnson Library, Austin, Texas.

Wheeler, Earle, G. Interview with Dorothy Pierce Mc Sweeney, Oral History Project Lyndon B. Johnson Library, Austin, Texas.

Author's Interviews

Busby, Horace, Interview with the Author, August 18, 1982.

Christian, George, Interview with the Author, August 16, 1982.

Clifford, Clark, M., Interview with the Author, August 18, 1982.

Ellsworth, Robert F., Interview with the Author, August 21, 1982.

Finch, Robert H., Interview with the Author, August 25, 1982.

Gans, Curtis, Interview with the Author, August 11, 1982.

Kleindienst, Richard G., Interview with the Author, August 25, 1982.

Mankiewicz, Frank F., Interview with the Author, June 23, 1982.

Mc Carthy, Eugene J., Interview with the Author, June 30, 1980.

Rauh, Joseph L., Interview with the Author, August 3, 1982.

Rostow, Walt W., Interview with the Author, December 22, 1982.

Schlesinger, Arthur, M. Jr., Interview with the Author, January 28, 1981.

Sears, John W., Interview with the Author, September 14, 1982.

Sorensen, Theodore C., Interview with the Author, June 16, 1980.

White, Theodore H., Interview with the Author, August 3, 1982.

Co-Author's Interviews

Bidault, Georges, Interview with the Co-Author, November 7 and 8, 1968.

Vasselot de Regnié, Colonel, Interview with the Co-Author, May 30, 1967.

d'Hérouville, Hubert, Interview with the Co-Author, December 1 and 2, 1968.

Ngo Dinh Trac, November 1963, Paris.

Newspapers

L'Aurore
Capital Times
Chicago Tribune
La Croix
Evening Star (Washington D.C.)
L'Express
France Observateur
France Soir
L'Humanité
Le Monde
Le Nouvel Observateur
Los Angeles Times
New York Times
Paris Match
San Francisco Chronicle
Wall Street Journal
Washington Post

Periodicals

Harpers
Life
Look
The Nation
National Review
New Republic
Newsweek
New York Times Magazine
Saturday Evening Post
U.S. News and World Report

Books, Memoirs and Special Studies

Ambrose, Stephen, *Nixon: The Triumph of a Politician 1962-1972* (New York: Simon and Shuster, 1991)

Bagby, Wesley M., *America's International relations since World War II* (New York: Oxford University Press, 1999)

Ball, George W., *The Past Has Another Pattern* (New York: W. W. Norton, 1975)

Bartholomew-Feis, Dixee R., *The OSS and Ho Chi Minh. Unexpected Allies in the War Against Japan* (Lawrence: Kansas, 2006)

Berman, Edgar, *The Triumph and Tragedy of the Humphrey I Knew* (New York: Putnam, 1979)

Berman, Larry, *No Peace, No Honor: Nixon, Kissinger and Betrayal in Vietnam* (New York: Free Press, 2001)

Bidault, Georges, *D'une résistance à l'autre* (Paris: Les Presses du Siècle, 1965)

Bodard, Lucien, *La Guerre d'Indochine*. Fiction (Paris: Grasset, 1963-1997)

Brocheux, Pierre and Daniel Hemery, *Indochina. An Ambiguous Colonization 1858-1954* (Berkeley: U. of California 2010)

Brodie, Fawn, *Richard Nixon: The Shaping of His Character* (New York: St. Martin's, 2002)

Brownell, Will and Richard Billings, *So Close to Greatness. A Biography of William Bullitt* (New York: Macmillan, 1987)

Bundy, William P., *A Tangled Web: The Making of Foreign Policy in the Nixon Presidency* (New York: Hill and Wang, 1998)

Caro, Robert A., *The Years of Lyndon Johnson: The Passage of Power* (New York: A. A. Knopf, 2012)

The Catholic Encyclopedia

Catton, Philip E., *Diem's Final Failure* (Lawrence: Kansas, 2002)

Clayton, Anthony, *The Wars of French Decolonization* (London; Longman, 1995)

Clifford, Clark, *Counsel to the President: A Memoir* (New York: Random House, 1991)

Chang, Jung and Jon Halliday, *Mao. The Unknown Story* (New York: A. Knopf, 2005)

Christian, George, *The President Steps Down* (New York: Macmillan, 1970)

Collins, Brig. General J. Lawton, *The Development and Training of the South Vietnamese Army 1950-1972* (Washington DC: Dept. of the Army, 1991)

Costigliola, Frank, *Roosevelt's Lost Alliances* (Princeton: Princeton UP, 2011)

Cronkite, Walter, *A Reporter's Life* (New York: Ballantine Books, 1996)

Crowley, Monica, *Nixon off the Record: His Candid Commentary on People and Politics* (New York: Random House, 1996)

Currey, Cecil B., *Victory at Any Cost. The Genius of Viet Nam's Gen. Vo Nguyen Giap* (Washington DC: Potomac, 1997)

Dallek, Robert, *Franklin D. Roosevelt and American Foreign Policy 1933-1945* (New York: Oxford, 1979)

———, *Flawed Giant: Lyndon Johnson and His Times 1961-1973* (New York: Oxford, 1998)

———, *Nixon and Kissinger: Patterns in Power* (New York: Harper Collins, 2007)

Dalloz, Jacques, *Georges Bidault. Biographie Politique* (Paris: L'Harmattan, 1992)

Dean, John W., *Blind Ambition* (New York: Simon and Schuster, 1976)

———, *Lost Honor* (New York: Harper and Row, 1982)

De Gaulle, Charles, *Mémoires de guerre* (3 Vols.) (Paris: Plon, 1954-1959)

De Gaulle et l'Indochine 1940-1946, Institut Charles-de-Gaulle (Paris: Plon, 1982)

Dellinger, David, *More Power Than We Know* (New York: Anchor Press, 1975)

Demery, Monique Brinson, *Finding the Dragon Lady. The Mystery of Vietnam's Madame Nhu* (New York: Public Affairs, 2013)

Donovan, Robert J., *Conflict and Crisis The Presidency of Harry S Truman 1945-1948* (New York: Norton, 1977)

———, *Tumultuous Years. The Presidency of Harry S Truman 1949-1953* (New York: Norton, 1982)

Duiker, William J., *Ho Chi Minh* (New York: Hyperion, 2000)

Duroselle, Jean-Baptiste, *Clemenceau* (Paris: Fayard, 1988)

Eden, Anthony, *Full Circle* (Boston: Houghton Mifflin, 1960)

Ehrlichman, John, *Witness to Power: The Nixon Years* (New York: Simon and Schuster, 1982)

Eisenhower, Dwight D., *Mandate for Change 1953-1956* (New York: Doubleday, 1963)

———, *Waging Peace 1957-1961* (New York: Doubleday, 1965)

Elgey, Georgette, *Histoire de la IVème République: Vol. I La République des Illusions; Vol. II La République des Contradictions* (Paris: Fayard, 1965, 1968)

Ellsberg, Daniel, *Secrets: A Memoir of Vietnam and the Pentagon Papers* (New York: Penguin, 2003)

Fall, Bernard B., *The Two Vietnams* (New York: Praeger, 1967)

——, *Street Without Joy. The French Debacle in Indochina* (Mechanicsberg, PA: Stackpole 1994) Reprint of the original 1961 edition.

Fleury, Georges, *La Guerre en Indochine* (Paris: Plon 1994-2003)

Folin, Jacques de, *Indochine 1940-1955. La fin d'un rêve* (Paris : Perrin, 1993)

Ford, Gerald, *A Time to Heal* (New York: Harper and Row, 1979)

Foreign Relations of the United States (FRUS)

Franchini, Philippe, *Les Guerres d'Indochine Vols. I-II* (Paris: Pygmalion, 1988)

——, *Les mensonges de la guerre d'Indochine* (Paris: Perrin, 2005)

Galbraith, John K., *A Life in Our Times* (Boston: Houghton Mifflin, 1981)

Gallup, George, *The Gallup Poll: Public Opinion, 1959-1971* (New York: Random House, 1972)

Vo Nguyen Giap, *Big Victory, Great Task* (New York: Frederick A. Praeger, 1968)

——, *The Military Art of the People's War: Selected Writings of General Vo Nguyen Giap.* Edited by Russell Stetler (New York: Monthly Review Press, 1970)

——, *People's War, People's Army* (New York: Frederick A. Praeger, 1968)

Girardet, Raoul, *L'Idée coloniale en France de 1871 à 1962* (Paris: la Table Ronde, 1972)

Goodwin, Doris Kearns, *Lyndon Johnson and the American Dream* (New York: St. Martin's, 1991)

Goldstein, Gordon M., *Lessons in Disaster. McGeorge Bundy and the Path to War in Vietnam* (New York: H. Holt, 2008)

Gras, Yves, *Histoire de la guerre d'Indochine* (Paris: Plon, 1979)

Haig, Alexander M., Jr., *Inner Circles: How America Changed the World. A Memoir* (New York: Warner Books, 1992)

Halberstam, David, *The Best and the Brightest* (New York: Ballantine, 1993)

Haldeman, H. R., *The Haldeman Diaries: Inside the Nixon White House* (New York: G. P. Putnam's Sons, 1994)

——, *The Ends of Power* (New York: Times Books, 1978)

Halstead, Fred, *Out Now! A participant's Account of the American Movement Against the Vietnam War* (New York: Monad Press, 1978)

Hammer, Ellen J., *A Death in November. America in Vietnam 1963* (New York: E.P. Dutton, 1987)

Héduy, Philippe, *Histoire de l'Indochine* (Paris: A. Michel, 1998)

Herring, George, *From Colony to Superpower: U.S. Foreign Relations since 1776* (New York: Oxford University Press, 2008)

——, *America's Longest War. The United States and Vietnam 1950-1975* (New York: McGraw-Hill, 1986-2002)

Higgins, Marguerite, *Our Vietnam Nightmare* (New York: Harper, 1965)

Hoffmann, Abbie, *Soon to be a Major Motion Picture* (New York: Putnam, 1980)

Hoopes, Townsend, *The Limits of Intervention* (New York: David McKay, 1970)

Ho, Hien V., *Alexandre de Rhodes and the Vietnamese Language* (advite.com/Alexandre de Rode.htm)

Humphrey, Hubert H., *The Education of a Public Man: My Life and Politics*, Ed. Norman Sherman (Garden City: Doubleday, 1976)

Hunt, Andrew E., *The Turning: A History of Vietnam Veterans Against the War* (New York: NYU Press, 1999)

Isaacson, Walter, *Kissinger* (New York: Simon and Schuster, 1996)

Jacobs, Seth, *Cold War Mandarin. Ngo Dinh Diem and the Origins of America's War in Vietnam 1950-1963* (Lanham, MD: Rowman and Littlefield, 2006)

Johnson, Lyndon B., *The Vantage Point: Perspectives of the Presidency 1963-1969* (New York: Holt, Reinhart and Winston, 1971)

Jones, Howard, *Death of a Generation* (New York: Oxford, 2003)

Journoud, Pierre, *De Gaulle et le Vietnam 1945-1969* (Paris: Tallandier, 2011)

Kaiser, David, *American Tragedy. Kennedy, Johnson and the Origins of the Vietnam War* (Cambridge: Harvard Belknap, 2000)

Kalb, Marvin and Bernard Kalb, *Kissinger* (Boston: Little Brown, 1974)

Karnow, Stanley, *Vietnam. A History* (New York: Penguin, 1981)

Kersaudy, François, *De Gaulle et Roosevelt* (Paris: Perrin, 2006)

Kimball, Jeffrey, *The Vietnam War Files* (Lawrence: Kansas UP, 2004)

Kissinger, Henry, *White House Years* (Boston: Little Brown, 1979)

——, *Diplomacy* (New York: Simon & Schuster, 1994)

Klein, Herbert G., *Making It Perfectly Clear* (Garden City: Doubleday, 1980)

Kolko, Gabriel, *Anatomy of a War: Vietnam, the United States and the Modern Historical Experience* (New York: Pantheon, 1985)

Lacouture, Jean, *Mendès-France* (Paris: Seuil, 1981)

Lawrence, Mark A. and Fredrik Logevall, *The First Vietnam War. Colonial Conflict and Cold War Crisis* (Cambridge: Harvard, 2007)

Le Page, Jean Marc, *Les Services Secrets en Indochine* (Paris: Nouveau Monde, 2012)

Logevall, Fredrik, *Embers of War* (New York: Random House, 2012)

Logevall, Fredrik, *Choosing War. The Lost Chance for Peace and the Escalation of War in Vietnam,* (Berkeley: California, 1999)

Louis, Wm Roger, *Imperialism at Bay* (New York: Oxford, 1974)

Maga, Timothy P., *The Vietnam War* (New York: Alpha Books, 2010)

Marangé, Céline, *Le Communisme Vietnamien (1919-1991)* (Paris: SciencesPo Les Presses, 2012)

Marr, David, *Vietnam 1945. The Quest for Power* (Berkeley: U. P. California, 1995)

McCarthy, Eugene J., The Year of the People (New York: Doubleday, 1969)

McGovern, George, *Grassroots: The Autobiography of George McGovern* (New York: Random House, 1977)

McCoy, Alfred W., *The Politics of Heroin. CIA Complicity in the Global Drug Trade* (Chicago: Review Press, 2003) Second revised edition.

McNamara, Robert S., *In Retrospect: The Tragedy and Lessons of Vietnam* (New York: Random House, 1995)

Miscamble, Wilson, *From Roosevelt to Truman: Potsdam, Hiroshima and the Cold War* (New York: Cambridge, 2006)

Morgan, Ted, *FDR* (New York: Simon and Shuster, 1986)

——, *Valley of Death* (New York: Random House, 2010)

Morris, Roger, *Richard Milhous Nixon: The Rise of An American Politician* (New York: Holt, 1990)

Moyar, Mark, *Triumph Forsaken* (New York: Cambridge, 2006)

Muelle, Raymond, *La Guerre d'Indochine 1945-1954* (Paris: Reportages de Guerre, 2004)

Newton, John, *Eisenhower. The White House Years* (New York: Doubleday, 2011)

Nouzille, Vincent, *Des secrets bien gardés* (Paris: Fayard, 2009)

Nguyen, Lien – Tang, *Hanoi's War* (Durham: UNC Press, 2012)

Nixon, Richard M., *RN. The Memoirs of Richard Nixon* (New York: Grosset and Dunlap, 1978)

——, *No More Vietnams* (New York: Arbor House, 1985)

——, *The Real War* (New York: Warner Books, 1980)

O'Brien, Lawrence F., *No Final Victories* (New York: Doubleday, 1974)

O'Sullivan, Christopher D., *Sumner Welles, Postwar Planning and the Quest for a New Order, 1937-1943* (New York: Columbia, 2003)

Paillat, Claude, *Dossier Secret de l'Indochine* (Paris: Presses de la Cité, 1964)

Pendar, Kenneth, *Adventure in Diplomacy* (London: Cassell, 1966)

The Pentagon Papers

Plaster, John L., *Secret Commandos: Behind Enemy Lines with the Elite Warriors of SOG* (New York: Simon & Schuster, 2004)

Prados, John, *The Blood Road: The Ho Chi Minh Trail and the Vietnam War* (New York: John Wiley, 1998)

——, *The Sky Would Fall* (New York: Dial Press, 1983) republished with new documents as *Operation Vulture* (New York: IBooks, 2002)

——, *Safe for Democracy. The Secret Wars of the CIA* (Chicago: Ivan Dee, 2006)

——, *Vietnam: The History of an Unwinnable War 1945-1975* (Lawrence: Kansas, 2009)

Rostow, Walt W., *The Diffusion of Power: An Essay in Recent History* (New York: The Macmillan Company, 1972)

Roussel, Eric, *De Gaulle Vol. I 1890-1945* (Paris: Gallimard, 2002)

Roy, Jules, *Dien Bien Phu* (New York: Carroll & Graf, 1963-2002)

Ruscio, Alain, *Les Communistes français et la guerre d'Indochine 1944-1954* (Paris: L'Harmattan, 1995)

Rust, William J., *Kennedy in Vietnam. American Vietnam Policy 1960-1963* (New York: Scribner, 1985)

Salan, Raoul, *Mémoires, Vols. I-II* (Paris: Presses de la Cité, 1970)

Schandler, Herbert Y., *The Unmaking of a President* (Princeton: Princeton UP, 1977)

Schlesinger, Arthur, Jr., *A Thousand Days* (Boston: Houghton Mifflin, 1965)

Schoenbrun, David, *As France Goes* (New York: Harper, 1957)

Schulzinger, Robert, *Henry Kissinger: Doctor of Diplomacy* (New York: Columbia UP, 1989)

Shawcross, William, *Sideshow: Kissinger, Nixon and the Destruction of Cambodia* (New York: Simon and Schuster, 1987)

Sherwood, Robert E., *Roosevelt and Hopkins. An Intimate History* (New York: Enigma Books, 2008) Reprint of the 1948-1950 edition.

Shultz, Richard H., Jr., *The Secret War Against Hanoi* (New York: HarperCollins, 1999)

Small, Melvin, *Johnson, Nixon and the Doves* (New Brunswick: Rutgers, 1988)

Smith, Richard Harris, *OSS* (Guilford: Lyons Press, 2005)

Sorensen, Theodore, *Kennedy* (New York: Harper, 1965)

Stavis, Ben, *We Were the Campaign* (Boston: Beacon Press, 1969)

Thomas, Evan, *Ike's Bluff: President Eisenhower's Secret Battle to Save the World* (Boston: Little Brown, 2012)

Toczek, David M., *The Battle of Ap Bac Vietnam* (Annapolis: Naval Institute, 2001–2007)

Tønnesson, Stein, *The Vietnamese Revolution of 1945- Roosevelt, Ho Chi Minh and De Gaulle in a World at War* (Oslo: PRIO, 1991)

Valenti, Jack, *A Very Human President* (New York: W. W. Norton, 1975)

Vaucher, Georges, *Sous les cèdres d'Ifrane* (Paris: Julliard, 1963)

Wainstock, Dennis, *Election Year 1968* (New York: Enigma Books, 2012)

Walker, Daniel, *Rights in Conflict* (New York: Dutton, 1968)

Wall, Irwin M., *The United States and Making of Postwar France 1945-1954* (New York: Cambridge, 1991)

Wedemeyer, Albert, *Wedemeyer Reports!* (New York: H. Holt, 1958)

Weiner, Tim, *Legacy of Ashes. The History of the CIA* (New York: Doubleday, 2007)

——, *Enemies: A History of the FBI* (New York: Random House, 2012)

Westmoreland, William C., *A Soldier Reports* (Garden City, N.Y.: Doubleday, 1976)

White, Theodore H., *The Making of the President 1968* (New York: Atheneum, 1969)

Wicker, Tom, *One of Us: Richard Nixon and the American Dream* (New York: Random House, 1991)

Wills, Garry, *Nixon Agonistes: The Crisis of the Self-Made Man* (Boston: Houghton Mifflin, 2002)

Winters, Francis X., *The Year of the Hare. America in Vietnam January 1963–February 1964* (Athens: Georgia UP, 1997)

Articles

Clifford, Clark M., "A Vietnam Reappraisal: the Personal History of One man's View and How it Evolved" *Foreign Affairs* 47 (July 1969), pp. 601-622.

Espinosa, William and John B. Henry, "The Tragedy of Dean Rusk," *Foreign Policy* 8 (Fall 1972), pp. 181-189.

Halberstam, David, "The Man Who Ran Against Lyndon Johnson," *Harpers*, December, 1968, pp. 47-66.

Hoopes, Townsend, "LBJ's Account of March 1968," *New Republic*, March 14, 1970, pp. 17-19.

Hughes, Emmett, Jr., "The Tormented Candidacies," *Newsweek*, February 5, 1968, p. 13.

McCarthy, Eugene J., "Why I'm Battling LBJ," *Look*, February 6, 1968, pp. 22-26.

McWilliams, Carey, "The Bitter Legacy of LBJ," *Nation*, September 9, 1968, pp. 198-201.

Newfield, Jack, "Kennedy's Search for a New Target," *Life*, April 12, 1968, p. 35.

Pearson, Drew, "The Ghosts that Haunted LBJ" *Look*, July 23, 1968, pp. 25-28.

Reddy, John, "Can Humphrey Hold His Party Together?" *Readers Digest*, July, 1968. pp. 105-110.

Reeves, Richard, "The Making of a Candidate, 1968." *New York Times Magazine*, March 31, 1968, pp. 25-27.

Sidey, Hugh, "Tortuous Road to Decision…and Lady Bird's Role" *Life*, April 12, 1968, pp. 32-33.

Stevens, Robert, "Disaster in Chicago?" *Commonweal*, August 23, 1968, pp. 550-551.

Wilson, Richard, "This Is Humphrey," *Look*, July 9, 1968, pp. 41-46.

Witcover, Jules, "Is There Really A New Nixon?" *Progressive*, March, 1968, pp. 14-26.

Government Documents

United States Congress. Senate Committee on Armed Services. Air War Against North Vietnam. Parts 1-5. Hearings before the Preparedness Investigative Subcommittee, 90th Congress, 1st Sess. August 1967.

United States. Department of Defense, United States—Vietnam Relations, 1945-1967. 12 Vols. Washington D.C.: United States Government Printing Office, 1971.

United States. President. Public Papers of the Presidents of the United States: Lyndon B. Johnson, 1967, 2 Vols. Washington D.C.: United States Government Printing Office, 1968.

United States. President. Public Papers of the Presidents of the United States: Lyndon B. Johnson, 1968-1969, 2 Vols. Washington D.C.; United States Government Printing Office, 1970.

United States. President. Public Papers of the Presidents of the United States: Richard M. Nixon 1969-1974, 6 Vols. Washington D.C.: United States Government Printing Office, 1971-1975.

U. S. Department of State. Foreign Relations of the United States: Foundations of Foreign Policy, 1969-1972, Washington D.C.: United States Government Printing Office, 2003.

U. S. Department of State. Foreign Relations of the United States: Foundations of Foreign Policy, 1969-1976: South Asia Crisis, 1971. Washington D.C.: United States Government Printing Office, 2005.

U. S. Department of State. Foreign Relations of the United States: Foundations of Foreign Policy, 1969-1976: United Nations, 1969-1972. Washington D.C.: United States Government Printing Office, 2004.

U. S. Department of State. Foreign Relations of the United States: Foundations of Foreign Policy, 1964-1968: Vietnam, 1967. Washington D.C.: United States Government Printing Office, 2002.

U. S. Department of State. Foreign Relations of the United States: Foundations of Foreign Policy, 1964-1968: Vietnam, January-August 1968. Washington D.C.: United States Government Printing Office, 2002.

U. S. Department of State. Foreign Relations of the United States: Foundations of Foreign Policy, 1964-1968: Vietnam, September 1968- January 1969. Washington D.C.: United States Government Printing Office, 2003.

U. S. Department of State. Foreign Relations of the United States: Foundations of Foreign Policy, 1969-1976: Vietnam, January 1969- July 1970. Washington D.C.: United States Government Printing Office, 2006.

Acknowledgements

Special thanks to all those who helped us in preparing this book and in particular: to the membership at the New York Military Affairs Symposium and Danny David for his excellent suggestions; to Paul Cardin for his encyclopedic knowledge of contemporary history and valuable insights into American and French politics and military affairs; to Prof. Denis Fadda, president of the Académie des sciences d'Outre-Mer de France, for his excellent insights into French colonial policy; to the late Marquis de Vasselot de Régnié, who served as an officer in the French armistice commission in Hanoi 1954-1955; and the late Colonel F. de Lignières, who served in Indochina before Dien Bien Phu, who both gave the author their impressions and insights on the Indochina War and its aftermath. Finally a very special tanks to the late former President of the Provisional Government of the French Republic and former premier and minister of foreign affairs, Mr. Georges Bidault, for his great patience during the many hours of interviews he was gracious enough to give me in 1968, long before the idea of writing *Indochina and Vietnam* even existed. And of course to Ngo Dinh Trac for the brief and wrenching assessment he gave at the Collège Stanislas in Paris, one evening in November 1963, shortly after losing his father and uncle in the military coup in Saigon. The lingering question 'How did it all happen?' was the spark behind this book.

Index